THE THEORY OF
UNIVERSALS

THE THEORY OF UNIVERSALS

BY

RICHARD I. AARON

SECOND EDITION

OXFORD
AT THE CLARENDON PRESS
1967

Oxford University Press, Ely House, London W. 1

GLASGOW NEW YORK TORONTO MELBOURNE WELLINGTON
CAPE TOWN SALISBURY IBADAN NAIROBI LUSAKA ADDIS ABABA
BOMBAY CALCUTTA MADRAS KARACHI LAHORE DACCA
KUALA LUMPUR HONG KONG TOKYO

FIRST EDITION 1952
SECOND EDITION 1967

PRINTED IN GREAT BRITAIN

PREFACE TO SECOND EDITION

THE whole of Chapter VI and large parts of Chapters VII and XI have been rewritten for this edition. In 1952 it was widely questioned whether the problem of universals was a serious philosophical problem, and it appeared necessary at that time to begin Part II with a chapter entitled 'Is there a real problem?' Today this is no longer necessary; instead I begin by explaining my approach to Part II. In Chapters VII and XI I present fresh accounts of general words and concepts. I have discussed some of the points in the new material with my colleagues at Aberystwyth, particularly Mr. Philip Walters, and am grateful for their help.

Minor corrections only have been made in Part I. Further references have been added in Parts I and II.

R. I. A.

Aberystwyth
Autumn, 1966

ACKNOWLEDGEMENTS

I OWE a great deal to two friends who were kind enough to read this book through in typescript, Sir David Ross and Professor Gilbert Ryle; I found their suggestions most valuable. I am also indebted to Mr. R. J. Spilsbury for reading Part II and discussing it with me, and to Dr. A. C. Ewing and Professor J. R. Jones for reading the sections on Kant and Spinoza. My chief debt is to my wife for much help throughout the production of this book.

I wish to express my thanks to the Officers of the Aristotelian Society for their kindness in permitting me to republish certain paragraphs of my paper on Hume's Theory of Universals (*Proceedings* of the Society, 1941–2). It was in studying Hume in the late thirties that I first realized the importance of dispositions for an adequate theory of universals and concepts.

R. I. A.

Aberystwyth
May Day 1952

CONTENTS

INTRODUCTION

There have been periods when the problem of universals was the dominating theme of philosophical speculation. One such period was the medieval; another was that of Plato and Aristotle. A strong case might be made, too, for the view that the crux and testing-point of the empiricist argument in the seventeenth and eighteenth centuries lay in its theory of universals and that Locke and Berkeley were well aware of this. It is the contention of this book that the problem is of equal importance in our own speculations. It is not denied that the contemporary attitude towards universals is frequently one of suspicion, nor that there are genuine grounds for suspicion. Yet the tendency to turn away from the problem and to ignore it because of a feeling that some of its formulations are unreal cannot be defended. The problem of universals, rightly posed, is still fundamental and urgent; for to understand universals is to begin to understand thinking.

It is from this angle that I approach the theory of universals, regarding it as a necessary part of the theory of thinking. What we call conceptual thinking involves the use of general words and no explanation of the successful use of the general word is possible without facing and solving the problem of universals. The conclusion of this book is that we must look in two directions for a solution, first, to natural recurrences and, secondly, to principles of classification, and I attempt to relate the two in order to present one theory of universals. During the course of the argument it will be necessary to examine such questions as the nature of common qualities and relations, of resemblances, of dispositions and concepts. It will be necessary, too, to test traditional theories in terms of contemporary thought. The theory in which the argument ends is neither realist, conceptualist, nor nominalist, and the reasons why none of these theories is acceptable as it stands must be made clear. Throughout, issues of fundamental importance both to contemporary empiricism and to formalism will have to be faced.

Such are some of the problems of Part II of this book. Part I is historical. When attempting to solve a philosophical problem it is unwise to ignore the history of that problem. In philosophy we never start from scratch; at best 'scratch' is something we may hope to work back to rather than begin from. But if Part I is historical it is necessary to add that no exhaustive history of the theory of universals will be found in it. I have merely selected certain theories which seemed worth thinking about, and worth thinking about even when they were erroneous. Part I is a sort of anthology from the history of philosophy with a view to the requirements of Part II. Or it might be likened to a predella. Painters of altar-pieces at one time used to paint under the centre picture a series of smaller pictures, usually illustrating the theme of the centre picture, and Part I of this book may be regarded as a predella to Part II.

PART I

I

PORPHYRY'S PROBLEM

1. If it is true that genius lies in posing problems as much as in solving them, then the title cannot fairly be withheld from Porphyry, the third-century disciple of Plotinus. He wrote a slim introduction (the *Isagoge*) to Aristotle's *Categories*. In the opening paragraph he says that he proposes to discuss what the Ancients taught on the predicables and the categories, but that he purposely avoids some of the deeper problems involved.

For the present [he remarks][1] I shall not discuss the question whether genera and species really exist (ὑφέστηκεν) or are in bare notions only (ἐν μόναις ψιλαῖς ἐπινοίαις); and if they exist whether they are corporeal things, or incorporeal; and whether they are separated (χωριστά) or exist in things perceived by the senses and in relation to them (ἢ ἐν τοῖς αἰσθητοῖς καὶ περὶ ταῦτα ὑφεστῶτα). For these questions are profound and demand other and more acute examination.

These words of Porphyry provided the medieval philosopher with his text. Not that medieval thinkers were diligent students of Porphyry; in the early period few of them had any knowledge of the Greek language in which he wrote, and fewer still would have the interest to consult an author of the Neoplatonic school had his works been available (though, through Augustine, they were more influenced by this school than they realized). But two centuries after Porphyry's death the *Isagoge* was translated and commented upon by Boethius, a writer whom medieval thinkers appreciated and understood.[2] Boethius was the bridge between

[1] *Commentaria in Aristotelem Graeca* ed. A. Busse, iv. 1, ll. 8–13.

[2] It was also translated by Marius Victorinus, cf. de Wulf, *Hist. Med. Phil.*, 3rd English ed., London, 1935, i. 63; but it was Boethius who popularized the work. Boethius's latinized version of the above quotation runs thus: 'Mox, inquit, de generibus ac speciebus illud quidem, sive subsistunt sive in solis nudisque intellectibus posita sunt sive subsistentia corporalia sunt an incorporalia et utrum separata a sensibilibus an in sensibilibus posita et circa ea constantia, dicere recusabo. Altissimum enim est huiusmodi negotium et maioris egens inquisitionis.' *Corpus Scriptorum Ecclesiasticorum Latinorum*, xlviii. 159.

the classical and the medieval; he had that skill in exposition which enabled him to present the teaching of the Ancient World to later thinkers not as a compendium of dead theories but as living thought of immediate interest and significance. This skill is seen in his *In Isagogen Porphyrii Commenta.* He quotes the passage given above, agrees that only the highest intellects could do justice to the problem set out in it, but yet tentatively and very guardedly ventures to open the discussion. It was a discussion that medieval philosophers found much to their liking.

Porphyry was fortunate in his commentator; and yet the true worth of Boethius's commentary lies not so much in the fact that it perpetuated the name of Porphyry but rather that it presented some part of the Aristotelian logic to the medieval world. After the Dark Ages the libraries of the early schools were woefully empty. The *Categories* and the *De Interpretatione* of Aristotle, a fragment of the *Timaeus* of Plato, scattered references in the works of the Fathers to Pythagorean, Epicurean, and Stoic philosophers—these provided the scanty fare of ninth, tenth, and eleventh century philosophers. There are grounds for believing that Boethius had translated the remaining books of Aristotle's *Organon* and possibly the *Physics*, *Metaphysics*, and *De Anima*, but these translations were unknown in these centuries. A commentary by Themistius on the *Posterior Analytics* seems to have been in circulation but not the text itself. Thus few of the riches of the Ancient World were available to the early medieval thinkers. In this situation Porphyry's question, asked in an off-hand incidental fashion, became of primary importance. For it brought the medieval world face to face with the central problem of Greek thought, not merely of its logic but also of its metaphysics. Boethius perceived its importance and devoted many pages of his commentary to this one sentence of Porphyry's. The medieval world was stirred and fascinated; discussion of the universal became the supreme and absorbing interest.

2. Since Porphyry's question was so influential it is necessary

to examine it carefully. Is it a correct statement of the problem of universals? There are critics who say that Porphyry posed the problem wrongly, and that as a consequence the medieval philosophers were led astray. To what extent is the criticism true?

The reader will not have failed to note that the word 'universals' does not enter into Porphyry's question. He speaks of genera and species; for instance, to give Porphyry's own instances, animal and man. These are universals in the sense that 'animal' is the name not of one but of many. They are substantival-universals or, more simply, thing-universals. But they are not the only universals. If I use the word 'blue' it also signifies not one but many. Yet it does not signify things; it signifies a quality possessed by things. Now, though Porphyry does not mention these in posing his problem they are certainly quite as important as thing-universals and some would say that they are more important being more primitive. For it is only because men have qualities in common, it is said, that we do group them together to frame the universal man. We need not discuss this point now but there seems to be no justification for omitting qualities. Moreover, if qualities are universals so are relations, for instance, being inside of and being to the right of. Most people today when discussing universals think of qualities and relations. It is strange to find Porphyry posing the problem in terms of thing-universals only.

If we are to expound Porphyry fairly, however, we must add that more seems to be implied in this sentence than is stated. He talks of species and genera only, but he appears to have in mind all the predicables which he mentions in the previous sentences. He does not, I believe, talk of universals as such anywhere in the *Isagoge*, but he makes it abundantly clear that just as the names of genera and species signify many and not one, so also do the names of differences, properties, and accidents. Referring to genera and species only, he none the less appears to include these other predicables as well. Boethius, it is interesting to note, assumes that this is the case; in discussing the passage he speaks of 'genera and species and the others' (*genera et species ceteraque*) where the 'others' are obviously differences, properties, and accidents.[1] Medieval philosophers usually followed Boethius in this matter, and in doing so it would not appear that they were falsely interpreting Porphyry.

Yet we should not lose sight of the fact that there is a difference between discussing the problem of universals with things predominantly in mind and discussing it with qualities predominantly in mind. Certainly if one substitutes the word 'qualities' for 'genera' and 'species' in Porphry's question it becomes a somewhat different question. It is not without significance for medieval speculation that Porphyry should talk of genera and species alone. It is said that he did so because he tended to think of the universal itself as a thing. He was a Neoplatonist. For the Neoplatonist the problem of universals was the problem of Forms. These eternal Forms or Ideas were more substantival than adjectival; the exemplars Bed, Table, even Beauty and Justice, were things rather than qualities. A Platonist discussing universals would be happier speaking of genera and species than of the accidents.

Hence Porphyry's bias and hence the tendency amongst the early Scholastics to discuss universals as if they were discussing things. Such criticism does not seem unfair, though too much should not be made of it. That Porphyry talks only of genera and species shows his bias, and this bias prevented him from presenting the problem fully. If he had stressed qualities and relations as he stressed genera and species the problem of universals would have appeared in a different light. All the same he does seem to have included the other predicables by implication. There is nothing to prevent the reader adding *et cetera* to genera and species if he so wishes, as Boethius did.

3. A deeper and more damaging criticism can be made of Porphyry. His book is an introduction to the *Categories*. Did he properly understand Aristotle? Would he have stated the problem of universals in different terms if he had understood Aristotle better? The charge is made that he completely failed

[1] *Corpus Scriptorum Ecclesiastuorum Latinorum*, xlviii. 163 and *passim*.

to understand him and so failed to hand forward the problem of universals as Aristotle left it. In this section I shall attempt to defend Porphyry on one point, for it is time that a word was said in his favour; none the less the main gravamen of this charge will remain.

To deal first with the point where he has, in my opinion, been unjustly treated, it is now the common practice to condemn Porphyry for including the species in the list of predicables, and some of the critics have been very scornful indeed at his expense. It is perfectly true that Porphyry lists the species with the predicables and that Aristotle in the *Topics* does not do so, but it is not difficult to defend the view that in doing this Porphyry is not misinterpreting Aristotle in any important particular. For Aristotle, it can be argued, meant the species to be grouped along with the genus, and when he says that the genus is a predicable he includes the species by implication. Porphyry simply makes the implication clear.

In *Topics*, i. 4–5 Aristotle makes a four-fold division of predicables according as such predicables are (*a*) coextensive with the subject or not, and (*b*) essential to it or not. Predicables listed as definitions are coextensive and essential; those listed as properties are coextensive but non-essential;[1] those as genera non-coextensive and essential; and finally those as accidents are non-coextensive and non-essential. Now from this point of view species and genus are all one; they both express a part of the essential nature of the subject, a part but not the whole. They are thus essential but non-coextensive. For the same reason the differentia is not distinguished from the genus in this passage, though Aristotle recognizes the difference between them elsewhere. There was thus no need for Aristotle to distinguish between genus and species at this point in his argument.[2] A further point to be noted is that, except in two cases, whatever is a species is at the same time a genus and whatever is a genus is a species. This is a matter which Porphyry in the *Isagoge* is at

[1] 'A "property" is a predicate which does not indicate the essence of a thing, but yet belongs to that thing alone.' *Topics*, i. 5, 102^{a}17–18.

[2] Later in the *Topics* he does discuss the relation between them, cf. iv. 4 (125^{a}5–^{b}14).

pains to emphasize. To give his example, 'body is a species of substance, but a genus of animated body'. The two exceptions are the highest genera (*summa genera*) which are not species, and the lowest species (*infimae species*) which are not genera. But with these exceptions what goes for the genus goes for the species as well. This is certainly the case when we consider their use as predicates. They then state a part of the essential nature of the subject. Consequently, when Aristotle spoke of genus in this passage he included species by implication, and Porphyry was not mistaken in saying that species as well as genera were predicables.

This was the main reason why Aristotle did not mention species, but there is an additional reason. In the *Topics* he is assuming that species are the subjects to which the predicates are applied. He is thinking there of dialectical reasoning such as the Sophists delighted in, and the subjects of their discussion were universals, species rather than individuals. In the same way the subjects of the scientific statements which Aristotle analysed in his *Posterior Analytics* were universal. The consequence was that species were assumed by Aristotle in the *Topics* to be subjects and were accordingly not included in a classification of predicates. But this should not be taken to mean that they are inevitably subjects and cannot be predicates. On the contrary, they frequently are predicates and in that case what would be said about them from the point of view of their relation to the subject is the same as is said of the genera.

If it were the case, as some of the critics say, that the species is always subject and can never be predicate, Porphyry would have erred radically in speaking of it as a predicable. But the error surely is the critic's. For when Aristotle does mention the species in works other than the *Topics*, as he often does, there is no suggestion but that they can figure as either subjects or predicates. This in itself should have given the critics pause. Consider the case of the *Categories* upon which Porphyry's exegesis is based. There is admittedly some doubt whether this book was written by Aristotle himself or by one of his pupils. If the latter it is clear from Aristotle's other works that the pupil is but echo-s rooted upon the apprehension of 'the universal attributes e species' possessed by individuals, and the sciences which with the universal are possible only because of this appre- nsion. The question, however, arises how the individuals do fact share these common attributes, and there is no satisfactory nswer in Aristotle. Is the quality one and the same in many ndividuals? Or do the qualities in different individuals resemble one another? The answer is not clear. Indeed in the *Categories* (1^{a}27) the author seems to be saying that the quality is as particular as the individual itself, so that just as we speak of primary and secondary substances so we ought to speak of primary and secondary qualities.[1] In such a case the primary quality could not be a predicate; the particular white, as is said in this passage, is 'never predicable of anything'. However, this is not Aristotle's usual position (and there is the further doubt whether Aristotle himself wrote the *Categories*). Nowhere else in Aristotle's work is the doctrine put forward. On the other hand the assertion of the uniqueness of the individual is part of Aristotle's permanent teaching. The individual, that which is, cannot be repeated, and cannot be common to many. Consequently that which is universal and is common to many cannot *be* in the sense in which the individual is. Now Porphyry misses this central point in Aristotle's teaching, and still asks whether the universal exists, without making it clear that it could not possibly exist in the sense in which an individual exists. He poses the problem of universals, we might almost say, as if Aristotle had never been—and this in a book expounding Aristotle's doctrines.

4. A somewhat different explanation of Porphyry's failure to understand Aristotle has been given recently.[2] Porphyry, it is

[1] This is a doctrine which we find held by certain modern thinkers, for instance, Reid, Cook Wilson, and Stout, cf. below p. 160 and J. R. Jones, 'Are the Qualities of Particular Things Universal or Particular?' *Philosophical Review*, March 1949, pp. 152 ff.

[2] By Mr. Ernest A. Moody and others. Compare E. A. Moody, *The Logic of William of Ockham* (1935), an interesting study of Ockham which throws considerable light on medieval thought in general. It seems to me, however, that Aristotle's logic is presented in this book in too Ockhamist a fashion. Moreover, I cannot see

ing his master when he asserts that species may be predicates. In the first page of the *Categories* the author remarks that the species *man* is predicable of the individual man, and he repeats the same point on the second page. A little later he remarks: 'It is true that inasmuch as primary substance is not predicable of anything, it can never form the predicate of any proposition. But of secondary substances, the species is predicated of the individual, the genus both of the species and of the individual.'[1] In view of these quite explicit statements does it any longer make sense to say that Porphyry completely misinterpreted Aristotle when he included species as a fifth predicable?

Yet, when this has been said in Porphyry's favour, the criticism still remains true, I believe, that he failed to grasp the whole of Aristotle's teaching about universals; more, that he missed the most essential point. That point is most clearly made in the *Metaphysics*, but it is also referred to in the *Categories*, the book which Porphyry was expounding, so that he has no excuse for not examining it. I refer to the distinction between primary and secondary substances and to the consequences of this doctrine for Aristotle's theory of universals. The distinction is mentioned in the passage I have just quoted from the *Categories*, and was made clear earlier in that work.

> Substance [he there says][2] in the truest and primary and most definite sense of the word, is that which is neither predicable of a subject nor present in a subject; for instance, the individual man or horse. But in a secondary sense those things are called substances within which, as species, the primary substances are included. . . . For instance, the individual man is included in the species *man*.

That is to say, the universal according to Aristotle is that which is common to many objects. It may be predicated of any of these objects; it may also be a subject since something may be said of it; but what it cannot be is to be a unique, individual thing. This is obvious since the universal is that which is common to many. It follows from this that we can never state fully what

[1] 3^{a}35–37.

[2] 2^{a}11–13, as translated in the Oxford edition. The reader may prefer to translate οὐσία as 'being' rather than 'substance' and to speak of primary and secondary being.

an individual is in terms of universals. The unique is not analysable into universals; and since we think in terms of universals the true individual eludes thought. This true individual is what Aristotle means by a primary substance. But it is also the case that we manage to speak and think about such individuals or substances so that the word 'substance' must have a secondary sense, namely, substance as object of thought. Hence the distinction between primary and secondary substance. The *Metaphysics* puts the point in this way;[1]

It seems impossible that any universal term should be the name of a substance. For, first, the substance of each thing is that which is peculiar to it, that which does not belong to anything else; but the universal is common, since that is called universal which naturally belongs to more than one thing. . . . Further, substance means that which is not predicable of a subject, but the universal is predicable of some subject always. . . . It is plain that no universal attribute is a substance, and this is plain also from the fact that no common predicate indicates a *this* but rather a *such* [not a τόδε τι but a τοιόνδε].[2]

Now if Porphyry had reflected upon this distinction between primary and secondary substance, and if he had realized its implications for the Aristotelian logic he was trying to expound, it is more than likely that he would not have included one of the alternatives present in his famous sentence, unless to point out that the alternative was from the first impossible. I refer to the alternative that the universal is a thing, whether corporeal or incorporeal. The universal, for Aristotle, could not exist as a thing, a primary substance, existed, and it could not exist

[1] 1038^{b}–1039.

[2] The implications of this doctrine for Aristotle's logic should be noted. It is true that he speaks, for instance, as if the two statements 'Man is an animal' and 'Swans are white' are of the same logical form, whereas in fact they are obviously different since in the first sentence we are saying that a certain class is contained in another class, and in the second that all the members of a class have a certain quality. Such criticism is fair, but it is then doubly important to emphasize the present point. Aristotle did at least realize that the statement 'Callias is a man', where 'Callias' is the name of an individual man, is a very different one from 'Man is an animal', or again from 'Swans are white'. Callias is the name of a primary substance and so the subject in the first sentence cannot be predicate, which is not the case with 'Man' or 'Swans'. The schools did Aristotle a great disservice when they linked the 'singular judgement' with the 'universal judgement' for greater convenience.

as the Platonic Forms, such as Bed,
supposed to exist.[1] For the Aristotelia
natives were ruled out from the beginn
metaphysics. And it would certainly have
ence to medieval thought if Porphyry had u
and, as a consequence, stated his problem
the end of the twelfth century the philosopher
discussion almost entirely to the one theme, wh
versal was a *thing*. But Aristotle had already an
question and it was unfortunate that Porphyry failed

It might appear from this account of the distinction
primary and secondary substances in Aristotle's philosoph
what is thought is completely different from what is. We t
the universal, that is, the secondary substance, whereas
individual, the primary substance, which alone exists, elude
thought. It might be supposed to follow from this that in thinking we are closed up within a thought-world wholly other than the real world. This, however, is not Aristotle's view, for he holds that though real individuals elude our thought, we do none the less think real qualities as real as the individuals themselves, and these qualities are shared in common by a number of individuals. It is because individuals have such common qualities that we can group and classify them and speak of them as members of species and genera. For instance, in the *De Partibus Animalium* Aristotle tells us:

The individuals comprised within a species, such as Socrates and Coriscus, are the real existences; but inasmuch as these individuals possess one common specific form, it will suffice to state the universal attributes of the species, that is, the attributes common to all its individuals, once for all, as otherwise there will be endless reiteration. [$644^{a}23$–27]

The Aristotelian doctrine of the 'common specific form' which gives the universal species and genus a real reference, in spite of the remoteness from thought of the real individual,

[1] Cf. *Metaph.* $1078^{b}30$–32: 'Socrates did not make the universals or the definitions exist apart (χωριστά); his successors, however, gave them separate existence and this was the kind of thing they called *Ideas*.' Also $1071^{a}19$ ff., where Aristotle tells us that the universals do not exist and that there is no universal man.

said, failed to realize that the problem of universals is primarily a logical problem rather than a metaphysical one, and 'that the word "universal" is not a metaphysical term but only a logical term'.[1] The outcome of Aristotle's philosophy, on this view, is that the universals are λεγόμενα rather than ὄντα and the consideration of their nature should be carried on at the logical level. Porphyry sets out the problem as a metaphysical one, because of his Platonism. He was too metaphysical. Medieval thought as a consequence lost itself in arid speculation about reifications of abstractions and was bogged in false problems. In a thousand years after Porphyry there was no advance beyond Aristotle in the understanding of universals; there was indeed no regaining of the ground which Porphyry had lost.

There is a good deal to be said for this view, nevertheless it needs modifying and is not correct as it stands. To begin with, any reader who sets out with the notion that Porphyry was too metaphysical and then turns for the first time to the *Isagoge* is likely to be considerably surprised by what he finds there, for anything less metaphysical it would be difficult to imagine. The charge might well be made that Porphyry in his concern for logic, or, indeed, for linguistics, that is, for words and their use in sentences, does not pay sufficient attention to the fundamental ontological considerations which go some way at least towards explaining our successful use of words. Porphyry, the reader might feel, is too little metaphysical, and if the schools are arid the aridity is to be assigned to Porphyry's lack of metaphysics rather than to too much metaphysics. The treatment of universals by the schools, on this view, is superficial, just because, as the result of Porphyry's influence, it is too logical. It would be interesting in this connexion to know how many of his contemporaries would have agreed with Roger Bacon when he says: 'I speak of universals with respect to their true being, as a metaphysician must consider them, not merely with

that the author succeeds in explaining away the fact that Ockham himself, in a passage cited by Moody (p. 95), expressly includes species as a fifth predicable.

[1] Moody, ibid., p. 76, cf. p. 18.

respect to the childish doctrine of Porphyry and the consideration of logic.'[1]

It might, however, be answered that we are not discussing the *Isagoge* in general here but rather the sentence at the end of its first section. Porphyry there sets out the problem of universals in too metaphysical a fashion, whereas Aristotle had come to see it largely as a logical problem. Even this statement, however, would need modification. It is true that we can observe in Aristotle a tendency to consider universals as objects for thought and it is obvious that in his discussion of universals certain logical considerations are very relevant. At the same time the realist strand in Aristotle must not be forgotten. Though universals are not real *things* they are none the less *in re*, and their being such is not a matter for logic but for metaphysics.

The important question to be asked in this context is this one: Was Porphyry's failure a failure to understand the *logic* of Aristotle? Was it not rather a failure to understand the metaphysical presuppositions of that logic? If the argument of the previous section is valid, the point which Porphyry missed in Aristotle is the distinction between primary and secondary substances. That distinction surely rests upon Aristotle's view of the nature of existence, and is a metaphysical issue. In other words what was wrong with Porphyry from Aristotle's point of view was not that he was too metaphysical but that his metaphysics was faulty. It was clear from the way in which he posed the problem of universals that he was thinking in terms of the Platonic metaphysics. But this is not the only metaphysics; it would be certainly erroneous to suppose that we touch metaphysical matters only when discussing the eternal Forms and the transcendent. Our question is equally metaphysical when we ask: how does it happen that though real things are individuals we can yet think universals, and our thought be about those individuals? Logic may help us to answer this question and so may psychology. But the final problem we have to face is epistemological and metaphysical, a problem in ontology.

[1] *Opus Majus*, I. ii. 6, cf. McKeon's *Selections from Mediaeval Philosophers*, London, 1930, ii. 35.

Thus the line of criticism which suggests that Porphyry's failure to state the problem of universals properly was due to his being too metaphysical and not sufficiently logical seems to me erroneous. Porphyry's failure was a failure to grasp Aristotle's metaphysics. On this question of universals Aristotle's own metaphysical teaching was an advance on Plato's and the charge that can be made against Porphyry is that he ignored this advance in setting forward his problem. He had the genius to pose a problem, but not the genius to understand Aristotle's doctrine and to develop it.

5. If this appraisal of Porphyry is correct it helps us to understand why, in spite of centuries of concentration upon the problem of universals, the Scholastics made so little advance on Aristotle. We may agree with Mr. Moody that certain aspects of the problem already grasped by Aristotle remained hidden from the earlier medieval philosophers and indeed were not fully understood until the end of the Scholastic period proper in the fourteenth century.

When the Western world in the ninth and tenth centuries began to recover from the stagnation of the centuries immediately preceding, the main influences were Augustinian and the first solutions of the problem set by Porphyry were markedly realist. John Scotus Erigena, the most considerable thinker of this period, while not as extreme a realist as some of his contemporaries, none the less accepted the view that the order from Being through Genera and Species to individual things was first a real order and only secondly one in thought. The universals existed first and the particulars were derived from them. A reaction came with Roscelin in the eleventh century though, since we have to depend upon his opponents for an account of his doctrine, it is not certain how far this reaction went. Anselm of Canterbury tells us that Roscelin and his school taught that 'universals were mere vocal utterances' (*flatus vocis*), that is to say, presumably, that they identified the universal with thc spoken general word. It seems clear that they emphatically rejected the Platonic realism of the earlier schools. Abelard who was for some time Roscelin's pupil followed him in his rejection of the earlier realism. Abelard reasserts Aristotle's definition: a universal is that which can be predicated of many individuals taken one by one. But if it is such it follows, says Abelard, that it cannot be a thing, since a thing is not predicable of many. Man as such, the specific man, does not exist. It cannot be true that there exists a universal essence, the same for all members of a species or a genus, differences between individual members being due to accidental additions over and above the common essence. If this essence exists as a complete thing in the man Plato, it cannot also be present in Socrates; on the other hand, if it is only partly present in both then neither, on this theory, is a whole man. Again, if the essence is the same in, for instance, all members of the genus, living being, then, *essentially*, Socrates and the ass are the same. But no theory which leads to such absurdities can be true. Thus far Abelard agrees with Roscelin, but he also criticizes Roscelin. If it is false to think of the universal as a thing it is equally false to think of it as a mere sound. (After all a sound itself is a concrete thing.) A name is more than a sound, it is a significant sound. *Nomen est vox significativa*. The general word is a word in a sentence, a term, usually the predicate term, of a proposition. But what exactly does it signify? The word 'man' does not signify man-ness as a thing, for we are agreed that this is false realism. It signifies, Abelard tries to say, a certain order or state (*status*), being man; but here Abelard's theory becomes so obscure that it is impossible to understand his answer. On the critical side Abelard is excellent, but when he himself attempts to give a positive theory he fails to do so.[1]

By the thirteenth century many more of the texts of the Ancient World, particularly of Aristotle, had become available

[1] Cf. McKeon's *Selections from Mediaeval Philosophers*, i. 208–58. In these pages Abelard discusses universals with much acuteness until we come to the obscure passage (pp. 235–7) referred to above. Following this passage there are some interesting psychological considerations and an attempt finally to answer Porphyry, but the answer suffers from the failure to explain what the universal term signifies. Mr. M. H. Carré on p. 58 of his useful study *Realists and Nominalists* (1946) draws our attention to the hint—it is scarcely more—given by Abelard (pp. 249–50) that universals must be involved in the conception even of an individual.

to philosophers, and they were not as confined in their thinking as were the earlier Scholastics. The problem of universals became one of many problems. Abelard's criticisms of the Augustinian realism were accepted fairly generally and there is little advance, for instance, in Albertus Magnus, the leading thinker of the middle thirteenth century and the teacher of Aquinas. His chief service was expository; he expounded clearly the various doctrines. Universals, he says, are regarded as *ante rem*, as 'formative causes' in the divine mind; or, again, as *in materia*; or, finally, as separated from things by intellectual abstraction. In certain senses Albertus was prepared to accept all three solutions. So also was Aquinas. For he believed that universals existed as Ideas in the mind of God and that pure intelligences, such as angels, were privileged to know these Ideas directly. But the human mind was not in this fortunate position. Man possesses intelligence but intelligence of the lowest order, co-operating with body. Man's experience begins with the sensible. Aquinas asserts as fundamental the empiricist doctrine: *Principium nostrae cognitionis est a sensu.* Now in the world revealed to the senses there are no existing things which are themselves universals. Abelard was justified in his condemnation of such a view. There exist individual, material objects only. None the less, Aquinas added, these individual things are such that the intellect of man when it is active (*intellectus agens*) can abstract the intelligible forms of material things from the phantasms gained in sense-experience. These 'quiddities' thus abstracted are the universals of human experience. The abstracting itself is more than mere selection, it is also the illuminating of the form, and that is why the active intellect, as opposed to the passive, alone can abstract the forms. It follows that the universal, in the case of human knowledge, is a product of human intelligence, but at the same time it is grounded on sense-experience.[1]

Thus the tendency in the thirteenth century was towards a

[1] Aquinas's theory of universals is found in the first part of the *Summa Theologica*, particularly in Questions 75 ff., as part of the general discussion of human knowledge.

modified realism with some suggestions of conceptualism, although Augustinian realism was still advocated by some philosophers, for instance, Bonaventura and his pupil Matthew of Aquasparta and, in a different way, by Duns Scotus. But I need not here expound the theories of these and other medieval thinkers; for my purpose is only to show, and that very briefly, how Porphyry's problem was handled in medieval times. Yet a word should be said about the fourteenth-century thinker William of Ockham, whose teaching was of very great significance. The universal, he holds, cannot be a real thing. The individual alone exists and the universal is essentially not an individual. It is true that the universal word 'man' exists as a token on paper, but in that sense it exists as an individual and it itself is not a universal. In the same way the concept *man* has psychological reality, yet as such it also is not a universal. Moreover, there may be Man as an exemplar in God's mind, but the existence of such a universal *ante rem*, if it does exist, is entirely irrelevant in the attempt to understand human knowledge, and this is what we do wish to understand. Once firmly grasp the principle that a universal cannot be a thing, then Platonic and Augustinian realism at once fail. Moreover, the universal cannot even be said to be part of a thing, for in that case it would be concrete, part of an individual, and so, again could not be universal. What, then, is the universal according to Ockham? We may begin by thinking of it as the word—not the token word, for instance, the word 'man' as it is here printed, but the word as a sign for many real individuals. We can begin with the word as a sign but cannot remain with it, for a word is a conventional sign and a conventional sign is only significant to an intelligence possessing a concept by which the significance of the word is established. In other words, as well as a conventional sign there is also a natural sign or the concept. The universal is the concept and has no being apart from the act of conceiving. A distinction must be made between two kinds of terms. The words 'man' and 'rose' signify things and may be called 'terms of first intention'. But there are, too, terms signifying terms themselves and these are 'terms of second intention'.

The terms of the natural sciences, for instance, are terms of first intention, those of logic are terms of second intention. *Universal* is a term of second intention in Ockham's opinion. A fruitful source of error is to regard it as a term of first intention, and so confound sign and thing signified.

Ockham, in a work entitled *Expositio Aurea Super Artem Veterem*, comments on Porphyry's *Isagoge* and it will be interesting to see what answer the last of the great medieval thinkers gives to Porphyry's problem. I quote from Ockham:[1]

> From what has been said above the solution of [Porphyry's three] questions is clear. As to the first question it must be held that genera and species are not substances outside the mind but are in the intellect in the sense that they exist only as intentions or concepts (*intentiones vel conceptus*) formed by the intellect and presenting the being of things and signifying them. They are not these things themselves, for the sign is not the thing signified. Nor are they parts of the things any more than the word is part of what it signifies. . . . Hence too the solution of the second question; for (not to speak of words) it must be held that genera and species and all such universals are not corporeal since they exist only in the mind, in which there is nothing corporeal. Finally the solution of the third question is plain, for universals are not in sensible things, neither in the whole of sensible things nor in parts of them.

[1] *Exp. Aur.* i. 9r. The original is cited by Moody, *Logic of William of Ockham*, p. 94.

II

THE CHARACTER OF LOCKE'S CONCEPTUALISM

6. The three centuries between Ockham and Locke witnessed the rise of the 'New Philosophy' with its stress on the observation of the particular and its revolt against the over-academic formalism and intellectualism of the schools. Its influence pervaded Western European thought. To be modern in the seventeenth century was to avoid, or at least to make a show of avoiding, abstract speculation. Literary men, such as Molière, poked fun at the jargon of the university-trained professional classes. The schools, it was felt, were out of touch with the real; concentration on abstractions and endless argument about them led nowhere; the new scientists were intent on being observers of nature in the concrete. And it was not merely professed empiricists who rebelled against the abstract; the revolt was general. Thus Malebranche, who stressed the Platonic and Augustinian elements in Cartesianism, nevertheless remarks in a passage characteristic of him and of the thought of his period:

> Just as blind men are only able to speak in general about colours, in a manner that is possibly entertaining but nevertheless ridiculous, having no distinct ideas of them . . . so those philosophers who possess only general ideas and ideas of logic, such as act, power, being, cause, principle, form, quality and the like, cannot argue successfully about the facts of nature. It is essential that they should avail themselves of distinct and particular ideas.[1]

The reasonings of the learned in the schools might possibly be entertaining and amusing but they were barren; the hope and the promise lay with the scientists observing nature in field and laboratory. It was in gaining particular ideas that we advanced knowledge; the universal belonged to the abstract and the effete.

It is consequently not at all surprising to find that the denial

[1] *Recherche de la Vérité*, III. iii. 9; *Oeuvres*, Genoude et Lourdoueix, p. 119.

of the reality of the universal was common amongst the leading thinkers of this period. The spirit of the age favoured conceptualism. It has frequently been pointed out that even in the thought of Descartes a strong conceptualist current is to be found. In some of the things he says, it is true, Descartes is almost a Platonist. His thought about universals has several facets. None the less the language of the *Principles of Philosophy*, for instance, is markedly conceptualist. 'Number,' he says,[1] 'when we consider it abstractly or generally and not in created things is but a mode of thinking; and the same is true of all that which is named universals.' The universal, that is to say, is not *in re*; it is a mode of thinking, something owing its existence to thinking and having no existence apart from it. And when in the next section he goes on to explain the origin of the universal it is the conceptualist explanation which he favours. 'Universals arise solely from the fact that we avail ourselves of one and the same idea in order to think of all individual things which have a certain similitude (*quae inter se similia sunt*); and when we comprehend under the same name all the objects represented by this idea, that name is universal.' A universal or general name, that is to say, stands for a group of similiar objects represented in the mind by one and the same idea. It does not stand for a real universal which the intellect apprehends.[2]

Conceptualism comes easily to the writers of this period and Descartes himself is no exception. As might be expected, too, there are suggestions of nominalism. A point of nomenclature

[1] i. 58.

[2] It is impossible to deny the conceptualist and empiricist side of the Cartesian teaching. One is sometimes surprised to find how characteristically empiricist Descartes can be. I do not refer merely to his emphasis on the need for observation and experiment but consider, for instance, his account of abstraction. Writing to Regius (A. and T. iii, p. 66) he remarks that the idea of which we avail ourselves, in order to think the individual things which resemble one another, is itself a particular or singular idea, *ideam ex se ipsa singularem ad multa refert*. Again, he makes the point, on more than one occasion, that abstracting is a very difficult procedure, as when, for instance, we try to abstract the shape in this coloured patch before us. The separation, Descartes thinks, is never carried out with entire success. The abstracted shape is confused, very vaguely the colour is still there. Compare the passage added in the French edition to *Principles*, i. 62. Compare also O. Hamelin, *Le Système de Descartes*, 2nd edition, Paris, 1921, p. 179, and J. Laporte, *Le Rationalisme de Descartes*, Paris, 1945, pp. 94–95.

arises which it would be well to clear up at once. The term 'nominalist' was frequently used in this period to describe a position that was in effect conceptualist. The term seems to have come into general use in the late fourteenth and fifteenth centuries. A realist was a person who gave an affirmative answer to Porphyry's question whether genera and species really existed outside the mind. Those who, for one reason or another, gave a negative answer to the question were all dubbed 'nominalist'. Yet most of them were in fact conceptualist.[1] Thus Ockham and his school were certainly described in the fifteenth and sixteenth centuries as nominalists in spite of the fact that the assertion of the concept, as we have seen, was the heart of Ockham's theory of universals. The distinction between conceptualist and nominalist must lie finally in this, that the former asserts the existence of a concept along with the name, whereas the latter denies the need for the concept and holds that the universal is merely the name. Undoubtedly much confusion was caused by the failure to distinguish between conceptualists and nominalists. Roscelin, perhaps, may have been a nominalist. If Anselm describes his theory correctly he certainly was so, but Anselm's account may have misrepresented his position.

It is but one step, however, from conceptualism to nominalism and, whatever be said of the Scholastics, nominalism in its true sense is certainly to be found in the thought of the seventeenth century. It is seen in its most explicit form, perhaps, in Thomas Hobbes. For instance, the following passages are authentically nominalist, as distinguished from both realism and conceptualism. 'The word *universal* is never the name of any thing existent in nature, nor of any idea or phantasm formed in the mind, but always the name of some word or name.'[2] Again, in the *Leviathan*[3] he remarks: 'There being nothing in the world universal but names, for the things named are every one of them individual and singular.' It might be argued that what Hobbes was attacking in the first quotation was imagism rather than

[1] De Wulf, *History of Mediaeval Philosophy*, pp. 138–9, goes so far as to say that there is no nominalism in medieval thought but only conceptualism.

[2] *Elements of Philosophy*, ed. Molesworth, London, 1839, i. 20.

[3] I. iv.

conceptualism, the notion that there must be an image before us whenever we universalize, and that he meant by the term 'idea or phantom' merely the image, and so does not really face the question whether a concept is necessary in universalizing. Yet it is more likely that he would also have included what we now call 'concept' under the term 'idea' in this context. In intention, it seems clear, Hobbes was a nominalist in the narrow sense of the term. Whether he was consistently a nominalist is another matter, for, in the same chapter of the *Leviathan*, to look no farther, what he says about the universal triangle seems hardly consonant with strict nominalism.

7. Thus, if we take the leading thinkers of this period, it appears true to say that in their case the conceptualist is the prevailing theory of universals, with even a suggestion of nominalism in the narrow sense, and we now understand how the spirit of the age lent itself to such views. Locke is consequently no isolated figure in his advocacy of conceptualism. He is of special significance, however, for two reasons. First, he is more whole-hearted in his conceptualism than several of his immediate predecessors and contemporaries—primarily, no doubt, because this theory conforms so well with the rest of his philosophy. In this latter respect, he differs, for instance, from Descartes, whose conceptualism, it may be argued, conflicts with certain elements in his rationalism. In the second place, Locke provides us with a thoroughgoing analysis of conceptualism and submits the theory to a rigorous examination. Moreover, the consequences of the theory are made clearer in the *Essay* than in any other work of the period. Thus Locke's treatment of the subject is of particular importance to us.

Empiricism is primarily a doctrine about our knowledge of the external world. When the empiricists took over the old adage *Nihil est in intellectu quod non prius fuerit in sensu* they were thinking of the external world and the *nisi intellectus ipse* of the critics was accordingly irrelevant. The heart of empiricism is the doctrine that we have no approach to the external world except through the senses. It was consequently very natural for empiricists to reject the realist theory of universals, particularly in the form that we know by pure intellect universal qualities of the real external world. But more than this, it was natural for them also to think that as they moved away from the sensibly given so they moved away from reality. Hobbes's strong phrase in this connexion reveals the general tendency; images for him were 'decaying' sensations, and concepts, apparently, were still more 'decayed'. On such a theory the closer one remained to the original sensation the better. Consequently the universal, which was supposed to be removed from the real, was suspect from the start, and the fact that it was thought to be the product of abstraction did not advance it in philosophical favour. It is thus possible to understand the tendency amongst empiricists to denigrate the general idea. Berkeley at one stage in his development goes to the extreme of holding that it would be best if we could avoid generalizing altogether. Locke never adopts this extreme position. Yet in spite of Berkeley's attack upon him in the introductory sections of the *Principles*, which might suggest that the two philosophers were poles apart in their teaching about universals, the fact is that the tendencies made explicit in Berkeley were already present in Locke. Locke, however, was conscious of certain other considerations which made it imperative for him to continue to affirm the necessity for general ideas and the inevitability of the universal.

The matter is discussed in the opening chapters of Book III of the *Essay*. Locke there argues that in spite of the fact that the use of general words is the cause of many errors we none the less find it essential to use such words. For, in the first place, it would be quite impossible for us to remember each particular thing experienced in its particularity, it would be impossible 'to frame and retain distinct ideas of all particular things we meet with'. Secondly, without general words the communication of thought would be far more difficult than it is and frequently impossible; in particular, it would be impossible to convey information by description. We should have to speak (if we could) in terms of proper names only, and if the hearer did not know what things were signified by our proper names we should be lost. Finally, generalizing is essential for the enlargement of our knowledge. Thinking in general terms helps to expand knowledge 'which though founded in particular things enlarges itself by general views'. If we learn a new truth about a whole class of objects, such knowledge is more valuable than is information about a particular object. Locke concludes that thinking would be almost impossible without generalizing, so would be the communication of our thoughts and our advance in knowledge. Consequently, though the material, in the case of our knowledge of the external world, is derived entirely from the senses, and though what we are given by the senses is particular, nevertheless, in Locke's view, we cannot remain with the particular but must pass forward to the universal.

8. But what precisely does Locke mean by a universal? We may begin by noting that in respect to species and genera he rejects both forms of the realist theory, both the Platonic and the Aristotelian. He will have nothing to do with the view that the universal exists separately as a Form. He dismisses it abruptly as obviously false.[1] At the outset of the discussion of universals he sets down a principle which at once rules out the Platonic theory. 'All things that exist are only particulars.'[2] He does not discuss this principle but introduces it as something that must be granted generally.[3] Had he reflected, however, he might have realized that there were elements in his thought which were not entirely consistent with this principle. For whilst he held that all knowledge of the external world is derived from sensation he also accepted the general view of scientists from Galileo onwards that the senses could deceive us. Why then should we not be deceived in supposing that the real consists of particulars? Why suppose that since things appear as particulars they really are particulars? Locke, however, remains convinced that in sense-perception we know the existence of tables and chairs, individual, particular things existing in reality. And so sure was he of

[1] In III. iii. 17. [2] III. iii. 6.

[3] Berkeley does the same: 'It is a universally received maxim that *every thing which exists is particular*' (First Dialogue: Luce and Jessop ed. ii. 192).

this that he took it as a fundamental principle that what existed in the external world was invariably a particular of this kind. Hence his conclusion that a universal could not possibly exist separated, as the Platonic Form is supposed to exist. Only particulars *exist*, no universal exists.

Thus far Locke's thought is in line with that of Aristotle, but he now proceeds to reject the Aristotelian theory, that is to say the traditional Aristotelian theory of his day, which Locke usually calls the 'Peripatetic' philosophy. According to this theory each species has its specific form, although the form does not exist separated. On the contrary, each object belonging to the species possesses this form as its essence, since it is shared in common by all objects pertaining to that species. For instance, there is the specific form of man which all men have in common, that real essence which makes them men rather than horses or apes. The universal man is this real essence common to all men.

Locke attacks this theory vigorously. He cites 'substantial forms' along with the 'soul of the world' of the Platonists as instances of the 'gibberish which, in the weakness of human understanding, serves so well to palliate men's ignorance and cover their errors'.[1] It is easy to prove that the Peripatetic theory is false, for but a little reflection will show that we do not know this real essence which is alleged to be common to all the members of a species. Locke brings forward two main arguments to prove this. First, if we knew the real essence in this sense we should, prior to experiencing it, have certain knowledge of what an object is and how it will behave; we could say of this piece of iron, for instance, before we examine it, that it must have such and such qualities and that it must behave in such and such a way. In fact, however, we cannot say this but have to wait upon experience. We possess, of course, a great deal of probable knowledge inductively established which enables us to say what the behaviour of the object is likely to be. But the very fact that this knowledge is probable only is itself proof that we do not know the real essence. If the real essence were revealed to us, 'scientifical' knowledge of the natural object,

[1] III. x. 14.

wholly certain and general, would be ours. But just because these essences, supposing them to exist, are hidden, our knowledge is probable only, until experience confirms it or fails to confirm it.

In the second place, if we knew the real essences we should know the precise boundaries of each species, we should have no difficulty with border-cases, individuals that is to say which do not appear to belong to one species but which fall in somewhere between two. Our troubles in classifying 'monsters and changelings' and border-cases of this kind, and the fact that we frequently force them arbitrarily, as we are well aware, into one species rather than another, show that in their case we do not discover the real essence allegedly common to all the members. Consider a species *S*; *a b c* are clearly members of it. But is *q* a member of it? We cannot be sure, it belongs more to *S* perhaps than to *T*. We decide it best to think of it as an individual pertaining to the species *S*. This is our predicament frequently in attempting to classify natural objects, and it shows that classifying does not consist merely in discovering those individual things which share one and the same real essence. It is not denied, of course, that classifications are suggested in the first instance by nature. Locke frequently makes the point that we set up our species and genera in accordance with the suggestions of experience. They 'have their foundation in the similitude of things'.[1] Nevertheless, they remain 'the workmanship of the understanding'. It is one thing to observe resemblances in objects and to classify accordingly, and quite another to discover a real essence common to all these objects and *thus* recognize them as instances of one and the same species. In the second case the species could not be regarded as the 'workmanship' of the mind, but rather as the mind's discovery. Yet this is a discovery, Locke holds, which never in fact occurs.

Locke would have us conclude, therefore, that we do not know the real essence allegedly common to each and every individual member of the species, and as the Peripatetic theory

[1] III. iii. 13.

of universals rests on the supposition that we do know this it must be false. Two comments may be made on this argument before we proceed to examine Locke's own account of universals.

In the first place, nowhere in the *Essay* does Locke discuss whether the real essences supposed to be common do in fact exist. He is convinced that we know no such essence, but are they there at all? He does not answer. The most interesting reference in his works is one in the controversy with Stillingfleet. Stillingfleet at one point in his argument had remarked that 'there must be a real essence in every individual of the same kind'. To this Locke replied, 'Yes, and I beg leave of your lordship to say, of a different kind too. For that alone is it which makes it to be what it is.'[1] Each individual, Locke seems to be saying, is essentially itself and not another. The real essence of an individual is what that individual is. This is a new account of the real essence, very different from the traditional account. But we should not take it too seriously since the passage is best viewed perhaps as an expression of impatience with the whole theory of real essences rather than as an attempt to set up a new theory. Locke was so dissatisfied with the Peripatetic theory that he does not bother to ask whether real essences do or do not exist.

In the second place it is important to note that Locke here denies the *In Re* theory in a limited context, namely, only as applying to species and genera. It does not follow from this that he would have denied the *In Re* theory in the sense, for instance, that a quality such as a shade of colour can be shared in common by two objects. This is a further position which Locke does not consider. He might possibly have accepted the theory in this sense,[2] but the matter is complicated by his representationalism. The secondary quality, in Locke's view, is not *in re*, if by *res* we mean the physical object, and so though the white of the first object appears to be identical with that of the second the white itself is not *in re* but 'in the mind'. For this reason it is difficult to group Locke with the supporters of the *In Re* theory

[1] *Works*, 4th ed., i. 399. [2] Particularly in the case of primary qualities.

even in respect of qualities which do appear to appertain to more than one object. Nevertheless, his explicit rejection of it refers only to the real essence alleged to be shared by all the members of a species. We do not know this essence and consequently, in this limited sense, the *In Re* theory is false.

9. Locke thus rejects what he took to be the Platonic and the Aristotelian theories of universals, that is to say, he rejects those two forms of the realist theory according to which the universal either exists separated or is the specific form or real essence of a species. Universals, he holds, are not discovered and are not in the world of particular existences, 'universality belongs not to things themselves which are all of them particular in existence'.[1] What kind of entities then (if we can call them 'entities') are they? In Locke's opinion they are creations of ours. 'It is plain by what has been said, that general and universal belong not to the real existence of things; but are the inventions and creatures of the understanding made by it for its own use, and concern only signs whether words or ideas.'[2] When dealing with universals, that is to say, we leave the realm of being, *τὰ ὄντα* and come to that of discourse, *τὰ λεγόμενα*. They 'concern' the signs of thinking, our language and our ideas. Locke it is clear, is reasserting the Ockhamist philosophy and his reference here to 'signs whether words or ideas' links him closely to that school.[3]

Now in this realm of discourse, what function does the universal play and what is its nature? The answer is to be found in Locke's doctrine of the nominal essence, a doctrine of great importance for him, since in it he finds his solution of the problem of universals. The nominal essence is contrasted with the real essence. We mistake the former for the latter, and that is why philosophers have assumed that we know the real essence when in fact we do not know it but merely think our

[1] III. iii. 11. [2] ibid.

[3] It would be interesting to trace the history and development of thought from Ockham to Locke, for we should then be tracing one of the sources of the theory that logic, and indeed philosophy, is primarily concerned with linguistical problems. It is noteworthy that Locke describes logic as the 'doctrine of signs' or *σημειωτική* (IV. xxi. 4).

nominal essence. But the nominal essence differs fundamentally from the real essence, for it is not discovered by the mind but made by it; it is not an essence in the real world but an essence in the world of discourse, something belonging to our ways of talking and thinking. At the same time it is not to be identified with the word. It is the concept for which the word stands. The term nominal essence should not mislead us into supposing that Locke is a nominalist; for him the general word always stands for a general idea.[1] In the case of the genus and species this general idea is the nominal essence. Thus the nominal essence must be distinguished both from the real essence and from the word.

10. We must next seek to understand how the nominal essence comes into being. It is a general idea, and to understand its origin we must understand how we generalize. This Locke considers in Book III. The account there grows and develops as he writes. It is fresh and alive; yet it is not always consistent with itself, since its guiding threads are many and they do not all lead in the same direction. I believe that at least three strands are to be found in his thought and I may discuss these briefly.

The first strand is the doctrine that what is actually before the mind when we are generalizing is a particular, but a particular used in a representative capacity. Such teaching is found, too, in Berkeley and Hume and was generally favoured by the empiricists. The reason is plain. They felt at home with particulars, for these were immediately given in sense-experience. But general ideas were more remote and mysterious. It would be useful and comforting if they too could be shown to be particular ideas, though, presumably, a very special kind of particular ideas. For instance, I take a particular triangle and let

[1] In the Stillingfleet Correspondence Locke states emphatically what it is clear he is assuming throughout. In the First Reply to Stillingfleet (*Works*, i. 369; 1801 ed. iv. 25): 'For he must think very oddly, who takes the general name of any idea to be the general idea itself; it is a mere mark or sign of it, without doubt, and nothing else.' Again, in the Second Reply (*Works*, i. 574: 1801 ed. iv. 430–1): 'You again accuse the way of ideas, to make a common nature no more than a common name. That, my Lord, is not my way, by ideas.'

it stand for all triangles. I still have a particular before me, but I use this particular to represent all other particulars of the same sort. In this way I bring into being a general idea of triangle.

The inadequacy of this acount of generalizing is patent. Even if it were the case that whenever I generalize what I have immediately before me is a particular—a very large assumption—the real problem of generalization would remain, namely, how the representative character of this particular is to be explained. It represents all particulars of the same sort. But how can a particular represent a sort? Locke saw the force of this question and he is more critical of this empiricist solution than is either Berkeley or Hume. It would be quite wrong to say, for instance, that this doctrine rules his thought in Book III. None the less it is a strand in his thought, and he is always anxious to emphasize the point that the general idea as occurring in thinking is a particular.

But there is a more important point here. What do we mean by a 'sort'? Locke explains that he uses this term instead of the more pedantic 'species' and 'genus' of the schools. A sort, he thinks, is suggested by experience but not discovered in it, and the difference is important for it means that the sort must be a fabrication of ours though suggested by experience. But how does the mind fabricate it? The answer will make clear the second strand in Locke's thought. Generalizing in the sense of fabricating sorts is the process of abstracting a core of qualities which we find to be common in many particulars and ignoring those which differ. Having seen many men I pick out rational behaviour, two-leggedness, ability to have sensations and so on, and frame an abstract idea of these common qualities. I omit tall, fair, wealthy, which vary from man to man. I thus 'make nothing new, but only leave out of the complex idea of Peter and James, Mary and Jane, that which is peculiar to each and retain only what is common to them all'.[1] The complex idea of man I thus gain is new in the sense that it did not exist before, but there is nothing new in its content. It consists of the

[1] III. iii. 7.

common qualities together with, in the case of the natural sort, one other ingredient, namely, the general notion of substance, with which Locke had notorious difficulties that need not be discussed here. The general idea of man is the idea of a substance having as qualities those which have been observed to be common to many men. Finally, we have to find a name for this general idea, either learning it from others, as is usually the case, or inventing one ourselves. The word 'man' signifies in the first place the general idea and, secondarily, all the particulars which are members of this sort. This general idea is Locke's nominal essence and it is thus that he explains the riddle of genera and species. They are nominal essences, framed by abstraction in the sense now explained.

The content of the nominal essence is derived from experience, but the fabrication is ours. It is we, and not nature, who set up the final boundaries. 'The boundaries of the species whereby men sort them are made by men.'[1] It is we also who decide what content each nominal essence is to possess. Thus the nominal essence is subjective, as being dependent upon the mind creating it. It can be objective only in the sense that the same word conveys the same general idea to more than one person. For instance, the nominal essence may be defined in terms which signify precisely the same ideas to all and so can be public. But it is never public in the sense of existing objectively so that all may discover it. Even in the narrow sense it is rarely that the word is fully objective. Indeed it is always possible that the term '*T*' signifying a nominal essence signifies for me *a b c d e*, whereas what you call '*T*', signifies for you *a b c f g*. We cannot assume that the same general word signifies precisely the same general idea to any two people.

Now this view of generalizing, according to which it is a framing of a nominal essence through abstracting common features from the many observed particulars and ignoring the differentiae is quite as open to criticism as is the first strand in Locke's thought. I may confine myself to two criticisms. In the first place, generalizing does not appear to be as difficult a

[1] III. vi. 37.

matter as Locke now makes it out to be. In the famous passage in IV. vii. 9, which Berkeley seized upon, Locke magnified the difficulty of fabricating the general idea. He there speaks in stronger tones than elsewhere in the *Essay*. Yet this business of choosing the common core, ruling out the differentiae, and giving the 'essence' so framed a name, is never regarded as an easy task by Locke. But can generalizing in fact be as difficult as Locke makes it out to be? After all, children generalize, and surely they do not have to carry out the difficult processes described by Locke in order to do so. There is point in Berkeley's criticism. Not that Locke's position means, as Berkeley says it does, that thinking of the general triangle, for instance, involves imagining a triangle which is at one and the same time isosceles and not isosceles. He expressly exhorts us when framing our universals to see that they 'contain no inconsistency in them'.[1] Fabricating universals is never for Locke—to use Berkeley's colourful language—the 'tacking together of numberless inconsistencies'. Yet he does depict it as difficult work, and the question remains whether it can be as difficult as Locke supposes it to be since children appear to frame general ideas with such ease.

Moreover, though Locke does not require us to tack together inconsistencies, he yet, it would seem, expects us to do something which is almost, if not quite, as difficult. He expects us to find qualities common to all the individuals belonging to a species. Now if all the individuals of a species happen to be known by us it would then not be impossible in principle to find what is common, if anything is common. But in the case of the species here under discussion, the natural species, few only of the individuals can possibly be known by us. How, for instance, can we select the common qualities in the case of the species horse when we have seen, comparatively speaking, so few horses? The very next instance we observe may lack a quality which we have always regarded as common to all horses. Thus, strictly speaking, it is impossible to discover in such cases that which is 'common to all'. But perhaps we should not press this criticism too far. It might be fairer to suppose that what Locke means is

[1] III. iii. 19.

that we should pick out the qualities that are constantly turning up in the individual instances of this species and ignore those which obviously vary from instance to instance. The procedure is not exact. It would follow that the common core would be chosen by each of us arbitrarily; and we know that there is an arbitrary element in the nominal essence anyway. These universals, as we have seen, are inevitably subjective, even though, as far as we can, we try through description and definition to make our general ideas tally with those of other people. We need not expect, therefore, to have found in generalizing what is common to all the members of a species. It will be enough if we take as the core what is usually experienced to be the common element. Yet, if we express the theory in these terms in order to save Locke from the above criticism, we do seem to be changing his theory. For it is then not the genuinely common elements, but what appear in a comparatively few instances to be the common elements, which make up the content of the nominal essence. Is this exactly what Locke wants to say? If he does wish to go farther, if he wants us to discover elements common to all members of the species, then he is setting us an impossible task. But it is not wholly clear what Locke's demands are in this connexion.

11. In the closing sections of III. iii the third strand in Locke's thought about universals is uppermost, and it is this strand, in my opinion, which is the most interesting of the three. The universal is conceived as a fixed, immutable meaning. We may think of a nominal essence, disregard its reference to individual things, that is, disregard the extension or denotation of the word which signifies it, and dwell solely upon its content. It is the connotation of the term alone that now concerns us, and we may arbitrarily fix this connotation. Once this is done, the essence is from this point forward 'ingenerable and incorruptible'. Things come into being and cease to be, but such essences as these 'are preserved whole and undestroyed, whatever changes happen to any or all of the individuals of those species'.[1]

[1] III. iii. 19.

From one point of view it might be thought unwise to fix the meaning in this way rather than to wait upon experience and change the connotation of the term as new features are noted. But it is not strange that Locke's thought should turn in this direction. For such fixity of meaning would give him objectivity, and we have seen that thus far objectivity is lacking in his account of the universal. If the universal were the real essence it would be objective enough, but Locke has denied this and substituted a nominal essence for it which is subjective. The only objectivity he can hope for is that of precise definition, and this becomes possible only if the essence to be defined is fixed and immutable. Thus conceiving the universal as a fixed, immutable meaning gives objectivity to Locke's thought.

But it does more; it liberates his theory from concern solely with natural species and genera. Up to this point Locke has been concentrating upon the natural sorts and seeking to explain the nature of such universals as man, horse, buttercup. But if we think of the universal as a meaning rather than as a selected common core we shall be freer to think of universals of another kind. When in the next two chapters[1] Locke discusses the universals which he calls modes, and particularly mixed modes, it is the third strand which is most evident in his thought. He discusses then such universals as murder, incest, stabbing, to give his own examples, and in dealing with these he is not concerned with the question whether instances of such universals exist, whether there are, or are not, murders, but solely with the concept of murder. When Locke is thinking in terms of this third strand his account of universals has little to do with existence and almost everything with discourse. It is the use of words that concerns him—though not the mere use of words, since he is never a nominalist—but the use of them as having meaning, and what they mean in Locke's opinion is the general idea or concept. Whether there is also a reference to existent things becomes now, when the third strand is uppermost, a point of secondary importance. There may or there may not be such a reference; what matters is that the concept

[1] III. iv and v.

should be as clear as possible, for it is the concept that we have in mind and it is about the concept that we are talking.

There is a passage in Russell's *Introduction to Mathematical Philosophy* which recalls Locke's position. Speaking of such propositions as 'I met a unicorn', Russell remarks:

> Thus it is only what we may call the *concept* that enters into the proposition. In the case of 'unicorn', for example, there is only the concept; there is not also, somewhere among the shades, something unreal which may be called 'a unicorn'. Therefore, since it is significant (though false) to say 'I met a unicorn' it is clear that this proposition, rightly analysed, does not contain a constituent 'a unicorn' though it does contain the concept 'unicorn'.[1]

Russell's position here, it seems to me, is identical with that of Locke when he is stressing this third strand. What enters into the proposition is the concept, the terms of our discourse are meanings; and our discourse can be significant irrespective of whether there exist entities in the world of existing things corresponding to these meanings. As long as I know what 'horses', 'murders', 'stabbings' mean, I can talk of them even if there are no horses, murders, or stabbings, just as I can speak significantly of unicorns though there are no unicorns.

This incidentally is not the only correspondence between Locke's philosophy and the philosophy of today. The influence of his empiricism on modern thought is obvious, but it is not so frequently noted that his view of the method of philosophy is also remarkably modern. He turns his back on metaphysics—not because he thinks it impossible or nonsense (he himself attempts a proof of God's existence)—but because he thinks that he has a prior task to perform. The task of the *Essay* is to clear away the rubbish before erecting the building. And the method he adopts in carrying out this task is the method of analysis. The apparatus of modern analysis is not used but the method itself is there. Sometimes in Book III when he is handling the universal as a meaning there are definite suggestions even of the apparatus. I may cite one instance. In the opening section of the eighth chapter Locke considers what it means to say: 'A man is white.' Both 'man' and 'white' are general; they are

[1] p. 168.

concepts or meanings. Yet, as Locke makes clear, when we say, 'A man is white' we certainly do not mean 'Humanity is Whiteness'. How, then, should we analyse this sentence? Locke's answer is as follows: ' "A man is white" signifies that the thing that has the essence of a man has also in it the essence of whiteness. . . . "A man is rational" signifies that the same thing that hath the essence of a man hath also in it the essence of rationality.' In other words: 'A man is white' should be analysed thus: there is a thing (x) that is human (ϕ) and also white (ψ) or $(\exists x).\ \phi x.\ \psi x$. Reference might be made to other detailed correspondences but it is more important to note that the whole tone of this third book is modern. It is a sort of seventeenth-century Theory of Descriptions.

Another interesting discussion in this book is that about the relation between the meaning and the name. Frequently it is necessary to use many words to express a meaning. Locke notes a tendency, however, to try to find one word for one meaning. For instance, we can go on talking of the murder of one's father if we choose, but we are happier when we have found one word for it, namely, 'parricide'. One word is more convenient than many, and the one word tends to tie the concept together. 'Though it be the mind that makes the collection, it is the name which is, as it were, the knot that ties them fast together.'[1] This theory that the word has an integrative function might be thought to be a modification of Locke's conceptualism, since the word's function is no longer regarded as being solely significatory. There is almost the suggestion that if we cannot find one name for the complex then it remains not one idea but many. The problem of the relation between thinking and talking is involved here, although it is one which Locke does not directly consider. His general standpoint is clear; thinking is not to be *identified* with the use of words, for if the word is a proper name it points to a particular individual object, and if it is a common term, to a concept. Yet in thinking we do most often use words and the thinking and the making use of words are not two separate processes. It is one process, namely,

[1] III. v. 10, cf. III. v. 4.

thinking by the use of words. That this would have been Locke's view seems clear from his theory that the word ties the concept together; the use of language, that is to say, is essential to the thinking process, though yet not the whole of it.

In concluding this brief discussion of the third strand in Locke's thought it should again be emphasized that it is merely a strand. No complete theory is given in terms of it. There is this link between it and the second strand that the complex made by selection of the common core in the case of species and genera can be, as it were, solidified, and, a word being given to signify it, it is henceforward a fixed and immutable meaning. But the discussion of modes also shows that there are meanings other than species and genera.

12. The general character of Locke's theory of universals is now plain. It is not a fully integrated theory, yet it points steadily in one direction, namely, conceptualism. Realism is rejected; the universal is never one entity amongst others in the world of existences, nor is it a real essence. Its being pertains to discourse; it is fabricated by us for our greater convenience in discourse and thought; it is a nominal essence. On the other hand, it is never merely the word; Locke's theory excludes nominalism as well as realism.

The consequences of Locke's conceptualism were disturbing; they led directly to a profound scepticism to which Locke himself gives utterance. He tells us[1] that there can be 'no science of bodies'. It is important to understand what he means by these words and how he came to this conclusion.

He uses the word 'science' here in the traditional sense and it has then two characteristics, namely, generality and certainty. 'It is a rainy day today' is not scientific since it is not general. 'Swans are white' is general but not certain. The schools concerned themselves with statements which were both general and certain, and sought by syllogism to deduce further statements from them equally general and equally certain. They dismissed the inductive reasoning of the natural scientists as a rule-of-

[1] IV. iii. 26.

thumb and refused to give it the dignity of the name 'science'. Locke, staunch empiricist as he was, agreed with the schools on this point, not because he shared their devotion to the syllogism, but because he found generality and certainty only in mathematics. He had learnt from the Cartesians that the ideal of knowledge was Euclidean geometry and, judging by this standard, he found the natural sciences defective.

But, in Locke's view, we do not understand the limitations of the natural sciences merely by referring to the fact that their method is inductive. There are deeper grounds for scepticism about them. Locke's scepticism arises from two facts, first, that all our knowledge of the external world is derived from the senses and, secondly, that through the senses we can never know real essences but are constrained to think nominal essences, though we frequently mistake these for real essences. All the defects of the inductive procedure follow from these facts. Not knowing the real essence we have to assume that nature is uniform, that if we gain information about a comparatively few individuals which belong to a species, that information will hold true of all individuals belonging to that species. We have to assume that the future will resemble the past. If we knew the real essence of this object and of other objects as they come into relation the one with the other we could know for certain what must happen. But we have no such knowledge and so we fall back on generalization from observations and on the fabrication of nominal essences. We do not then attain certainty. We cannot be sure that these species exist or that there is a real essence, such as horse. There is indeed much to suggest that nature is not uniform, even in this limited sense, as Locke points out in the following passage:

> That which, I think, very much disposes men to substitute their names for the real essences of species, is the supposition before mentioned, that nature works regularly in the production of things, and sets the boundaries to each of those species by giving exactly the same real internal constitution to each individual, which we rank under one general name. Whereas any one who observes their different qualities can hardly doubt, that many of the individuals called by

the same name are, in their internal constitution, as different one from another as several of those which are ranked under different specific names.[1]

Thus the fundamental trouble is our ignorance of the real nature of objects in the external world. Our acquaintance with them in sense-perception is superficial only. It is because this is so that we cannot speak of them generally and with certainty at the same time, but are constrained to resort to the nominal essence and to the assumptions of induction. Hence Locke's scepticism and the conclusion that there can be 'no science of bodies'. Hence also the opening chapters of Book IV of the *Essay* in which Locke, in order to find certainty, turns away from our knowledge of the external world. We cannot answer with certainty when we ask ourselves whether our nominal essences, our species and genera, correspond to anything in reality. Conceptualism destroys the very possibility of such 'science'. We must therefore search for certainty elsewhere. Now the content of our thought is finally determined by what is given in sensation and reflection (or introspection), but out of such content we create our universals. Is it then possible to perceive, to intuit, connexions between these universals or fixed meanings? If it is, we may still have a knowledge which is certain; it would be intuitive and general at the same time. We should not then require to concern ourselves with a reference outwards, for we should be handling what Locke describes as 'ideas which are their own archetypes'; the nominal essence would be the only essence and so real as well as nominal.

In this way Locke frees himself from that dualism of real and nominal essences which leads to scepticism. Thus we may find a certainty which is general without pretending to know the real essence of natural objects, and without compromising the conceptualism which Locke believed to be inevitable, since sense-perception is what it is. Locke himself sums up the position in these words:

So that, as to all general knowledge, we must search and find it

[1] III. x. 20.

only in our own minds, and it is only the examining of our own ideas that furnisheth us with that. Truths belonging to essences of things (that is, to abstract ideas) are eternal, and are to be found out by the contemplation only of those essences, as the existence of things is to be known only from experience.[1]

Can we apprehend a connexion between two fixed meanings? That connexion will itself be fixed and unalterable, and knowledge of it will be certain and eternal; but the knowledge is only of the *ideal*; it cannot be a 'science' of the external world. Locke finds such knowledge in mathematics and in mathematics alone, though he also throws out the suggestion that it may too be found in morals.

13. Locke's reflections upon universals thus led him to a profound scepticism. Man's only knowledge of the external world is by way of the senses and the senses do not reveal that world except in a superficial manner. If he is to think of it in general terms at all, that is to say, if he is not to be limited to statements about particular observations, he has to frame concepts. But he can never then be sure that what he is thinking about has anything corresponding to it in the real world. This is Locke's conceptualism, with scepticism as an inevitable attendant. We could be saved from the latter by a realist theory of universals. But Locke challenges us to produce that theory. Can we, if we do justice to the facts, claim that we ever know the essences of species and genera? Is it not obvious that these universals, man, horse, buttercup, and rose, however much the framing of them may be suggested by experience, are yet the 'workmanship of the understanding'? In Locke's view conceptualism is the only possible theory, but then we must pay the price for conceptualism and admit the sceptical conclusions about our knowledge of the external world.

It is unnecessary at this stage to consider whether Locke was justified in his general conclusion; this is a problem to which I shall return later. I may content myself instead with a brief reference to certain gaps in Locke's account of universals, which

[1] IV. iii. 31.

may none the less have a bearing on the weightier matter of his scepticism.

First, there is the tendency to concentrate upon the problem of species and genera to the exclusion of other problems. This is not surprising when one considers the course which reflection upon universals had taken up to this point. None the less this tendency causes Locke to neglect two classes of universals which are of great importance, namely, qualities and relations. He does not neglect them entirely. When speaking of abstraction in Book II *white* is his example. Again, we have noted the discussion of modes, and these include the all-important universals of mathematics, such as triangle. But the angle of approach in Book III is determined by his interest in species and genera and by his desire to explain what these universals are. Now it may prove to be the case that what is true of these universals is not true of universals of quality and of relation. In particular, Locke might have denied that we knew real essences in the case of species and genera and yet have affirmed that we knew universals in the realist sense in the case of the universals of quality. But he never considers this point.

The second defect is that he takes altogether too sophisticated a view of generalizing. He concentrates on the scientific universal and seems to forget that men and women with no pretence to science, and again very young children, manage the general word quite successfully. What is the universal in these cases? Locke rarely considers them. Yet a satisfactory theory of universals must take this generalizing, too, into account, the more so since reflection upon it may throw light on the nature of those universals with which Locke is very much concerned. For example, is 'fabricating' what Locke takes it to be, namely, the self-conscious act of putting ideas together and building up a complex out of them as the builder puts brick on brick to build up a wall? Reflection on the origins of the unsophisticated universal might have led him to consider the nature of 'fabricating' more carefully, though possibly still holding to his general account of the matter.

There are thus gaps in Locke's account of universals and

there are no doubt errors in his theory. None the less his contribution is a very real one, for he provides a valuable introduction to the modern theory of the universal, and in what follows we shall find ourselves frequently reverting to Locke's patient and skilful discussion of these difficult matters.

III

BERKELEY'S CRITICISM

14. It will be easier to understand Berkeley's contribution to the theory of general ideas and universals if we turn first to the concluding sections of the celebrated *Introduction* to the *Principles of Human Knowledge*. He there points out that what Locke had assumed to be the truth is not the truth but a source of error, namely, that a general word invariably stands for a general idea. This is false in the first place because it ignores the ends and function of language. Language is not solely descriptive or communicative; it may, for instance, express emotion. Secondly, even when its end is descriptive the account which Locke gives of it is still erroneous. Locke assumes that whenever a general word is used there is a precise, determined idea in the mind. Berkeley denies this. Men use general words descriptively, in thinking or in communicating their thoughts, without having such precise, determined ideas annexed to them. It is not the case that whenever we use the words 'justice' or 'democracy', or even 'cat' or 'house', precise ideas corresponding to these words exist in our minds. Words are used vaguely; general words in Berkeley's opinion refer not to a precise idea but signify vaguely many particular things. If we assume that they signify precise ideas we are led into frequent error about the nature of particular things. We need, says Berkeley, to 'draw the curtain of words' and look at the things themselves. We are more likely to advance in true knowledge if we cease to think in terms of our generalizations and abstractions, expressed in general words, and concentrate instead on the particular ideas given us in experience. 'So long as I confine my thoughts to my own ideas divested of words, I do not see how I can be easily mistaken' (section 22).

All this is effective criticism of Locke and of many other philosophers in and before Locke's day. If Locke is successful in his criticism of realism, his own form of conceptualism is certainly too narrow. But what account of universals does Berkeley put in its place? And how does he explain our use of general words?

The answer which the *Introduction* to the *Principles* gives is far from clear. The main concern of the *Introduction* is with abstracting, a *part* of the problem of generalization certainly, but not the whole, nor perhaps the most important part. The argument against the abstract idea is presented by Berkeley with so much brilliance that it has an unusual effect upon the reader's mind. It does not convince him—indeed when carefully considered it turns out to be a weak argument—yet it makes him suspicious and uneasy about abstraction. It is less refutation than innuendo; it is effective in prejudicing the mind even when it fails to convince the reason.

Moreover, the reader expects a more broadly based discussion, one that includes the discussion of common qualities, of natural classes or 'sorts', as well as a discussion of the psychological process of generalizing. Berkeley tends to confine himself to the latter, and even to a part of it, namely, to the abstracting which is alleged to take place in generalizing. At the end of the *Introduction* (section 21) he tells us that what he has proved is 'the impossibility of abstract ideas'. Why does he make this his main task? A reading of certain preparatory reflections of his in the *Commonplace Book* and in the *Draft*, which he wrote in preparation for the *Introduction*, provides the answer, namely, that in the *Introduction* he was of set purpose avoiding certain problems within the main problem because he had already examined them and failed to solve them. In the *Introduction* he purposely narrows his field of inquiry; in doing so his treatment of universals is inevitably partial; indeed it might be argued that he never comes to grips with the central issues.

15. It is sometimes said that the sole aim of the *Introduction* is to show that matter is an abstract idea and that since abstract ideas are a myth, matter is a mere figment in the philosopher's mind, a mere hypostatization having no reality of its own. Now this was certainly one of the aims of the *Introduction*, though not,

I think, the sole aim. It would be well to clear away this point first before turning to the other questions involved.

Already, at the beginning of the *Commonplace Book*, the reader will find reference to 'the immaterial hypothesis'.[1] Berkeley's feeling for the reality of the spiritual, his strong dislike of materialism in all its forms, his reflections on the dilemmas and paradoxes of the new philosophy, all combine to lead him to the denial of the ultimate reality of the material world. He does not know as yet precisely what form his immaterialism will take, but he sees it as the base and foundation of the new philosophy stirring within him. For what is *matter*? And how do we know it? In Locke's philosophy, upon which Berkeley had pondered a great deal, matter is a 'substratum'; yet it is unknown, a something-I-know-not-what. At the beginning of the *Commonplace Book* Berkeley himself still thinks of physical qualities as being grounded in an *unknown* substratum. Thus, in L. 80, he thinks we may have demonstrative and not merely sensitive knowledge of the existence of bodies—presumably by their effects, that is, the effects of their qualities, their 'powers', but these powers, he holds, pertain to an 'unknown substratum'. This unknown substratum, however, is not matter. At this stage Berkeley does not know what it is. Some thirty folio pages later, however, a new thought strikes him with considerable force, a thought which transforms his immaterialism into an idealism. He sees now that 'our simple ideas are so many simple thoughts or perceptions and that a perception cannot exist without a thing to perceive it or any longer than it is perceived, that a thought cannot be in an unthinking thing'.[2] The unknown substratum is accordingly that which perceives and thinks, that is, mind. Only mind and its ideas exist. Bodies are ideas. This, he now realizes is the solution of his fundamental difficulty and he blames himself for his slowness in finding it. 'I wonder not at my sagacity in discovering the obvious though amazing truth, I rather wonder at my stupid inadvertency in not finding it out before.'[3]

[1] Cf. L[uce] 19. All references are to A. A. Luce's edition (1944). Prof. Luce prefers the title *Philosophical Commentaries*.

[2] L. 280.

[3] L. 279.

But if mind is the one reality and the only true substratum, what is matter? In explaining how men fall into the error of supposing that a material substratum exists Berkeley has recourse to the theory of abstraction. We know mind directly, we directly experience our own activity as living beings, but *matter* is a mere abstraction. Thus the argument on abstraction becomes a most useful weapon in Berkeley's armoury, and can be effectively used against the materialists. Yet it would be wrong to suppose that the whole attack on abstraction was carried out for this purpose alone. More is involved and Berkeley understood this well enough.

Thus when we first find him discussing the abstract idea it is extension, succession, and motion which concern him and not matter. He gives considerable attention to extension in the opening third of the *Commonplace Book*. In particular he questions the presumption that we abstract extension from the visible experience and abstract the *same* extension from the tangible. Once the New Principle is established, that *esse* is *percipi*, he then stresses the need for thinking of extension concretely. The only extension we know is the shape seen or the shape felt. But as the result of our experience visible extension and tangible extension are so closely connected and associated in our minds that experiencing the one we are inevitably led to think the other. But what we think of is *experienced* extension, that is, seen or felt extension. The extension of the scientists is not experienced and so, on Berkeley's New Principle, it does not exist. What cannot be perceived does not exist.[1] Therefore extension in itself or absolute space, succession in itself or pure time, the perfect absolute circle,[2] the ideal triangle, absolute motion, the infinitesimals of the mathematician, and so on—all of these are 'nothings', the figments of the philosopher's creation. 'I say the invisibles are nothings.'[3] If we think concretely they at once cease to exist. What exists is extension as one of the qualities

[1] Cf. L. 392: 'There are men who say there are insensible extensions, there are others who say the wall is not white, the fire is not hot, etc. We Irishmen cannot attain to these truths.'

[2] Cf. L. 235, 238: 'No idea of circle etc. in abstract.'

[3] L. 464.

along with for instance, colour in the visible object, or as a quality along with, for instance, smoothness in the tangible object.

These reflections in the *Commonplace Book* lead us up to the posing of the fundamental question, 'Qu. is it not impossible there should be general ideas?'[1] The answer which he intends is obviously the affirmative one, that it is indeed impossible that there should be general ideas. If we do, none the less, insist that there are general ideas then, appearances to the contrary, they must somehow exist as concrete particular ideas, for they cannot exist in any other way. On this point L. 497 is positive enough: 'All abstract ideas whatsoever are particular. I can by no means conceive a general idea.'

16. It is clear that Berkeley at this time was passing through a phase in which he came near to denying the very possibility of a general idea. He had passed through this phase before he began to prepare the *Principles of Human Knowledge* in its final form; nevertheless its influence on his thinking was profound. By way of illustration I may refer to two passages; first to the interesting speculation about the Solitary Man and, secondly, to a passage in the *Draft* of the *Introduction* and its subsequent correction in the published *Introduction.*

The Solitary Man is mentioned in several of the jottings of the *Commonplace Book*,[2] but the conceit is stated most fully in the *Draft*. 'Let us conceive', he there says,[3] 'a solitary man, one born and bred in such a place of the world and in such circumstances, as he shall never have had occasion to make use of universal signs for his ideas. That man shall have a constant train of particular ideas passing in his mind.' Let us suppose also that he has leisure to contemplate and gain knowledge. 'Such a one I should take to be nearer the discovery of certain great and excellent truths yet unknown, than he that has had the education of the schools. . . . It is true, the knowledge of our solitary philosopher is not like to be so very wide and extended, it being confined to those few particulars that come within his own observation. But

[1] L. 318. [2] e.g. L. 592, 607, 648 and cf. L. 566, 588, 600.

[3] Fraser, iii. 379, Luce and Jessop, ii. 141 (hereafter cited as F., and L. and J.).

then, if he is like to have less knowledge, he is withall like to have fewer mistakes than other men.'

Berkeley appears to approve of the state of the Solitary Man and to think it a more hopeful one from the point of view of gaining true knowledge than our own. A man in this predicament would be the more likely to trust to observation, and that is an obvious point in his favour in the eyes of an empiricist. But this is not what the conceit stresses. He would also be less prone to generalization. Perhaps generalization could not be entirely ruled out; but there would be much less of it, and there would be *no* abstract thinking.

The moral of the story seems to be that the moment we begin to generalize and to abstract we are making difficulties for ourselves. Our best state would be one in which these processes are absent. Now there is no direct reference to the Solitary Man in the published *Introduction*, and that in itself is significant of a certain change. Yet the plea in the final sections for a consideration of one's 'naked, undisguised ideas' is in line with its teaching. There is an echo of it in the third of the *Dialogues between Hylas and Philonous.*[1] But the conceit, as we find it in the *Draft*, does not appear in Berkeley's later work. Having come to see the necessity of some abstraction and generalization, he probably felt that the conceit went too far. Its presence in the *Commonplace Book* and the *Draft* is, however, a very interesting illustration of how near Berkeley was to denying abstraction and generalization altogether.

The second illustration also comes from the *Draft.* Berkeley is discussing the question whether abstract ideas are necessary for the enlargement of knowledge, and concludes that they are not. In the course of the discussion he remarks: 'For though it be a point much insisted on in the Schools, that all knowledge is about universals, yet I could never bring myself to comprehend this doctrine.' It is not immediately clear whether Berkeley wishes to imply that no knowledge is about universals or that only some is, but if we judge by the context the point seems to be that all true knowledge is about particulars. However, on

[1] F. i. 467.

re-reading the *Draft* later, he seems to have felt that these words were too strong, for according to Fraser[1] he erased 'could never bring myself to comprehend' and corrected the sentence so that the final clause reads: 'Yet I can by no means see the necessity of this doctrine.' He still seems to be denying the need for universals in the enlargement of knowledge, although he is not now suggesting that the doctrine is nonsense. But the general standpoint remains the same: generalization and abstraction are unnecessary for the enlargement of knowledge.

Perhaps the most interesting point in connexion with this passage lies in the sequel, for in coming to prepare it finally for the published *Introduction* he found it necessary to alter it radically in view of a fundamental change in his general position. Indeed he says now the exact opposite of what was said in the *Draft*. For the sentence in section 15 of the *Introduction* reads: 'It is I know a point much insisted on that all knowledge and demonstration are about universal notions, to which I fully agree.' This is an obvious volte-face that calls for explanation.

17. How did this opponent of generalization and abstraction yet come to admit, in spite of himself, the value and the necessity of such processes in human life and thought? It is interesting to read through the works of 1707–10 with this question in mind. His reflections upon mathematical reasoning, upon reasoning in general and upon 'sortal' knowledge, led him, I believe, to a position in which denial of generalization and abstraction was impossible.

(*a*) Thus in respect to geometry, much as he would like to say that the only object we think about is this particular triangle now before us in its particularity, he never quite manages to say this. For clearly in geometry, even if we say that what we have concretely in mind is this particular triangle, we are not thinking of *it* in its particularity and concreteness, but rather of what holds good of it as well as of any other triangle. In 1734 in the second edition of the *Principles* he affirms that we can abstract triangularity and make it the subject of geometrical speculation.

[1] F. iii. 368.

He is not so explicit in the first edition, but it is clear even there that the triangle under consideration if particular is also more than particular. The case is the same with number. He stresses the particularity of number,[1] but it is always more than the bare particular. In Berkeley's opinion the sign '7' has corresponding to it no abstract *idea* of seven. It itself is a particular, but it is a particular functioning in a representative capacity; it stands for this group of seven objects and that group and all groups of seven. Thus if we are to retain arithmetic and geometry there is inevitably some generalization.

(*b*) Again, Berkeley's reflections about reasoning in general led him ultimately to the same conclusion. In this connexion I find a comment in the *Commonplace Book* interesting. Berkeley is reading Locke's chapter on reasoning in Book IV of the *Essay* and comes across Locke's own statement that whenever we reason our ideas are in fact particular (IV. xvii. 8). Such a theory is naturally a welcome one to Berkeley. But he asks himself whether Locke has really worked out its implications and whether he (Berkeley) can accept them? An acute jotting in the *Commonplace Book* is worth quoting:[2]

> Locke says all our knowledge is about particulars, if so, pray what is the following ratiocination but a jumble of words *Omnis Homo est animal, omne animal vivit, ergo omnis Homo vivit* [Locke's example]. It amounts (if you annex particular ideas to the words *animal* and *vivit*) to no more than this: *Omnis Homo est homo, omnis homo est homo, ergo omnis homo est homo*. A mere sport and trifling with sounds.

And surely Berkeley is right.[3] Reasoning without universals is impossible. But on realizing this he does not at once admit universals. He rather attempts to deny the need for mediate reasoning, asserting that 'proving by intermediate ideas comes to nothing'.[4] The Solitary Man, it would seem, would not infer mediately. Yet Berkeley soon realized that this was an impossible position. There *is* reasoning and if so what we are thinking about is not the bare particular. Hence the significant

[1] Cf. *Principles*, section 13 and sections 120–2. [2] L. 668.

[3] Compare the discussion about the dog 'Melampus' in the *Draft*, F. iii. 373–4, L. and J. ii. 136. [4] L. 729.

admission in the *Principles* that demonstration is about universal notions.

(*c*) Thirdly, Berkeley had to admit the existence of 'sorts'. For the most part he is silent about them in the *Introduction* to the *Principles*, but this does not mean that he denies them. Groupings and kinds are at least suggested by our experience even if they are not *in* nature. In the next section I propose to consider what Berkeley has to say about 'sorts'. But, once admitted, they can be spoken of only in general terms. Generalization is inevitable.

For such reasons as these Berkeley found it impossible to assert that the use of general words is entirely without value or to suggest that it were best not to generalize. Yet his opposition to abstraction had not weakened. His first attack was upon general ideas, but then he had to admit that some general ideas had their uses and that they were necessary to knowledge. He consequently found it difficult to settle upon the precise form which his attack upon abstraction should take. Quite suddenly, however, as we can see from the *Commonplace Book*, his difficulties were resolved. About this time he was working through Book IV of the *Essay* and jotting down his observations.[1] He finds Locke speaking in IV. vii. 9 of abstract general ideas which are framed only with great difficulty. He thinks that Locke says they involve inconsistencies within them, and at once the main lines of his future criticism of abstraction and generalization become clear to him; henceforth his polemic must be directed against this 'abstract, general idea'.

18. Before we examine in detail the polemic against abstract ideas in the *Introduction* we have still to answer one further question, namely, why Berkeley has nothing to say in it about the 'sorts'. It was not that he was unaware of the problem involved. There is a discussion of 'sorts' in the *Draft*, and there are references also in the *Commonplace Book* and in the *New Theory of Vision*. The *Draft* discussion in particular reveals Berkeley's

[1] Cf. L. 561.

failure to solve the problem involved and in my opinion explains the silence of the published *Introduction.*

During the years 1707–10 Berkeley was in a hurry. Having written the mathematical papers of 1707, prepared himself for and taken the Fellowship Examination at Trinity College in the summer of 1707, in the following autumn, winter, spring, and summer he appears to have given himself over to the reflections and preparations which are recorded in the *Commonplace Book.* On 15 November 1708 he began to write the *Draft*, finishing it on 18 December 1708.[1] In 1709 the *Essay Towards a New Theory of Vision* was published and the *Principles* prepared, the latter appearing in May 1710. During these years Berkeley was obviously working rapidly and at great pressure. He was anxious to get his ideas before the public as speedily as possible. Now suppose that in this period Berkeley comes across the problem of the 'sorts' and finds it very difficult to solve. He particularly wants to discredit abstraction, in order, for instance, to be able to explain that 'matter', 'extension', &c. are *merely* abstract ideas: yet he does not wish to be held up by a prolonged discussion of a most difficult topic. It would not be surprising in these circumstances if he set himself to consider ways and means of by-passing the difficulty, discrediting abstraction without first having to develop a satisfactory doctrine of the 'sorts'. I want to suggest that this is what happened and that this explains his silence about the 'sorts' in the published *Introduction.*

Berkeley means by the 'sorts' what Locke meant by them, primarily, the natural 'sorts'. Things in nature are grouped in sorts—or appear to us to be so grouped. Can we say that the sorts are objective existences, as this dog, this cat, this table, are objective existences? In other words, are there natural classes?

The answer of the *Commonplace Book* is confused. In an early jotting[2] Berkeley notes, referring to Malebranche's position: 'he does not prove, nor can it be proved on his principles, that the sorts are the work of the mind and only in the mind.' Later, he links the problem with that of abstraction. Are 'sorts' abstract ideas? And are they the abstract, general ideas to be

[1] Cf. Luce's *Philosophical Commentaries*, p. xxxi, note 2. [2] L. 288.

condemned? It is interesting that when he first singles out the abstract general idea for attack he expressly excludes genera and species: 'certainly genera and species are not abstract general ideas.'[1] But genera and species are soon grouped along with abstract general ideas (in L. 566 and again in L. 703). Abstract general ideas are mere figments of the mind. Are genera and species such also, and are the sorts such? No clear answer emerges from the *Commonplace Book.*

In the *Draft*, however, he is more explicit. He first sets out the theory of abstract general ideas and expressly identifies genera and species with them: ' . . . abstract ideas, genera, species, universal notions, all which amount to the same thing.'[2] He says of these ideas that they 'equally represent the particulars of any sort and are made by the mind which, observing that the individuals of each kind agree in some things and differ in others, takes out and singles from the rest that which is common to all, making thereof one abstract general idea'. On this account genera and species are very plainly abstract general ideas 'made by the mind' by singling out elements common to the particulars. But it is not clear whether the 'sorts' are also such abstract general ideas. Apparently this is not the case. But we may quote farther: 'To this abstract general idea thus framed the mind gives a general name, and lays it up and uses it as a standard whereby to judge what particulars are and what are not to be accounted of that sort, those only which contain every part of the general idea having a right to be admitted into that sort and called by that name.'[3] The name of the general abstract idea is also the name of the sort. Does this mean that they are identical? Or should we use the language of extension and intension and say that the sort is the extension and the abstract idea the intension? The passage obviously needs further clarification, but Berkeley does not clarify it. What he did when he came to read it later was to erase it.

Farther on in the *Draft* he is explaining what he means by a general word. It is a sign not of an abstract general idea but 'of a great number of particular ideas, between which there is some

[1] L. 561. [2] F. iii. 360, L. and J. ii. 123. [3] F. iii. 360.

likeness and which are said to be of the same sort'. At this point he realizes that he has to explain what he means by a 'sort'. The first answer that he gives is as follows:

> But these sorts are not determined and set out by Nature, as was thought by most philosophers. Nor yet are they limited by any precise, abstract ideas settled in the mind, with the general name annexed to them, as is the opinion of the author of the *Essay*, nor do they in truth seem to me to have any precise bounds or limits at all. For if they had I do not see, how there could be those doubts and scruples, about the sorting of particular beings, which are observed sometimes to have happened. Neither do I think it necessary the kinds or species of things should be so very accurately bounded and marked out. Language being made by and for the common use of men, who do not ordinarily take notice of the minuter and less considerable differences of things.[1]

This passage is the nearest thing we have in Berkeley to a discussion of the traditional problem of universals. In it he first rejects the realist view. The sorts are not objective, not 'set out by nature'. But he also rejects the second alternative, what we should call conceptualism, that the sorts are limited by 'precise abstract ideas' which we have framed. The argument that he urges against the second alternative is that since the mind formulates 'precise abstract ideas' then whenever we speak of a sort we should know precisely what we are speaking about. But this, Berkeley holds, is certainly not the case. The realist view that precise sorts exist and the conceptualist view that the mind makes them are both false theories.

Here is the beginning of an interesting discussion but unfortunately it is one which Berkeley does not develop. If the realist and the conceptualist accounts of the 'sorts' are rejected what other account, we ask, is to be put in their place? There is no answer in the *Draft*. On rereading it Berkeley erased this passage as well as the other quoted above. For this passage he substituted on the opposite page the following sentence:

> Every one's experience may convince him that this is all that is meant by general names [signs for many particulars 'said to be of the same sort'] and that they do not stand either for universal natures

[1] F. iii. 365–6, L. and J. ii. 128.

distinct from our conceptions as was held by the Peripatetics and generality of the Schoolmen, nor yet for universal notions or ideas as is the opinion of that sort of Schoolmen called Nominals and of the author of the *Essay*.

It is noteworthy, in passing, that Berkeley here terms Locke's conceptualism a 'nominalist' doctrine, thus lending support to the view that the traditional nominalism of the Schools was nearer to what we today call conceptualism than to nominalism, and that he himself rejects such nominalism. But in respect to the central point, it will be observed that the argument is in no way developed, the same points are made as in the passage erased, but the word 'sort' is avoided. The only conclusion we can come to is that Berkeley found it impossible to develop the argument.

A passage about sorts is to be found in the *New Theory of Vision* which at first arouses hopes that something more positive is going to be said. I refer to section 128. 'When, upon perception of an idea, I range it under this or that sort, it is because it is perceived after the same manner, or because it has a likeness or conformity with, or affects me in the same way as the ideas of the sort I rank it under.' But as the paragraph develops no clear doctrine emerges and our hopes are once again dashed. As Professor A. A. Luce justifiably comments: 'Nothing clear issues, and the paragraph leaves the reader with the impression that the mind both makes the sorts and finds them.'[1]

The evidence points to the fact that Berkeley found this problem of 'sorts' too difficult to solve in the short time at his disposal. Realizing this he might have dropped the *Introduction* altogether, since it was to deal with generalization, for the proper understanding of which a satisfactory theory of 'sorts' appeared essential. But he was most loth to do so. The attack on abstraction was to be the spearhead of the general attack on materialism. Could it be carried out in any way *without* solving the problem of 'sorts'? He was already resolved not to introduce the latter problem into the *Principles*. Could he still retain the *Introduction*?

[1] *Berkeley and Malebranche*, p. 152.

The use of general words involves abstracting and this is a process wherein the mind 'takes out and singles from the rest that which is common to all'.[1] The problem of 'sorts' is bound up with this notion of something common to all. But suppose instead of concentrating on the common element, the universal, one concentrates instead on the 'singling'. Suppose it could be shown that there was something wrong with the account of 'singling'. The theory of abstraction would then be equally well discredited. Is 'singling' psychologically justifiable? Can the common element, whatever its nature, *be* abstracted? Indeed, can any one quality of an object be abstracted or singled out from another of its qualities, for example, colour from extension? Berkeley had concerned himself with this problem at the opening of the *Commonplace Book* and it is present in the *New Theory of Vision.* Why not concentrate on the 'singling'? Now this is precisely what happens in the *Introduction.* Berkeley is silent about the 'sorts'; his criticism falls on the 'singling'.

One finds confirmatory evidence in the *Commonplace Book.* Early in that work he had seen the possibility of, and the need for, an introductory discussion of 'sorting'. L. 139 runs: 'Preliminary discourse about sorting, simple ideas.' The interesting point is that sometime later he crossed out 'sorting' and substituted for it the words 'singling and abstracting'.

19. Thus we see that when Berkeley comes to write the *Introduction* to the *Principles* several influences are at work on his mind. In the first place, he deeply distrusts the use of general words and of abstraction but has yet, almost in spite of himself, to admit their necessity. Secondly, he realizes that he has no satisfactory solution to put forward to the problem of universals and that in particular he cannot say with any confidence what the sorts are. Nevertheless, he is still sure that the best way of opening his book is by attacking the general and abstract idea. It was a fashionable line of attack at the time and he could use it to discredit the abstract idea of matter. But he decides, as far as possible, to avoid some of the most awkward questions and in

[1] F. iii. 360, L. and J. ii. 123.

any case to put forward only the briefest possible answers to these, whilst emphasizing what he took to be psychological errors in Locke's account of abstraction.

The *Introduction* begins by pointing out that while there are natural limitations to our cognitive powers a good deal of our ignorance is due to a misuse of our talents, 'we have first raised a dust and then complain we cannot see'. This misuse of talents in turn is in the main the consequence of our abuse of language leading us to 'innumerable errors and difficulties'. Finally, the abuse of language can be attributed almost entirely to our supposing 'that the mind hath a power of framing *abstract ideas* or notions of things'.[1]

By what process is it supposed that these abstract ideas are formed? First, by considering a quality in an object, which itself has many qualities, singly and apart (Section 7). I see a moving, circular, red object and I concentrate on the circularity and abstract it. Secondly, I 'consider apart or single out by itself' that which is 'common and alike' in several observations, for instance, the quality of being extended. So I get 'a most abstract idea of extension which is neither line, surface nor solid nor has any figure or magnitude, but is an idea entirely prescinded from all these' (Section 8). Finally, I can frame abstract ideas 'of the more compounded beings'. For instance, I take the abstracted common qualities observed to be in man and frame the abstract idea of man:

> wherein it is true there is included colour, because there is no man but has some colour, but then it can be neither white, nor black, nor any particular colour; because there is no one particular colour wherein all men partake. So likewise there is included stature, but then it is neither tall stature nor low stature, nor yet middle stature, but something abstracted from all these. And so of the rest [Section 9].

Such are the powers of abstraction which the mind is supposed to possess and such is the theory of abstraction which Berkeley now proposes to demolish. He opens the attack in Section 10. 'Whether others have this wonderful faculty of *ab-*

[1] Section 6.

stracting their ideas, they best can tell: for myself I dare be confident I have it not.' Now what precisely has Berkeley *not* got? First, he does not find in himself the ability to imagine, for instance, a hand, which lacks determinate colour. 'Whatever hand or eye, I imagine, it must have some particular shape and colour.' Nor can he frame an idea of a man who is coloured and yet has no particular colour. 'Likewise the idea of man that I frame to myself, must be either of a white or a black or a tawny, a straight or a crooked, a tall or a low or a middle-sized man. I cannot by any effort of thought conceive the abstract idea above described.' In other words, the singling or mental separation which is alleged to give the abstract idea of man who is coloured and yet has no precise, particular colour, is, Berkeley finds in his own case, psychologically impossible. In the second place, he remarks: 'It is equally impossible for me to form the abstract idea of motion distinct from the body moving, and which is neither swift nor slow, curvilinear nor rectilinear; and the like may be said of all other abstract general ideas whatsoever.' I cannot single out a general quality common to many objects, such as motion or being coloured. If I think of motion it is always the motion of a particular body moving quickly or slowly as the case may be.

In these respects Berkeley thinks his experience to be that of most other men. Perhaps the learned, by some difficult process unknown to the vulgar, can fabricate such universals, but Berkeley cannot.

We have now to ask whether this psychological criticism is valid? In the first place, it seems quite safe to say that I cannot *imagine* a man who has height but is neither tall nor short nor medium-sized, or again that I cannot imagine a hand that has shape and colour without having some particular shape or colour. But does this justify the view that to think of man is always to imagine a man of a particular height and to think of a hand is always to imagine a hand of particular shape or colour? Critics have spoken of Berkeley's imagism, the suggestion being that he thought of conceiving in terms of imagining and failed to distinguish between the two. In view of certain passages in Berkeley's works,[1] however, this view can hardly be sustained, for he does distinguish quite freely between imagining and conceiving. None the less, what he says in sections 7–10 of the *Introduction* would appear to be appropriate to imagining only and not to conceiving. The fact that I cannot imagine a particular man who is neither black, white, nor tawny does not at all prove that I cannot speak of 'man' meaning white, black, and tawny men at one and the same time. We shall consider the nature of such a conception later; it is enough to point out that Berkeley's criticism applies to imagining and not to conceiving.

The point that Berkeley makes is that I cannot single out the movement from the body moving. The body moving has other qualities along with motion, it has quality and shape. I cannot single out motion. So in Section 99 of the *Principles* he argues that extension cannot be abstracted from the other sensible qualities coexistent in a thing. It is psychologically false that we can thus separate motion or extension from the other qualities. If this is so, Berkeley argues, the alleged 'singling' of Sections 7 and 8 is psychologically unsound. No quality *can* be singled out in the way in which this false theory of abstraction asserts.

But, again, is Berkeley's psychological analysis correct? Here is a rectangular piece of brown paper before me. Can Berkeley seriously hold that I cannot think of the rectangularity of the paper and neglect its brownness? No doubt when I first think of the rectangularity the other qualities will also come to mind and as long as I am seeking to recall *this* rectangularity I can, perhaps, never entirely rid myself of them. They remain vaguely in the background. Yet I can certainly proceed to talk significantly of rectangularity as such without talking of the other qualities.

Berkeley himself seems to have been apprehensive of this section (section 10) even before it was published. For he adds a passage in the *Errata* to the first edition in which he admits that one can after all consider some particular qualities separated from another, that 'mental separation' or 'singling' is possible in

[1] Cf. *Alciphron*, 1st ed. vii, sections 6–8.

some cases. He adds however: 'I deny that I can abstract from one another, or conceive separately, those qualities which it is impossible should exist so separated.' Unfortunately he gives us no instance of such qualities, and until we understand which qualities he has in mind it is difficult to measure the value of the qualification. If he is thinking of the colour, extension, and motion of an object, as he seems to be doing, surely the mind can abstract, say, the shape from the colour and movement and concentrate on it alone. As we shall see, he himself admits as much in 1734.

Thus Berkeley's criticisms up to this point are unconvincing. (1) He has shown that I cannot *imagine* a man who is neither white nor black nor any particular colour and is yet coloured. (2) He claims to have shown that 'singling' in certain cases is a psychological impossibility. (3) If the abstract general idea *man* is a fabrication of such 'singled' ideas, and if the 'singling' is impossible, the abstract general idea is impossible. But if 'singling' *is* possible then, of course, this argument against the abstract general idea does not hold.

20. We may now proceed with the polemic, and we shall find that little new is attempted on the destructive side, Berkeley seeming to think that the criticisms already made are adequate.

Since, in Berkeley's opinion, few men ever conceive abstract general ideas Locke's teaching can hardly be true, namely that the having of them is man's distinguishing mark. Unlike the brutes men use words, but this is not a sign of the existence of general abstract ideas in their minds, for 'a word becomes general by being made the sign, not of an abstract general idea but of several particular ideas, any one of which it indifferently suggests to the mind' (section 11). For instance, supposing I say *Whatever has extension is divisible*, then there is no abstract general idea in the mind corresponding to the word *extension*, but there *is* some idea there none the less, namely, a particular line, a surface or a solid, of which the axiom holds. But no abstract general idea corresponds to the word.

This point is developed in section 12. It begins by setting

down the distinction which we have seen emerging in the *Commonplace Book* between 'general ideas' whose existence Berkeley does not deny and 'abstract general ideas' whose existence he does deny. It then explains what the valid general idea is; 'an idea which considered in itself is particular becomes general by being made to represent or stand for all other particular ideas of the same sort.' I may be using a triangle drawn on paper to illustrate a theorem in geometry, the theorem, however, holds of all triangles. I use this particular triangle (an idea in my mind) in a representative capacity.

This twelfth section should have been the most important in the *Introduction*. Berkeley's positive theory of generalization is being put forward, namely that it is taking a particular and letting it stand for many particulars. But he fails to ask one essential question. What particulars is this particular to stand for? What marks them out for grouping? Why do we choose a particular to represent just these? Inevitably Berkeley must say more than that a particular stands for many particulars. The particular idea, he says, represents 'all other particular ideas of the same sort'. Berkeley has to introduce the notion of 'sort' here, in order to make sense of his theory. But once he does introduce it the important element in his theory is no longer the using of the particular to represent the sort, but the sort itself. It is at this point that we should expect an adequate discussion of sorts; but, as we know, Berkeley cannot provide such a discussion. The consequence is that the section fails. What is a matter of secondary importance is put in the forefront, whilst the really important question is begged.

Being unable to develop the positive theory, Berkeley falls back on his polemic. He now brings forward the 'killing blow' which had been in his mind from the first. Locke in IV. vii. 9 describes the general idea of triangle as 'neither oblique nor rectangle, neither equilateral, equicrural, nor scalenon; but all and none of these at once. In effect, it is something imperfect, that cannot exist; an idea wherein some parts of several different and inconsistent ideas are put together.' This means, says Berkeley (interpreting Locke wrongly, as I believe), that to think the abstract, general idea is to think that which involves a self-contradiction within itself, an impossibility. Surely Locke's theory is the height of absurdity. And yet it is alleged that these are the ideas we use in communicating our thoughts. When, Berkeley asks, did we frame these ideas? When did we learn to carry out this most difficult and complicated procedure? Since we are not aware of learning to do so as adults we must have framed them first in childhood. But, as Berkeley says, 'Is it not a hard thing to imagine that a couple of children cannot prate together of their sugar-plums and rattles and the rest of their little trinkets, till they have first tacked together numberless inconsistencies, and so framed in their minds *abstract general ideas*, and annexed them to every common name they make use of' (section 14).

Nor are such ideas necessary for the *enlargement* of knowledge. Berkeley now admits, in stark contrast to the passage in the *Draft*, that knowledge and demonstration are 'about universal notions'.

> But [he adds] it doth not appear to me that these notions are formed by *abstraction* in the manner premised, *universality*, so far as I can comprehend, not consisting in the absolute, positive nature or conception of any thing, but in the relation it bears to the particulars signified or represented by it: by virtue whereof it is that things, names or notions, being in their own nature *particular*, are rendered *universal* [section 15].

Here again, as in the *Draft*, we find the denial that the universal is objective in the realist sense; nor is it a conception framed by the mind. So much in the quotation is clear, but the remainder is difficult. Universality consists 'in the relation it bears to the particulars signified or represented by it'. What he has in mind is seen more clearly, perhaps, in the example he gives. When I prove something of *triangle* I do have a universal idea of triangle 'in view', though not an abstract general idea; I have *immediately* in view a particular triangle which represents all triangles. The universality of this particular idea lies in its representative capacity *vis-a-vis* those particulars represented by it.

Berkeley himself feels that a fundamental objection can be

made to this account of the universal, and in section 16 he tries to face it. A demonstration made of any particular triangle holds of *that* triangle, but why should it hold of any other? Berkeley answers that while he is reasoning immediately about a particular triangle with sides of determinate length and so on, nevertheless the differentiating features of this triangle are not 'concerned in the demonstration'. 'It is true, the diagram I have in view includes all these particulars, but then there is not the least mention made of them in the proof of the proposition.' Therefore what is true of *this* triangle is true of all.

Now this line of argument obviously leaves a good deal unsaid. Berkeley is now in fact affirming that our real object after all—though we make use of a particular triangle—is not that particular triangle but rather that which is common to all triangles and present in this one. He does not say this openly in the first edition, but how else can the paragraph be interpreted? His argument only holds if it is the case that we are now aware of triangle in general. But in that case it is essential that Berkeley should explain to us exactly what the triangle in general is; to say that it is a particular triangle having a representative capacity is not to explain its nature.

It is significant that in 1734 in the second edition Berkeley thought it necessary to add a few sentences to this section. 'And here it must be acknowledged that a man may consider a figure merely as triangular, without attending to the particular qualities of the angles, or relations of the sides. So far he may abstract: but this will never prove that he can frame an abstract general inconsistent idea of a triangle.' We may grant the final point. What is important is that Berkeley now says we can abstract the triangularity. This seems to imply that looking at these shaped coloured patches before me I *can* abstract ('single out') the shape triangle, and concentrate upon it, neglecting other shapes, neglecting the colour, neglecting the movement, or lack of movement, of the patches. I can fasten upon the triangularity of certain of the patches and think about it as such. This is the abstract idea of triangularity. And triangles are particulars which make up one sort because they all share triangularity. So much seems to be admitted in this addition to section 16.

Thus Berkeley's polemic against abstract ideas ends with the admission of abstract ideas, with the acknowledgement of the universal abstract idea *triangularity*. But it is one thing to acknowledge the existence of such ideas; it is another to give an account of them. We find no satisfactory account of these ideas in Berkeley's *Introduction*.

21. Thus what should have been the most important sections of the *Introduction* turn out to be hopelessly inadequate, and we return to the point with which we began, namely that the most valuable sections of the *Introduction* come at the end (18–25). Here Berkeley puts forward, though in a very tentative fashion, some highly interesting suggestions. These cannot but be tentative because they lack the solid foundation which a successful theory of universals would have given; none the less they contain some very pertinent and penetrating observations.

They have to do with language. Berkeley finds the source of the erroneous theory of abstraction in language. For it is supposed that whenever we use a general word it stands for a precise determinate general idea. 'Whereas, in truth, there is no such thing as one precise and definite signification annexed to any general name, they all signifying indifferently a great number of particular ideas' (Section 18). This is Locke's mistake. He thinks there must invariably be a precise general idea. He does not realize that the general word can stand for many ideas and stand loosely for them all. And Berkeley, it is interesting to note, goes farther than this. He holds that the general word never stands for a precise idea. For instance, he will not allow that the most strictly defined term signifies a precise idea. A triangle is defined as a plane surface comprehended by three straight lines. But 'in the definition it is not said whether the surface be great or small, black or white, nor whether the sides are long or short, equal or unequal, nor with what angles they are inclined to each other; in all which there may be great variety, and consequently there is no one settled idea which limits the signification of the word *triangle*' (section 18). Thus a general word, however carefully I use it, signifies a wide variety of ideas rather than one precise idea.

Moreover, it is not even true that whenever we use a word it must at least signify some particular idea or other. Words can be used which signify no ideas. This doctrine of Berkeley's has sometimes been assumed to be nominalist in character. In fact he is saying something which a realist might well admit.

> A little attention [he says] will discover that it is not necessary (even in the strictest reasonings) significant names which stand for ideas should, every time they are used, excite in the understanding the ideas they are made to stand for; in reading and discoursing names being, for the most part, used as letters are in *algebra*, in which, though a particular quantity be marked by each letter, yet to proceed right it is not requisite that in every step each letter suggest to your thoughts that particular quantity it was appointed to stand for [section 19].

That is to say, though words do stand for ideas (but not precise, determinate general ideas), these ideas need not always be in the mind when the words are used.[1]

Finally, we should not assume that the sole end and purpose of language is to communicate ideas. 'There are other ends, as the raising of some passion, the exciting to or deterring from an action, the putting the mind in some particular disposition', and we may seek these ends without even attempting to communicate ideas (section 20). It thus seems entirely false to suppose that whenever we use a general word we are at that time conceiving some general idea signified by it; and this is the erroneous supposition made by Locke.

Because words do signify such a great variety of ideas and because we tend to think they signify a precise idea, Berkeley counsels us to abjure their use as far as possible. 'Since, therefore, words are so apt to impose on the understanding, whatever

[1] In the *Alciphron*, Seventh Dialogue (1st ed.), sections 7 and 8, Berkeley makes a like point. But here he adds that words can be used for indistinct as well as distinct ideas. Not all our ideas are distinct; words can be used vaguely. The general discussion of abstract ideas in the *Alciphron* while clear and explicit adds little if anything to the main argument of the *Introduction*.

ideas I consider, I shall endeavour to take them bare and naked into my view, keeping out of my thoughts, so far as I am able, those names which long and constant use hath so strictly united with them' (section 21). The Solitary Man is not introduced into the text at this point, but he is clearly much in the author's mind.

22. When we now attempt a final assessment of Berkeley's polemic and of his teaching on the abstract and the general, the following conclusions suggest themselves.

Berkeley is fully justified in ruling out the 'abstract general idea' which includes within itself an open contradiction. The use of such ideas in thinking would lead to disastrous consequences. The question that arises, however, is whether Locke or anyone else ever held such a theory of abstraction. There may be concealed contradictions in our thinking, but no philosopher would consciously welcome and retain them. Berkeley's interpretation of Locke is surely mistaken.

In the second place, what Berkeley says about 'singling' seems doubtful psychologically, for he himself ends by admitting that one can single out triangularity.

Thirdly, the charge can be made against Berkeley that in the *Introduction* he turned his back upon the main problem, that of the status and nature of what he called the 'sorts'. In the *Commonplace Book* and *Draft* he had touched on the problem but found it too difficult. Yet the argument of the *Introduction* is incomplete without a discussion of this matter and lacks a foundation.

The concluding paragraphs dealing with language are none the less very valuable. They suggest that the conceptualist view of universals in the Lockean form, which was fast becoming the prevailing view, itself needed correction. It was not true that a general word invariably signified a general idea. Perhaps, it never did so. There were certainly occasions when it did not signify any idea whatsoever, and occasions when we used words merely to arouse emotions or incite to action. The prevailing theory of language was too narrow.

Valuable, too, is the logical implication which may fairly be drawn from Berkeley's denial of general abstract ideas. To say that a man is coloured is to say that he has some colour, white, black, tawny or some other colour; it cannot mean that he has no colour. To be triangular is to be scalene or equilateral or isosceles; it is absurd to say that something is triangular but is neither scalene, equilateral, nor isosceles. In other words, the determinable or generic character, to be significant, must be a disjunction of determinates or specific characters. What pretends to be a determinable and is yet not a disjunction of determinates is logically impossible. It does not follow that we must be acquainted with all the determinates before we can use the determinable, nor need we have precise knowledge of any one determinate. We may and do use these determinable predicates in somewhat indefinite ways. If I say that certain objects are blue I may not know the precise shade of blue, but I do not mean that they are blue without being any precise shade of blue. The logical point that a determinable is invariably a disjunction of determinates is an important one and it is present by implication in the *Introduction*.

These are valuable points in Berkeley's discussion and yet the *Introduction* as a whole, viewed as a positive contribution to the theory of universals, is disappointing. It can be said in its favour that it asked some very relevant questions. Berkeley says of Locke that he 'bantered' the notion of substance; in the same way we may say of Berkeley that he 'bantered' the general idea. His real criticism of Locke was a deeper one than that we cannot think inconsistencies. It was regrettable that he was carried away by his desire to inflict 'the killing blow', particularly since the blow does not seem to have been as mortal as Berkeley thought it would be. His real and effective line of attack was rather that Locke throughout presented his theory of universals in too narrow and too academic a manner. Here Berkeley was undoubtedly on safe ground and subsequent philosophers did not fail to notice some of his criticisms. Yet he himself, we must conclude, did little to solve the general problem.

IV

RESEMBLANCE AND DISPOSITION IN HUME'S THEORY

23. There is much that is novel and revolutionary in Hume's account of our use of general words. His fullest and best discussion of the matter is to be found in the *Treatise of Human Nature* in the section on abstract ideas.[1] In this section the novel features do not at once emerge. Indeed a hasty reader may easily jump to the conclusion that the author has nothing fresh to say but merely wishes to restate a doctrine put forward earlier by Berkeley. To some extent Hume's innate modesty, possibly even a little inexperience in the presenting of his argument—for the *Treatise* is an early work—help to create this mistaken impression. But there is also a deeper explanation. Hume himself, it is clear, is not fully aware of the importance and significance of the new suggestions he is making. In his later works he never develops the teaching of this early passage. In the somewhat superficial treatment of abstraction in the *Inquiry Concerning Human Understanding* (sections 122—6) he all but omits the new elements in his theory.

This is not the only instance of a failure on Hume's part to realize the worth of his own achievements, as witness his disavowal of the *Treatise* in later life and his wish that he should be judged by works which are undoubtedly inferior to it, namely, the *Inquiry Concerning Human Understanding* and the *Inquiry Concerning the Principles of Morals*. In the section on abstraction, beginning with the Berkeleian theory that whenever we generalize we have before us a particular idea, Hume develops the argument in a highly original manner, setting forward the important Disposition or Propensity theory. This theory fills a gap left unfilled in Locke's theory of universals and provides the solution of a difficulty in Locke which had considerably disturbed Berkeley but which Berkeley had not succeeded in

[1] I. i. 7.

solving. Furthermore, in a note added in the Appendix referring to this section, Hume sets forward the Resemblance theory, not in its fullness it is true, but none the less in its essentials. In other words, outlined in these pages are two theories of outstanding importance for the psychology of generalizing. And yet the impression Hume first leaves upon his reader is that the only doctrine of importance which he has to convey is Berkeley's doctrine that we cannot generalize without having in mind a particular image.

24. In considering Hume's theory it would be best to begin with this latter doctrine and with Hume's formulation of it. Essentially it consists in the assertion that generalizing involves concrete imagery. As Hume states the point: 'Abstract ideas are in themselves individual, however they may become general in their representation. The image in the mind is only that of a particular object, though the application of it in our reasoning be the same as if it were universal.'[1] General ideas are 'nothing but particular ones annexed to a certain term, which gives them a more extensive signification, and makes them recall upon occasion other individuals, which are similar to them'.[2] Hume attributes the doctrine to Berkeley and describes it as 'one of the greatest and most valuable discoveries that has been made of late years in the republic of letters'. He will endeavour, he tells us, to 'confirm it by some arguments'.

It is not difficult to see why Hume ranked this theory so highly. In the first place, as we have already seen, it was in accord with the contemporary revolt against abstraction. The general idea itself was held to be a particular concrete individual. Secondly, Hume in the opening pages of the *Treatise* sets down the principle that 'all our ideas are copied from our impressions', and allows no exception to the principle.[3] What, then, of the general idea? It must somehow be shown to be a copy of an impression. Hume cannot admit that it is an intel-

[1] Selby-Bigge, p. 20; Everyman, pp. 27–28 (hereafter cited as S-B., and E.).

[2] S-B., p. 17; E., p. 25.

[3] The 'one contradictory phenomenon' he mentions (S-B., p. 5; E., p. 15) is hardly an exception.

lectual idea apprehended by reason. We may rationally intuit a relation between ideas, where this relation 'depends entirely on the ideas'.[1] But the ideas themselves will be derived from impressions, and if the ideas so derived do not permit of such relationships no intuition and no certain knowledge are possible. A consequence is the surprising account of geometry which we find in the opening section of the third part of the *Treatise*, an account which shows how far Hume carries his empiricist principles. Now, the more thorough-going the empiricism, the more difficult it is to explain the general idea, and the more welcome is any account of it consistent with empiricism. Hence Hume's commendation of Berkeley's theory, and hence also his confident rejection of all universals and abstract ideas other than the Berkeleian, i.e. particular ideas used in a representative capacity.

It is easy to see [he says, speaking of the other kind of universals] why philosophers are so fond of this notion of some spiritual and refined perceptions; since by that means they cover many of their absurdities and may refuse to submit to the decisions of clear ideas, by appealing to such as are obscure and uncertain. But to destroy this artifice, we need but reflect on that principle so oft insisted on, *that all our ideas are copied from our impressions.*[2]

Here we find both the general criticism that 'refined and spiritual' universals (or, as he also calls them, universals 'comprehended by a pure intellectual view') are merely a means for disguising absurdities and obscurities, and also the special empiricist criticism that such ideas cannot really exist since the only ideas which exist are those which copy impressions.

Hume offers three arguments in support of the view that ideas are concrete or, in his language, 'that the mind cannot form any notion of quantity or quality without forming a precise notion of degrees of each': (1) To talk of such abstractions as pure line, pure extension, &c., involves the absurdity of abstracting (and so separating) an 'essential part' of a thing from that thing itself.

It is evident at first sight that the precise length of a line is not

[1] Cf. I. iii. I.

[2] S-B., p. 72; E. p. 76.

different nor distinguishable from the line itself; nor the precise degree of any quality from the quality. These ideas, therefore, admit no more of separation than they do of distinction and difference. They are consequently conjoined with each other in the conception; and the general idea of a line, notwithstanding all our abstractions and refinements, has in its appearance in the mind a precise degree of quantity and quality.[1]

This quotation, particularly the last sentence, reveals, what Hume of course does nothing to hide, that he has in mind an image. He thinks it true beyond all doubting that we cannot have an image of a line which is not of some particular length. Whether this is so or not—and it is a debatable question—it in no way proves the assertion that the abstract idea is always an image, nor does it prove that the mind cannot form a 'notion', which is not an image, of line in general. Yet these are the points which really need to be proved. Moreover, it is questionable whether Hume's words here are consistent with his account a few pages farther on of the so-called 'distinctions of reason', for he there admits that we may in one sense at least think of a globe without thinking of its colour, and this suggests that we may also think of a line without thinking of its precise length. (2) Since all ideas copy impressions and since an impression is determinate, ideas, including abstract ideas, must be equally determinate. In criticizing this argument we can, on the one hand, query the determinateness of all impressions.[2] On the other, the fundamental question whether abstract ideas are in fact images is still being assumed and has not been proved. (3) Everything in nature is 'individual', i.e. in this context, a precisely determined particular. Now, since existence is not a predicate, or, in other words, since there is nothing more in respect of ideal content in the idea of an existing thing than in the idea of the thing, an idea of a thing has precisely the characteristics of a thing. Consequently, since it is absurd to suppose that any individual thing 'in fact and reality' should not be precisely determined, it is equally absurd to suppose that the idea should not be so

[1] S-B., pp. 18–19; E. pp. 26–27.

[2] Laird aptly quotes W. E. Johnson (*Logic*, I. xxix): 'Neither images nor perceptions reflect the concreteness and particularity of the individual thing.'

determined. This third argument rests on very questionable premisses. In what sense is it true that everything existing is individual? Secondly, is every idea an exact copy of the thing in the sense supposed; more especially, is the *general* idea such an exact copy of an individual thing?

Such are the arguments which Hume brings forward in support of Berkeley's position. They hardly convince the reader, nor do they greatly strengthen Berkeley's case. Critics have held that these pages are badly argued and that anyhow the position they set forth is indefensible. It is contended that Hume contradicts himself and cannot but contradict himself the moment he admits, as he must, genuine instances of abstraction, for instance, the 'distinction of reason'. Moreover, the most elementary introspection, not to mention the careful work of introspective psychologists to which I must refer later, shows that sometimes we certainly generalize *without* having concrete, precisely determined imagery in mind. To say the least, the imagery is frequently very vague. Sometimes no imagery whatever seems to be present. Criticisms of this sort in respect to Hume's teaching seem to me valid. Having admitted them, however, the point I immediately wish to make is that such criticisms when urged against Hume's theory of universals are not final. For though Hume begins by accepting the position outlined here and speaks at first as if he had nothing to add to it, he does in fact work out a theory of his own which cannot be refuted merely by refuting the present theory. The neglect of this point, I venture to think, is the main defect in the contemporary criticism of Hume's theory of universals.

25. Before we consider the main contribution which Hume makes in this connexion it would be wise to consider his account of resemblance and the celebrated note in which the Resemblance theory emerges. There are two accounts of resemblance in the *Treatise*: first, what may be called the traditional account according to which two things resemble when they have one or more elements in common and, secondly, Hume's additional theory which provides the foundation for the Resemblance

theory proper, that resemblance may occur where there are no elements in common.

Hume begins with what was the traditional theory in his day, and were it not for one circumstance it is plain that the second theory would never have entered his head. In the language of composites, which was Hume's language, the traditional theory could be set out thus. Two composites may be said to resemble each other if amongst the simples out of which one composite is formed and amongst the simples out of which the other is formed at least one simple will be found common to the two groups. Thus, if there is a composite *A* consisting of *a b c d* and another *B* consisting of *a b e f*, the composites *A* and *B* may be said to resemble each other, having the simples *a* and *b* in common. Our task in generalizing, as Locke taught, consists in seizing the common element or elements in these resembling wholes. Professor Laird cites[1] a passage from one of Hume's essays which expresses Hume's general standpoint in respect to this matter: 'General reasonings seem intricate, merely because they are general; nor is it easy for the bulk of mankind to distinguish in a great number of particulars that common circumstance in which they all agree, or to extract it, pure and unmixed, from the other superfluous circumstances.' It is not easy to find the common element or elements nor easy to isolate it or them, yet this, Hume takes for granted, is what we have to do. If, further, we ask what is meant by a *common* element, the answer which appears to be assumed by both Locke and Hume is that it is an identical quality, for instance, the red shade of this flower is identical with the red shade of that flower. They assumed this, without, however, being fully aware of the problem implicit in the assumption they were making.

Now Hume did become aware of this problem, and puts forward a new account of resemblance, in reflecting upon another problem which Locke had posed in this connexion. Locke had realized that if we begin with the theory that resemblances can be observed only where composites possess common components in the sense explained above, then it ought to

[1] *Hume's Philosophy of Human Nature*, p. 58.

follow that simples cannot resemble each other and that consequently we cannot generalize in their case.

> The reason whereof is that the lowest species being but one simple idea nothing can be left out of it, that so, the difference being taken away, it may agree with some other thing in one idea common to them both; which, having one name, is the genus of the other two; for example, there is nothing that can be left out of the idea of white and red to make them agree in one common appearance and so have one general name.[1]

And yet simples do resemble each other and we do generalize in their case. The solution proposed by Locke to this difficult problem, is other than Hume's. Locke sought for a common characteristic extrinsic to the simples, for instance, white and red are both *visibilia*, they 'get into the mind' in the same way, and so may be said to resemble each other in this respect. But would not the consequence of this be that the entities with which he now deals are in fact composites and not simples, consisting of two characteristics, for example, (*a*) being white and (*b*) being a *visibile*? If so, his problem remains unsolved.

When writing the *Treatise* Hume did not have this problem of Locke's in mind, but he reflected on it later and added the note on resemblance in the appendix.[2] In the text of the *Treatise* he merely remarks: 'When we have found a resemblance among several objects, that often occurs to us, we apply the same name to all of them.' He attempts no analysis of the process of 'finding a resemblance'. However, in the note he realizes that something must at least be said about resembling *simples.*

> It is evident [he writes] that even different simple ideas may have a similarity or resemblance to each other; nor is it necessary that the point or circumstance of resemblance should be distinct or separable from that in which they differ. *Blue* and *green* are different simple ideas, but are more resembling than *blue* and *scarlet*: though their perfect simplicity excludes all possibility of separation or distinction. It is the same case with particular sounds and tastes and smells. These admit of infinite resemblances upon the general appearance and comparison without having any common circumstance the same.

[1] *Essay*, III. iv. 16.

[2] S-B., p. 637; E. p. 28.

Here is a very definite suggestion of the Resemblance theory. We may generalize not by discovering a common element or elements, but by noting resemblances where there are no identical common qualities, or at least no known identical common qualities. Blue and green are more resembling than blue and scarlet. This shade of blue and that shade of blue, though different, none the less resemble one another more than do this shade of blue and this shade of green. This is a sufficient basis for generalization, even if we know no such identities as are assumed in the theory that we know common elements. Hume has thus put forward quite a new account of finding resemblances and of generalizing, and the modern Resemblance theory is merely the development of this suggestion. It has developed it by applying Hume's suggestion not merely to simples but also to complexes. Even in the case of composites, is it so necessary as we supposed to find identities before we can generalize? Must we first make quite certain that the quality a^1 in A is identical with the quality a^2 in B, before we can group A and B for purposes of generalization? The demand for absolute identities raises awkward questions. Would it not be enough to say that these qualities resemble one another? This is a matter to which it will be necessary to return later. It is enough now to note that the solution proposed by the adherents of the Resemblance theory is already suggested in Hume's note.

Yet it is also worth recalling that the new theory of resemblance emerges as Hume is dealing with what he, like Locke, would regard as the exceptional case, namely, resemblances between simples. There is no evidence to suggest that Hume would have applied his findings in the sense of the previous paragraph to resemblances between complexes, although there was nothing to prevent his doing so as his successors realized. But Hume did not develop his own suggestion. Moreover, even this note is not free from ambiguity, for it might be urged that in its concluding sentences he slips back into speaking of even these simples as resembling one another in respect of an identity. Here he asks what it is that enables us to group all simples together and to talk of them, for instance, under the abstract term *simple idea.* He finds the explanation in the fact that they 'resemble each other in their simplicity'. Now, if we continue to interpret the note in terms of the 'similarity' theory this would mean that the simplicity of the one simple idea *a* resembles, or is similar to, but is not identical with, the simplicity of the second simple idea *b.* Yet this hardly seems to be Hume's meaning. He surely means that the simplicity in both cases is identical.[1]

Thus Hume's position is ambiguous even in the note and it would be wrong to suggest that the Resemblance theory emerges fully fledged in the *Treatise.* None the less, the explicit suggestion of it is present.

26. We now turn to consider the most important element in Hume's discussion of our use of general words, namely, the Disposition or Propensity theory. It is novel; nothing quite like it is to be found in Locke or Berkeley or in the works of any contemporary continental philosopher. It is, furthermore, bound up with what is most original in Hume's teaching in general, namely his particular interpretation of the association of ideas on the one hand and of belief on the other. It rests upon the theory of the association of ideas as do so many other doctrines of the *Treatise.*

Hume illustrated the Disposition theory by certain 'analogies', and we may begin with an examination of these. I am convinced that the analogies are meant to illustrate this theory rather than, as some of the critics have assumed, the other theory that in generalizing we always have a particular in mind. They will be found towards the end of the section on abstract ideas.[2] They are three in number and 'a fourth reflection' is added noting the manner in which the 'act of mind'

[1] This is the view taken by Dr. R. W. Church in his *Hume's Theory of the Understanding*, London, 1935, chap. i, section i. Cf. also his interesting 'Hume's Theory of Philosophical Relations', *Phil. Rev.* July, 1941. But Church goes farther and holds that this is Hume's invariable meaning. In Hume's philosophy, he holds, 'a resemblance is any case of a qualitative identity that exists in at least two cases of itself' (p. 356 of the article in *Phil. Rev.*). In my opinion Hume sometimes seems to mean this by 'resemblance'. At other times his words demand a different interpretation.

[2] S-B., pp. 22–23; E. pp. 30–31.

illustrated by the analogies is greatly facilitated by the readiness with which the imagination recalls resembling ideas. Now of these analogies one of the commentators, Dr. Maund, says, they 'are not strictly speaking "analogies" at all, but merely instances or illustrations of the point he is trying to make',[1] and Professor Kemp Smith holds that they are 'not really analogous in any helpful manner'.[2] Both commentators come to this conclusion, it appears to me, because they assume that the analogies are meant to illustrate the use of a particular idea or image to represent all ideas 'of the same sort'. But Hume, I think, is trying to illustrate something else with their aid.

We may be helped to understand what he has in mind if we consider each of these analogies in turn.

> First, then [he says], I observe that when we mention any great number, such as a thousand, the mind has generally no adequate idea of it, but only a power of producing such an idea, by its adequate idea of the decimals under which the number is comprehended. This imperfection, however, in our ideas is never felt in our reasonings, which seems to be an instance parallel to the present one of universal ideas.

Now this is not meant as a thorough-going analysis of number, still less of mathematics. Hume is merely pointing to a phenomenon familiar to anyone who understands how to use the decimal system. By using a certain technique we can frame an idea of a very large number. In one sense the number is clear enough, in another it is not but is somehow imperfect. For instance, when astronomers compute the number of stars in the skies or physicists the number of atoms in a cupful of water, and mention a number, we find it difficult to comprehend the number because of its largeness. Yet we handle the largest numbers successfully and our abilities in this respect prove most useful. Just so with generalizing; it is a most useful technical accomplishment without whose aid we could not reason nor, indeed, live out our full, human life; and yet, Hume thinks, the general idea has in it something 'imperfect' and 'inadequate'.

[1] *Hume's Theory of Knowledge*, London, 1937, p. 173.
[2] *The Philosophy of David Hume*, London, 1941, p. 262.

Consider next the second analogy. 'We have several instances of habits which may be revived by one single word; as when a person, who has by rote any periods of discourse or any number of verses, will be put in remembrance of the whole, which he is at a loss to recollect, by that single word or expression with which they begin.' This is no analogy, says Professor Kemp Smith, for while 'the opening word is part of the discourse or poem, a particular image is not a part (at least not in this manner) of the abstract idea'.[1] But why assume that the analogy is meant to illustrate the relation between a particular image and an abstract idea? Does it not rather illustrate the way in which a person, once conditioned in a certain way, can be stimulated to the appropriate reaction by hearing or seeing a word? Hume suggests that a like sort of occurrence is present in the whole mental act we call generalizing.

He uses the third analogy to show how 'we do not annex distinct and complete ideas to every term we make use of'. Take such words as 'government', 'church', 'negotiation', 'conquest', 'we seldom spread out in our minds all the simple ideas of which these complex ones are composed'. Yet we manage to use these words intelligently, and quickly perceive any fundamentally absurd use of them. The critics here question Hume's right to call such ideas complex ideas. That is not an uninteresting point in itself, but it seems to me largely irrelevant in this context and to stress it is to miss the analogy. Hume is merely pointing out that we ordinarily use such words as these with a fair amount of success, even though they are not exactly defined by us. The ordinary man's use of these words has a certain imperfection, but yet he does not use them foolishly. By conversation and reading he has accustomed himself to the proper use of the words, and he generally uses them correctly, though he is not able to define them precisely. This, Hume thinks, illustrates the manner in which general words are used successfully although we do not have precisely in mind at the time all the possible instances covered by the general word.

From these three analogies we can conclude that Hume wants

[1] *The Philosophy of David Hume*, p. 263.

to establish the following points in connexion with the use of general words: (1) In order to use general words successfully we have to learn a certain technique, the technique of using a word to cover a vast amount of material, much of which is not strictly speaking in our thought when using the word. (2) The general word acts as a stimulus and, in Hume's language, 'revives a habit'. We shall see in the next section what the habit is and how it is revived. (3) The meaning of this general word cannot be said to be fixed when we use it; it is used with a certain degree of looseness and is not precisely defined. None the less we use it significantly in thinking and in the communicating of our thought to others. These, it seems to me, are the points which the analogies are meant to illustrate.

27. We now turn to consider Hume's development of this theory.[1] We begin with the finding of resemblances, and we have already seen that Hume thought it possible to observe a resemblance without discovering a common character. The next step, therefore, need not be the abstraction of a common character or common characters. Instead of such explicit abstraction Hume substitutes custom and the natural association of ideas acting, as he has said earlier,[2] 'as a gentle force which commonly prevails'. This is not to deny that we may occasionally make the explicit abstraction—always supposing that we can find the common characters—but ordinarily the process is very different.

> When we have found a resemblance [he says] among several objects that often occur to us, we apply the same name to all of them, whatever differences we may observe in the degrees of their quantity and quality and whatever other differences may appear among them. After we have acquired a custom of this kind, the hearing of that name revives the idea of one of these objects. . . .[3]

Hume here may be charged with over-simplifying the business of naming, for it is more correct to say that we usually learn *the* name than that we apply a name—and much is involved in learning the appropriate name. Nevertheless, his purpose is not

[1] S-B., pp. 20–22; E. pp. 28–30.
[2] Section 2. iv.
[3] S-B., p. 20; E. p. 28.

to explain the nature of naming. He wishes rather to explain the whole process of becoming accustomed to a recurrence of resembling entities in experience, and of associating a name with the recurrence, in such a way that henceforward the hearing of that name, or the seeing of it in writing, stimulates the mind to certain activities. In the first instance, he holds, following the Berkeleian theory, it 'revives the idea of one of these objects and makes the imagination conceive it with all its particular circumstances and proportions'. In addition, however, it revives something else, which Hume finds difficult to describe. 'The word raises up an individual idea, along with a certain custom, and that custom produces any other individual one, for which we may have occasion.' It 'raises up a custom' or 'revives a habit'. This is puzzling language. Hume seems to be saying that something which was dormant is awakened and the consequence is that the mind becomes taut, ready to recall any one of the ideas of the resembling entities which it has experienced. In a sense, the hearing of the name brings them all before it, but potentially rather than actually. 'They are not really and in fact present to the mind, but only in power; nor do we draw them all out distinctly in the imagination, but keep ourselves in a readiness to survey any of them, as we may be prompted by a present design or necessity.' Usually only a few ideas are recalled; indeed, 'the production of all the ideas, to which the name may be applied, is in most cases impossible'.

The mind becomes prepared also in another way. Just as it is ready to recall, so it is ready to reject. It is ready to reject that to which it is *not* accustomed. It is on its guard, waiting to denounce any attempt to include within the 'compass of the collection', i.e of the experienced collection, an entity which does not belong to it, or to exclude from the collection an entity which *does* belong to it.

Thus, should we mention the word triangle, and form the idea of a particular equilateral one to correspond to it, and should we afterwards assert *that the three angles of a triangle are equal to each other*, the other individuals of a scalenum and isosceles which we overlooked at first, immediately crowd in upon us, and make us perceive the falsehood of this proposition, though it be true with relation to that idea which we had formed.

We may even recall one and the same particular idea in response to different terms, as when we recall the same particular equilateral triangle an inch high when the words 'figure', 'rectilinear figure', 'triangle', and 'equilateral triangle' are mentioned, and yet not be muddled in our use of these words, if the custom and habit which determine the 'compass of the collection' be strong enough. Moreover, Hume adds, where the habit is not 'become entirely perfect... the mind may not be content with forming the idea of only one individual, but may run over several, in order to make itself comprehend its own meaning, and the compass of that collection, which it intends to express by the general term. That we may fix the meaning of the word *figure* we may revolve in our minds the ideas of circles, squares, parallelograms, triangles of different sizes and proportions, and may not rest on one image or idea.'[1] Here the mind, it would seem, is consciously and explicitly doing what custom for the most part does for it unwittingly; it consciously sets out to notice what the habit brings forth and so 'fixes' the meaning of the word 'figure'. But this last quotation in particular shows how we can no longer say that taking one particular and making it stand for all of the same sort is the central feature of the theory now emerging. The taking of one particular is not the important element; what is important is this custom-induced suggestibility of the mind, this habit, or 'propensity'.

28. The theory of universals and of the use of general words found in these pages, which I have called the Disposition or Propensity theory, is not fully worked out here, nor is it further developed by Hume elsewhere. But enough is said to enable us to see its main outlines. Basically, it may be regarded as a protest against the view that prior to the use of general words there is always, or even usually, a conscious selection of common characteristics followed by the framing of a universal. This, it holds, is bad psychology, being too sophisticated an account of

[1] S-B., p. 22; E. pp. 29–30.

the process in question. We cannot suppose that children set out to isolate common characteristics, and abstract them to frame the universal. In their case, as in the case of adults, for most of the time, custom is king; familiarity with a world in which certain resemblances recur creates within the mind, almost without our knowing, a customary grouping whose links are strengthened by the learning of the common name. And if later the name is used for an entity which does not resemble members of the group, the mind is disappointed in its expectation. By the time we reach maturity these expectations of ours have been abundantly confirmed and have a powerful influence on our thought. Such Hume thinks is the more 'natural' account of this process at the level of daily life.

Or we may look at Hume's theory from another angle, and think of it as a protest against the 'refined' concept of the schools. Not that, having rejected this concept, Hume merely substituted for it a particular idea having a representative capacity. Such a theory would have been equally unsatisfactory. Hume, however, shows that a concept must be thought of in terms of the conceiving of a concept; that logic cannot be wholly divorced from psychology; and that, frequently at least, conceiving a concept is having this expectation on hearing a name, this readiness to recognize an instance and to reject what is not an instance. A universal in so far as it is something permanent possessed by the mind should not be regarded as invariably a solid core of ideal content but rather as sometimes a readiness and expectation, which has in addition to a cognitive side an emotional side, although occasionally the latter may be in abeyance. Just as William James has talked of 'the feeling of *but*', and Bertrand Russell of 'either . . . or' in terms of the feeling of hesitation or indecision, so also Hume would seem to think of the universal as a psychological state that is 'sensitive' as well as cognitive. Universals, that is to say, cannot be adequately described in terms of bare ideas, or even of images; we must also think of them in terms of tendencies and states of mind.

Hume's theory may be elaborated farther by borrowing certain notions from psychology. Thus the notion of *set* may help us, a notion derived in the first place from the psychologist's laboratory. In reaction-time experiments the observer is prepared for a certain occurrence and warned to be ready for it. His state is then described as one of *set. Set* is a state found, of course, outside the psychologist's laboratory, and what Hume seems to have in mind here may be said to be an instance of it. For he describes us as 'keeping ourselves in readiness' once we hear the word. Hearing the word takes the place of the psychologist's warning and we are then prepared and waiting. If this, however, is *set*, the great difference between it and the psychologist's is that it is not created artificially but is an empirically produced custom. It is the offspring of experience.

Again, Hume's theory may be held to anticipate that of the introspectionist Würzburg school, particularly that of Marbe. This school a generation ago developed the doctrine of 'imageless thinking', proving by psychological experimentation that thinking did not necessarily involve the use of images. Marbe went further and held that thinking did not necessarily involve intellectual concepts either, but consisted largely in expectations, states of uneasiness or of hesitation, conscious attitudes, which he called *Bewusstseinslagen*. This seems to be very much the sort of thing which Hume has in mind.

Unlike Marbe, however, Hume would hold that a particular concrete image is present together with the mental state. We have seen some ground for doubting whether this insistence on concrete imagery is the really essential element in his theory. He might, particularly in view of what he says about the possibility of many concrete images being in the mind rather than one, have developed this side of his teaching so as to anticipate still a third theory of psychology, that of the 'generic image'. According to this theory familiarity with objects having features in common provides the observer in due course with a generic image, in which the common features of these objects tend to stand out and the variable tend to disappear. The mind is presented with a composite photograph of the group. Now Hume might have developed this part of his theory in this way, yet it is necessary to add that no 'generic image' theory is ever suggested by him, whereas the suggestion of a *Bewusstseinslage* theory is quite explicit in what he says.

29. In concluding we may consider the value of Hume's achievement. His immediate contribution, and it is an important one, was the solution of the outstanding difficulty in the empiricist theory of universals. Locke had made the use of general words so difficult that one almost needed to be an intellectual giant to use them at all. Yet ordinary people and children spoke in general terms apparently without difficulty. Hume, approaching the problem from a new angle, steeped in reflection upon custom and habit, showed that learning to use general words is not normally a conscious act. We use general words long before we consciously frame concepts, and we are able to do so because experience has familiarized us with certain recurrences and so habits have been formed. The process of coming to use general words is to be described in terms of these habits. Hearing a word we tend to think so and so and we are ready to reject what we are not disposed to think. These are the child's 'concepts' and these the 'materials' of his thought. The mass of our universals are of this kind; but it is not Hume's position that all universals must be of this kind, for he would clearly have no objection to the explicit analysis of what we are so disposed to think and the fabrication of a possibly more precise universal, a concept in Locke's sense. Locke's trouble was that he thought of the general idea solely in terms of this latter process, whereas, Hume holds, most often it is something very different. Hume was the first of the empiricists to explain our use of general words at the level of daily life, below the 'scientific', and this in itself was a considerable accomplishment.

But he not merely solved the problem which Locke had left outstanding, he gave us also the first clear indication of a new theory of thinking. In saying this we have in view not merely his account of abstract ideas but also his wider philosophy and his general account of the mind's activities as set forth in the *Treatise*. Hume's work is a challenge to those who ignore the habitual in their account of human life. A general discussion of Hume's philosophy from this point of view would be out of place here, but a reference to an interesting note in the section on belief[1] may be permitted.

In this note Hume remarks that it is usual to distinguish between *conception*, *judgement*, and *reasoning* as if they were three distinct processes. Hume believes that this is a faulty practice.

> What we may in general affirm concerning these three acts of the understanding [he adds] is that, taking them in a proper light, they all resolve themselves into the first and are nothing but particular ways of conceiving our objects. Whether we consider a single object or several; whether we dwell on these objects or run from them to others; and in whatever form or order we survey them, the act of the mind exceeds not a simple conception; and the only remarkable difference which occurs on this occasion is when we join belief to the conception and are persuaded of the truth of what we conceive.

Thus for Hume judging and reasoning are forms of conceiving. Now, of course, in so far as we think of judging as involving an *asserting*, it is not then identical with conceiving—and it would not be so for Hume, since it involves belief. So also with reasoning, if we suppose it to involve an explicit assertion of the conclusion. But Hume is not thinking of judging and reasoning in these terms. He is thinking of the way in which we can entertain a judgement without believing it, or a piece of reasoning without asserting the conclusion. I may entertain the judgement that England's days of prosperity are over; I may consider the argument that since comparatively poor states cannot in the long run win a modern war and since Germany was poor as compared with the states opposed to her, it was inevitable that Germany should lose the war. In these cases, Hume thinks, the conceiving, judging, and reasoning, are all finally of one character. As we saw in discussing Locke, the murder of one's next-door neighbour is as much a concept as parricide is, so is England's-days-of-prosperity-being-over. We do not usually call the latter a concept, but it is of the same nature as a concept, Hume thinks, and so also is the complicated piece of reasoning.

Now conceiving, judging, and reasoning in this sense are

[1] *Treatise*, I. iii. 7.

constituents of thinking for Hume, although this is not to be taken to mean that thinking may not also include something different, namely, believing and even knowing. But in so far as thinking is a sort of conceiving then the account given by Hume of the latter applies also to the former. Conceiving must sometimes be explained in terms of empirically formed habits, and so must thinking. Philosophers are too prone to speak of thinking in terms of one species of it, namely, that pondering on a problem when the mind is alert and fully active, when nothing is assumed, when every truth is grasped afresh and the whole ordered logically. But normally we do not reach this ideal. The main characteristic of normal thinking is a reliance on habit. There are acts of insight and there is some purposive steering, but mostly we follow the familiar tracks. Some of these have been laid down consciously. They are principles which we first consciously accepted and which now habitually rule our thoughts. But most of them are the consequence of all we have experienced and learnt; they came into being almost without our knowing and for the most part we follow them blindly.

Such is the theory of thinking suggested in the *Treatise*. We should add that the explanation of believing itself is on the same lines. The constant recurrence of a certain phenomenon in our experience leads us to associate a lively idea with a present impression. Not that all knowing is a believing of this kind, for Hume asserts that we have intuitive knowledge in certain fields, but much of what we call 'knowing' is in fact this sort of believing. So that in so far as our thinking involves knowing, the latter, as likely as not, is a believing, to be explained in this way. Hume explains it in terms of the association of ideas. One of the principles which habitually ruled Hume's own thought was the mechanistic gravitational principle of Newton's physics transcribed into a theory of the association of ideas. It is interesting to speculate what form his explanation of believing and of conceiving would have taken if the notions of growth and development, the biological as opposed to the mechanistic, were uppermost in his mind.

V

THE RATIONALIST RECOIL

30. The differences between empiricists and rationalists at the beginning of the modern period have undoubtedly been exaggerated in the past, and the tendency nowadays is to minimize them. It is clear that both schools began with the same general presuppositions and the consequent philosophies had more in common than the authors themselves or subsequent historians realized. None the less there remain differences, and an important difference between the two schools lies in their attitude to universals.

The empiricists, speaking generally, and not forgetting the demurrers of Berkeley and Hume, elaborated a bold, simple theory according to which the universal is identified with the concept. This is the 'workmanship of the mind' and is fabricated out of materials given in experience. The rationalists were not prepared to accept this theory, and it is instructive to understand why. In the first place, it should be noted that though realist tendencies are occasionally found in their writings, their protest is not that of realists affrighted by a thorough-going conceptualism. On the contrary, the doctrine that the source of universals was the mind itself could not be but acceptable to them, for it was in line with a conviction of theirs that what was in the mind was to be explained solely in terms of the mind. The dualism between body and mind central to their philosophy allowed of no extraneous source of ideas. What was thought emerged from within. It is true that some of these ideas represented things outside which were corporeal and other than mind. But the ideas themselves were mental. The empiricists had not emphasized the dualism of body and mind to the same extent, but they did share the belief that the idea can only represent the corporeal. The table is represented in idea, but not directly known. Consequently both schools begin with the assumption that whatever is directly perceived and whatever is thought, including universals, are 'ideal' and in the mind.

Thus the rationalists had no quarrel with the conceptualism of the empiricist theory. They protested, however, against its empiricism. They could not agree that all universals were fabricated out of empirically derived material. Some universals, no doubt, were fabricated in this way but not all; and the empiricist theory particularly failed in the case of a group of universals of outstanding importance, since they were basic and fundamental in human knowledge. The empiricists had over-simplified the position; their theory, true up to a point, was yet misleading because it was superficial. A deeper analysis of universals was essential.

All this is brought out very clearly by Leibniz, particularly in his examination and criticism of the relevant portions of Locke's *Essay* in the *Nouveaux Essais*. He admits the value of Locke's work on universals but argues that Locke is blind to some of the issues involved. In doing so Leibniz repeats Descartes's criticism of the Gassendist position. Kant, whilst agreeing with the rationalists in finding Locke inadequate, finds their own solution dogmatic, and attempts a solution of his own which we must briefly consider. Nor can we neglect the special case of Spinoza. His analysis of the way in which we first come to conceive universals is most valuable and the criticism of the empiricist standpoint implied in his position, though it differs from that of Leibniz, none the less deserves attention. It would be best to begin with him and then follow the main line of development of the rationalist critique in Descartes and Leibniz.

31. According to Spinoza's theory the universals with which the empiricists are concerned are gained by the mind at the level of Imaginatio. But there is another level or grade of knowledge and it also has its universals, namely, Ratio. Any account of universals which neglects the latter is incomplete, and empiricism is defective in so far as it attempts to conceive the universal in terms of Imaginatio alone. Thus Spinoza's position is rationalist. It differs, however, from the rationalism of Descartes and Leibniz in certain respects, two of which may

be immediately mentioned; first, Spinoza does not stress the innateness of Ratio's knowledge of universals as do Descartes and Leibniz, though such knowledge still remains intellectual and non-empirical for Spinoza; secondly, Ratio itself has its defects in Spinoza's view and is not the highest and most perfect grade of knowledge.

Universals, Spinoza explains in the famous Scholium to Proposition 40, come about at first almost haphazardly. The mind-body dualism is such that my mind always represents my body in idea and any changes in my body, brought about, for instance, by other bodies, have corresponding changes in my mind, corresponding *imagines.* Now supposing the number of these modifications be very great, then the mind fails to represent all the changes and the *imagines* become confused. Only those elements which are frequently repeated tend to be represented, only characters which constantly reappear and are common; it is these accordingly which make up the nucleus of a somewhat vague general image with which is associated a general name. This is the universal of Imaginatio. The mind has no full control of the situation in which it comes into being; the universal is the outcome of modifications which happen to have occurred in my body; it is accordingly private to me and subjective, and yet is not consciously produced. No wonder that philosophers disagree when the universals they use in seeking to understand nature are universals of this kind.[1]

These empirical universals, as we may call them, such as man, horse, rose, are the consequence of a generalization through omission, but the omission, Spinoza holds, is not conscious. There is here a foretaste of Hume's later theory; in our whole variegated experience features constantly recur together, and by force of habit the mind is led to concentrate on these and to neglect those other features which do not constantly recur. What is of further interest in Spinoza's theory, however, and indeed remarkable in a rationalist, is that he includes in universals of Imaginatio not merely man, horse, rose, but also certain very general universals such as being and thing, which

[1] Cf. *Ethics*, ii. 40, Scholium 1.

according to Descartes and Leibniz cannot possibly be described in empiricist terms. Spinoza expressly asserts that such *transcendentales termini*, as he calls them, come about in the same way as other universals of Imaginatio. Thus it is not Spinoza's criticism, as it is Leibniz's, that the empiricists fail to explain the source of certain basic notions such as being and thing, for he obviously thinks that an account of their origin is possible without going beyond Imaginatio. This does not mean that these universals cannot be known at the higher level of Ratio, although first known in Imaginatio. Nothing in Spinoza's account of universals rules out the possibility that a universal known at the level of Imaginatio may also be known, in a profounder manner, at the level of Ratio. Advance in knowledge lies in the substitution of the rational for the imaginative, and we cannot rest content with universals of Imaginatio. Nevertheless, on Spinoza's showing, we find amongst the latter not merely concepts such as dog, horse, and so on, but also the traditional transcendentals, which other rationalists would say could only be gained in a non-empirical fashion.

Spinoza's position, as outlined in Proposition 40, is thus itself remarkably close to empiricism. But it is important to bear in mind that this passage is written in order to show the deficiency and inadequacy of imaginative knowledge and of the universals of Imaginatio. The universals of Ratio possess two characteristics absent from those of Imaginatio; they are clear and distinct, as contrasted with the confusedness of the imaginative, and they are pervasive. Ratio is the mind's conscious and explicit effort to gain clear and adequate knowledge of universals; Imaginatio is primarily concerned with the particular and, as it were, only accidentally with generalizations and universals.

Spinoza's discussion of Ratio in the *Ethics*, however, is unfortunately meagre. He tells us in Proposition 40 that it is knowledge of common notions (*notiones communes*) which he considers not so much in the sense of mathematical axiomata, as had become the custom, but more generally as synonymous with the 'adequate ideas of the properties of things'. These are ideas of pervasive features of reality. In an earlier passage[1] instances of these features are given: 'All bodies agree in this that they involve the conception of one and the same attribute and again that they may be moved now more quickly and now more slowly and absolutely be in motion or at rest.' This passage suggests that extension and motion and rest are pervasive features of the corporeal world and are thus possible objects of rational knowledge. We are, of course, aware of spaced objects and of moving objects in Imaginatio, but we do not then realize, first, the true nature of space and motion, nor, again, their pervasiveness throughout the corporeal. At the level of Ratio we do gain this further knowledge.

Ratio is knowledge of a universal which is fully explicit, in no way confused. I know the universal Extension as it is everywhere and as it must be known by all who know it truly. It is objective and adequate knowledge, nothing is hidden but all is clear and distinct. And as a consequence of the distinctness of the knowledge on the one hand and its pervasiveness on the other, to know it is also to know the necessary, so that necessity is a further characteristic of this universal: 'it is not the nature of Ratio to contemplate things as contingent, but as necessary.'[2] Moreover, I can perceive relations between these universals and so deduce whatever is implied in them and my deductions have equal certainty and necessity.

It has been said that Spinoza's own philosophical work exemplifies such 'rational' knowledge, though it can be questioned whether he did in fact possess so adequate and final a knowledge of, for instance, the nature of space and of motion. We need not here consider the difficulties in his system, but merely note his dissatisfaction with empirical, contingent universals and his demand for universals which are distinct, adequate, and necessary. Yet possibly Spinoza's most significant contribution to the discussion of universals is his further doctrine that even rational knowledge is not the highest kind, just because it is of universals and because knowledge of universals is always partial even when in Ratio it reaches the ideal

[1] *Ethics*, ii. 13, Lemma 2. [2] *Ethics*, ii. 44.

of its own kind. Higher than Imaginatio or Ratio, the *Ethics* teaches us, is Scientia Intuitiva. In the *Tractatus de Intellectus Emendatione*[1] Spinoza affirms that we do not know a thing when we know its properties, however accurate our knowedge, for 'the properties of things are not understood as long as their essences (*essentiae*) are unknown'. In Scientia Intuitiva, however, we know the essences themselves, and to know the essence for Spinoza is to know concrete individual things in their essential being in the Attribute to which they belong. Now it is true that we know the Attribute in one sense at the level of Ratio, but formally and abstractedly; we do not then know the concrete existences which make up the real being of that Attribute. We need to pass 'from the adequate idea of the formal essence of certain attributes of God to the adequate knowledge of the essence of things',[2] and this we do in passing from Ratio to Scientia Intuitiva. Thus the latter alone is true knowledge of things, and Spinoza becomes the critic not merely of empiricism but of rationalism as well.

This criticism of rationalism is better understood if it is viewed as the outcome of that deep distrust and suspicion of the abstract which, as we have seen, characterized Spinoza's generation and the generation which followed. Warnings against taking as real what are in fact merely abstractions are frequent in Spinoza's writings. It is Peter and Paul who exist, not the universal Man; Bucephalus and not Horse. And it is interesting that just as later Berkeley was to argue that Matter, being an abstraction, did not exist, so Spinoza holds that the Will is a mere abstraction and that, therefore, it does not exist. In the *Korte Verhandeling* he warns us against those 'who are accustomed to keep their understanding busy with things of Reason more than with particular things which really exist in nature and through doing this, come to regard a thing of Reason not as such, but as a real thing. For because man has now this, now that, volition he forms in his soul a general mode which he calls Will . . . and because he docs not adequately distinguish the real things from the things of Reason, he comes to regard the things

[1] Section 95.

[2] *Ethics*, ii. 40, Scholium 2.

of Reason as things which really exist in Nature and so he regards himself as a cause of some things.'[1] We should not confuse an *ens rationis* with an *ens realis*. Universals are *entia rationis* and so, however adequate our knowledge, we are not knowing things as they are in knowing them; the generalized knowledge of Ratio must give way to the apprehension of the concrete in Scientia Intuitiva.

Yet nothing of the understanding gained in Ratio is to be lost. Imaginatio is knowledge of the concrete, but Scientia Intuitiva is no return to Imaginatio. It is not knowledge of particulars in their apparent isolation, but of the concrete ultimate realities which are pervasive and which finally explain the particulars of Imaginatio. In the *Tractatus* these are termed *res fixae et aeternae* and their description there is interesting. 'Whence these fixed and eternal things, although they are individual, yet on account of their presence everywhere and their widespread power, will be to us like universals.'[2] It is difficult to know precisely what Spinoza meant by these 'fixed and eternal things', but they are clearly the highest objects of knowledge and the objects of the highest degree of knowledge; it is accordingly significant that they are *singularia* which are yet *tamquam universalia*. Scientia Intuitiva appears to be a knowledge of what is universal, yet not as abstracted but as existing concretely; it is consequently the final stage in the knowledge and understanding of universals as well as of individual things. And universals themselves are concrete not, as some Idealist commentators on Spinoza have held, as being organic wholes, for I do not take this to be Spinoza's meaning, but as being at one and the same time pervasive and yet concrete and real, universal and yet *entia realia*.

32. The more orthodox rationalist answer to the empiricist theory of universals will be found in Descartes's reply to Gassendi and Leibniz's reply to Locke. In his fifth *Meditation*

[1] *Korte Verhandeling*, ii. 16; cf. *Ethics*, ii. 48S, 49D, and Cor. S.

[2] Section 101: 'Unde haec fixa et aeterna, quamvis sint singularia, tamen ob eorum ubiquè praesentiam, ac latissimam potentiam, erunt nobis tanquam universalia.' Vloten and Land, i. 33.

Descartes held that the geometrical triangle was 'an immutable and eternal nature' known independently of sensation. Gassendi demurred.[1] The geometrical triangle, which both Gassendi and Descartes take to be a universal, is known, says Gassendi, in the same way as we know other universals. We observe through the senses that particular triangles resemble one another, having certain features in common; we abstract the common features and so fabricate the universal. It is in no way necessary to suppose we begin with knowledge of an ideal triangle prior to all experience of triangles.

Gassendi is prepared to admit with Descartes that we use the universal triangle as a standard whereby to recognize particular triangles when we see them, but this he holds does not mean that the universal is known *a priori*. It is incidentally noteworthy that Gassendi puts forward here quite explicitly the theory that the universal is a rule, and assumes that Descartes would accept this view of its function.

> The triangle [he says] is indeed a sort of mental rule which you employ in discovering whether something deserves to be called a triangle. But there is no necessity for us on that account to say that such a triangle is something real and a true nature over and above the understanding, which alone, from beholding material triangles, has formed it and has elaborated it as a common notion.[2]

The doctrine that the universal functions as a rule is sometimes stated as a distinctive and original contribution of Kant's but, as we see, it is at least as old as Gassendi, and he puts it forward as something beyond dispute that empiricists and rationalists alike would accept. The point he then makes is that an empirically derived universal may function as a rule quite as effectively as any alleged *a priori* universal.

In replying to Gassendi, Descartes protests against the suggestion that he is a 'dialectician' holding a Platonist theory of universals.[3] It is plain that he would admit the existence of empirical universals brought about in the manner described by Gassendi; yet he is also convinced that not all universals are

[1] *Objection V, Works of Descartes*, Haldane and Ross, ii. 182 ff.

[2] Ibid., p. 184.

[3] Ibid. ii. 226.

of this kind. He therefore repeats what he has said in the Fifth Meditation that certain universals are known in a non-empirical manner and that these are 'immutable natures'. Examples of these are mathematical objects. His case, it becomes clear, rests upon two arguments—the first of which is a very doubtful one. It is impossible, it runs, to derive the universal triangle from observed triangles, since in fact I never do observe a genuine triangle. For do I ever perceive in sense-perception any strictly rectilinear figure? Do I ever see a straight line? 'It will be quite impossible', he says, 'for any really straight part of the line to affect our senses, because when we examine with a magnifying glass those lines that appear to us to be most straight, we find them to be irregular and bending everywhere in an undulating manner.'[1] Yet surely if I first see a straight line, and if what I see then through a magnifying glass held over this line is not straight, it does not follow that I did not see a straight line in the first instance. The second visible object admittedly is not straight but the first is, and this is enough to give me the idea of a straight line. The second argument asserts that our knowledge of the geometrical triangle is a pure intellectual intuition of 'a simple nature'. It is simple because though the triangle has sides and angles it is 'seen' or intuited as a whole. And if one intuits the simple nature, a three-sided rectilinear figure, in this manner, then one already possesses the concept of the geometrical triangle. Whether triangular objects exist in the real world or not, and whether one has chanced to see such objects or not, matters nothing; the essence has been apprehended. This essence is necessary; the interior angles of the intuited triangle cannot be more or less than two right angles, equi-angular triangles must be equilateral, and so on. But if the triangle is known by an intuition of this kind, it follows that it is not known by abstracting the common features of observed triangular objects and framing an empirical universal. Gassendi must be wrong.

This argument is complicated, however, by a further consideration. Knowledge of the triangle is not empirical, says Descartes, but intuitive; yet sometimes he argues that it is not

[1] Haldane and Ross, ii. 227.

empirical because it is innate, and the question arises how intuitive and innate knowledge are related. This is a difficult question to answer because it does not seem possible to give a straightforward and consistent account of Descartes's theory of innate knowledge. Does saying that an object is known innately rule out the possibility that it is known intuitively, and *vice versa*? Or is innate knowledge a later substitute for intuitive knowledge? Descartes sometimes speaks as if innate knowledge was a specific kind of knowledge with special objects that could not be known in any other way—not by *intuitus*, or *inspectio*, for instance, since they would then be acquired and not known innately. In a letter to Mersenne he speaks of 'God, Mind, Body, Triangle and all true essences' as ideas known innately,[1] and in another letter explains that such innate knowledge 'involves no affirmation or denial'.[2] In the *Meditations*, however, he speaks more vaguely. Innate knowedge does not originate outside the mind,[3] nor is it the product of an act of judging on my part, but it arises from my own inner knowing power.[4] This might make it one with intuitive knowledge. The clearest statement of this point of view comes in the well-known passage in *Notes against a Programme* which Descartes wrote late in his life.

I never wrote or concluded [he there says][5] that the mind required innate ideas which were in some sort different from its faculty of thinking; but when I observed the existence in me of certain thoughts which proceeded, not from extraneous objects nor from the determination of my will, but solely from the faculty of thinking which is within me, then, that I might distinguish the ideas or notions (which are the forms of these thoughts) from other thoughts *adventitious* or *factitious*, I termed the former *innate*. In the same sense we say that in some families generosity is innate, in others certain diseases like gout or gravel, not that on this account the babes of these families suffer

[1] Adam and Tannery, iii. 383. [2] Ibid., 418.

[3] It does not originate in sense-experience, though since sense-experience is mental it too is within the mind together with its objects. But then it is difficult to understand the distinction between adventitious and innate ideas.

[4] Cf. a passage in the *Third Meditation*, Haldane and Ross, i. 160: 'for, as I have the power of understanding what is called a thing, or a truth, or a thought, it appears to me that I hold this power from no other source than my own nature.'

[5] Haldane and Ross, i. 442.

from these diseases in their mother's womb, but because they are born with a certain disposition or propensity for contracting them.

Here knowledge is innate in so far as one is disposed to this knowledge from the outset, though it is gained in the course of one's life and experience. Notions of Deity, substance, circularity, triangularity are natural to us; our endowments are such that we naturally think in terms of these notions. This is accordingly not knowledge we acquire from an extraneous source but part, as it were, of what we are.

This view of the matter is, however, admittedly different from that given elsewhere. Descartes is dissatisfied with Gassendi's account of how we gain universals, yet his own account is far from clear. The position he is striving to attain is defined more clearly by Leibniz and we need not discuss Descartes further. But one thing stands out very clearly, namely, the sharpness of Descartes's recoil from Gassendi's empiricism. Influenced by contemporary science Descartes is well aware of the need for observation through the senses; nevertheless he is convinced that empiricism may be taken too far and that Gassendi has been led by it to ignore elements in our knowledge which cannot be derived from experience, and universals which can only be 'drawn from the thought itself'.

33. In Leibniz's *Nouveaux Essais* the treatment of Locke's theory of universals, particularly in Book III, is fair and even sympathetic, and Leibniz himself observes at the end of a discussion of III. vi. of the *Essay* that his own position accords very well with that of Locke. The main difference is that Leibniz believes in innate knowledge and that Locke does not.

In the course of his discussion Leibniz makes interesting minor criticisms of Locke before coming to the major criticism that certain universals must be known innately if they are to be known at all. Some of these minor points are worthy of attention. Locke is too ready, he thinks, to assume the invariability of the sequence: observation of individuals, formation of species, formation of genus. The fact is that our experience may lead us direct to the generic. Linguistic considerations confirm this conclusion; few who use the general word *cow* are aware of the various species of cows.[1]

In the second place, he argues that Locke's conceptualism rests on an unacknowledged realism. The universals are not entirely the workmanship of the mind, they are also discoveries in the real. 'Generality', says Leibniz, 'consists in the resemblance of separate things among themselves and this resemblance is a reality.'[2] Locke acknowledges that the mind does not frame its concepts in an entirely arbitrary fashion, but he is so anxious to establish his conceptualism that he ignores the realist elements implicit in his theory. The mind generalizes on the strength of observed resemblances; yet these resemblances are discovered by it, they are not the workmanship of the mind. Thus Locke's conceptualism, Leibniz argues, rests on a realism.

This leads Leibniz to his third point of criticism. He rejects Locke's distinction between nominal and real essences. If the species and genera depend on observing resemblances, and if these resemblances are real, why not seek the essence of species and genera in the resemblances?[3] Why speak of the essence as if it were merely a mental construct or fiction? If genera are grounded in reality, why think of them as merely nominal? Can the assertion that the general is merely a nominal essence and in no way a real essence be justified? The essence of gold is what it is. It is quite true that your description of gold may differ from mine, and we may proffer different explanations of how we use the name 'gold'. But 'if men differ in the name, does it change the thing or the resemblance?' Leibniz thinks of the essences as so many possibilities in nature; it is nonsensical to speak of nominal as opposed to real *essences*. Locke is confusing essence with definition. Supposing that the essence of gold were indeed unknown, in that case if we say that gold is yellow, malleable, and so on, we do not state what the nominal essence is, we merely explain how the word 'gold' is being used. The

[1] Leibniz's example is *wormwood*: 'We are contented with the general name, wormwood, although there are so many species of it that one of the Bauhins has filled a book with them.' III. iii. 5, *Opera*, ed. Erdmann 303b, *New Essays*, tr. Langley 308.

[2] III. iii. 11, Erdmann 305*a*, Langley 313.

[3] III. iii. 13 ff., Erdmann 305*a* ff., Langley 313 ff.

essence throughout is unknown; there are not two essences, one of which, the nominal, is known.[1] Consequently Leibniz concludes that the distinction between nominal and real essence is quite unjustified. It is questionable, however, whether he thereby rejects, or intends to reject, anything vital in Locke's theory. It is a disagreement about terminology. Leibniz does not object to the view that we can frame a concept of, for instance, gold without knowing the essence of gold, and this is the central point of Locke's theory. Perhaps Locke should not have termed such a concept an essence, even a nominal essence; we may accept the criticism without feeling that his theory has been changed in any fundamental sense.

34. In respect to Leibniz's main criticism, however, the difference between the two philosophers is profound. Locke denies innate knowledge and in doing so, Leibniz thinks, makes a satisfactory theory of knowledge impossible; for he deprives the mind of those fundamental and logically primitive universals on which the rest of its knowledge depends. These universals are known innately and can only be so known; they cannot be derived from sense-experience. Sense-experience cannot tell us what must be. Thus experience may show that such and such entities share such and such qualities, and occasionally, when all the members of a class are set out before us, we learn directly that all the members share these qualities. Most often, however, we do not meet all the members and we cannot be sure that the qualities are shared by members not met. In such cases experience cannot provide the necessarily universal. Yet we possess knowledge of the necessarily universal properties of things. 'Experience', Leibniz concludes, 'never assures us of a perfect universality and still less of necessity'.[2] This is the theme of the

[1] Leibniz does not agree with Locke that we never know the essences of substances, though we do know those of qualities. 'We have a knowledge of true substances or unities (as God and the soul) as intimate as we have of the most of the modes. Besides, there are some predicates as little known as the contexture of bodies; yellow or bitter, for example, are objects of simple ideas or imaginations, and yet we have only a confused knowledge of them.' III. iii. 18.

[2] *Specimen of Thoughts upon the First Book of the Essay on Human Understanding*, Langley, p. 22.

opening section of the preface to the *Nouveaux Essais*. Incidentally, it is noteworthy how completely Kant's position is foreshadowed in this preface. Human knowledge begins with sense-experience, but it cannot be explained entirely in terms of it. 'The senses, although necessary for all our actual knowledge, are not sufficient to give it all to us.'[1]

Some of our knowledge, Leibniz holds, is innate and *a priori*. Now what does he mean by innate knowledge? Not knowledge of which we have always been conscious; he does not seek to defend the view that children are born knowing certain principles. He means rather that the mind itself comes to experience prepared and disposed to think in certain ways. Locke and the empiricists were misled by their analogy of a *tabula rasa*. In fact, prior to all sense-experience, the mind has a life of its own and what it later knows must be explained partly in terms of this inner life. This is the significance of the celebrated *nisi ipse intellectus* of the *Nouveaux Essais*.[2] If we neglect the mind itself we neglect half the explanation of knowledge. Locke failed to study the mind with sufficient attention. His account of 'reflection' is an afterthought and superficial. If he had looked into his own mind he would have found there the answers to many of his difficulties. He never understood, for instance, how we gain the notion of substance. Leibniz thinks we know it in so far as we are aware of ourselves: 'it is in the consciousness of self that we perceive substance'.[3] It is in this way, too, if we are to believe the preface of the *Nouveaux Essais*, that we become aware of 'being, unity, duration, change, action, perception, pleasure and a thousand other objects of our intellectual ideas'.[4] Our first knowledge of such 'transcendentals' is not gained empirically, but by the mind's reflection upon itself. Now this active mind, which has a life of its own, orders the given of experience in its own way. Space, figure, motion and rest, and such notions, are consequently to be finally understood in terms of the mind's own nature. They, too, are known innately and it

[1] *Nouveaux Essais* Avant-propos Erdmann, 195*a*, Langley 43.

[2] II. i. 2, Erdmann 223*a*, Langley 111.

[3] *Specimen of Thoughts upon the Second Book*, Langley 23–24. Cf. *Nouveaux Essais*, I. iii. 18, Erdmann 221*a*, Langley 105.

[4] Erdmann 196*a*, Langley 45.

is in this fact that we must search for an explanation of the necessity, the universality and the adequacy[1] of such a science as mathematics.

But does this mean more, we must now ask, than that we possess innately a power or a faculty to know such universals as being, substance, duration, and the rest? Locke never denied that we had such a power, and held that it could rightly be described as innate. Is this all that is involved in affirming innate knowledge? Leibniz replied that much more is involved. What we possess from the outset is more than 'a naked faculty which consists in the mere possibility of understanding them [the "transcendentals"]; it is a disposition, an aptitude, a preformation which determines our soul and which makes it possible for them to be derived from it.'[2] The mind is disposed from the outset to think in certain ways and this disposition lies at the base of all subsequent knowledge. We are determined to think thus by our very nature as intellectual beings. Thus Leibniz puts forward a disposition theory, as do Spinoza and Hume; but the disposition in this case is not the product of experience, a custom-established trend; it is innate, a disposition of the mind itself independent of experience. Leibniz makes use of a suggestive analogy. Certain blocks of marble lend themselves to certain figures, as the good sculptor well knows; they are veined in the right way. It requires skill and labour to bring out the figure, but it is there from the outset. So the mind is intellectually disposed to certain principles and truths.[3]

Leibniz accordingly distinguishes between 'truths of fact' and 'truths of reason'. The former are 'drawn from the experience of the senses'.[4] The latter are known by the understanding itself and are independent of experience. Now 'truths of reason' underlie human knowledge as synthesizing principles. In a passage which again reminds us of Kant, he remarks: 'The general

[1] 'J'appelle adéquate celle où il n'y a plus rien à expliquer', *Reflexions*, Erdmann 138*a*, Langley 17.

[2] *Nouveaux Essais*, I. i. 11, Erdmann 210*a*, Langley 81.

[3] Preface to *Nouveaux Essais*, Erdmann 196*a*, Langley 46.

[4] Yet even sensory ideas are ideal and so within the mind. In I. i. 1, Erdmann 206*a*, Langley 71, Leibniz having explained that truths of fact are drawn from the experience of the senses adds 'and even from those confused perceptions which are in us'.

principles enter into our thoughts, of which they form the soul and the connexion. They are as necessary thereto as the muscles and sinews are for walking, although we do not at all think of them. The mind leans upon these principles every moment.'[1] They thus play a most important function in human knowledge, and yet Locke denies that such innately known principles exist but tries to derive them from experience, not seeing that their nature is such that they cannot be so derived.

A question still remains to be asked, however, namely, how Leibniz justifies the assumption that principles derived from within apply to the natural world discovered in experience. He seeks to do so by holding that a Pre-established Harmony exists between all the parts of the real so that principles which are 'the sinews of thought' are also the laws of the natural world. Leibniz and the rationalists in general maintain their central position, that the mind of itself can think the truth about the real, only by assuming that, as Spinoza puts it, 'the order and connexion of ideas is the same as the order and connexion of things'. But any justification they attempt of this assumption rests on a dogmatic metaphysics and Kant is right in maintaining that the assumption is in fact never justified by them. Locke's method of waiting upon experience at least saves him from dogmatism.

35. One way of viewing Kant's work is by thinking of it as an attempt to rid philosophy of rationalist dogmatism whilst yet reasserting in essentials the Leibnizian protest against the empiricists. Kant is the critic of rationalists and empiricists; the former because they fail to see how essential sense-experience is to knowledge, the latter because they disregard the *a priori*. As he puts it in the *Critique of Pure Reason*:[2]

> Leibniz *intellectualised* appearances, just as Locke . . . *sensualised* all concepts of the understanding, that is, interpreted them as nothing more than empirical or abstracted concepts of reflection. Instead of seeking in understanding and sense two sources of ideas, which while quite different can supply objectively valid judgments of things

[1] *Nouveaux Essais*, I. i. 20, Erdmann 211*b*, Langley 74.

[2] A 271 = B 327.

only *in conjunction* with each other, each of these great men holds to one only of the two.

Kant cannot admit that all knowledge is empirically derived, for 'pure concepts of the understanding' play an important part in human knowledge and they are not empirically derived.[1] But neither can he admit that all knowledge is derived from within, for, in the case of human knowledge at least, sensory intuition is essential.

Since the concept plays so important a part in the theory of knowledge which Kant himself puts forward one would expect a very thorough analysis of it in Kant's works, and since, as we shall see, he tends to identify the concept with the universal such an analysis would provide us also with a complete theory of universals. But no such theory is to be found in Kant. In the *Critique* his concern is with pure concepts and what he says of empirical concepts and of concepts in general is somewhat incidental. His problem in the *Transcendental Deduction* is to justify the use we make in knowledge of such pure concepts as substance, relation, being, causality, and so on. But he says expressly that no justification (or 'deduction') of empirical concepts is necessary. Thus he does not think it necessary to set forward a full theory of concepts. We may, if we choose, seek to explain the origin of empirical concepts and he praises Locke for his attempts in this direction. But he does not feel obliged himself to further this study.[2] In his *Logic*, however, Kant does deal with concepts in general although in this latter book he is stating the position of the Leibniz-Wolff school, which he accepts as his own, rather than thinking out afresh the nature of the concept. Nevertheless, a study of the *Logic* is interesting if only as revealing what Kant takes for granted in the *Critique*.

36. One may begin with two general points. The *Logic* is

[1] Locke, it is true, attempted to deduce them from experience but merely managed to contradict himself: 'The illustrious Locke . . . meeting with pure concepts of the understanding in experience, deduced them also from experience, and yet proceeded so *inconsequently* that he attempted with their aid to obtain knowledge which far transcends all limits of experience.' B 127.

[2] A 84–85 = B 116–17.

explicitly representationalist in its teaching—more so than the *Critique*. The objects of knowledge are invariably ideas (*Vorstellungen*, a term that carries with it a suggestion of representationalism); these, he explains in the introduction,[1] are of two kinds, sense-presentations (*Anschauungen*) and concepts (*Begriffe*). There is no suggestion that sense-presentations in any way copy a real thing outside in the crude representationalist manner, but it is understood that there *is* a thing-in-itself and that it is never the object of human knowledge since we know the phenomenal only. The second point is that Kant thinks in terms of two kinds of knowledge and presumably only two kinds, namely, sense-experience and discursive knowledge involving concepts; for every possible object of knowledge is either an *Anschauung* or a *Begriff*. It follows from these two points that the field of theoretical knowledge is doubly limited; it is the phenomenal, and it includes only sense-experience and discursive knowledge in which concepts are used.

If we now ask what the concept is, the answer in the *Logic* is quite explicit. The text opens with a section distinguishing between intuition and concept: 'The intuition is a single idea (*representatio singularis*), the concept a universal (*representatio per notas communes*) or reflective idea (*representatio discursiva*).' In a note he adds that the concept is an idea 'which is common to many objects'. The content of the concept is simply the common character. It will be noted that he identifies the concept with the universal idea (*allgemeine Vorstellung*), and as ideas are the sole objects of knowledge, it follows that the only universal for human knowledge is the universal idea. Thus the universal is the concept. The distinction between an objective universal in the sense of a real common quality of real things and a subjective concept is not possible for Kant. In the introduction to the *Logic*[2] Kant speaks of these universal ideas as 'partial' only, *Partialvorstellungen* and *Teilbegriffe*, since they contain only the shared characters of things and ignore differences.

Just as the *Logic* then reveals the representationalism which lies at the base of Kant's thought so also it reveals his con-

[1] Section 5, opening paragraphs. [2] Section 8.

ceptualism. It is a conceptualism which rests on two assumptions, namely, that identically the same character can be observed to belong to two or more phenomena and, secondly, that there are no universals where there are no common characters. The latter makes it difficult to account for relations, which appear to be universals, and also for what might be called thing-universals, such as dog, man, table, and so on. But these matters are not considered in the *Logic*.

The *Logic* proceeds to discuss the difference between the matter and the form of concepts, and the distinction between empirical and pure concepts. On the first question the discussion is not very illuminating. 'The matter of concepts is the object (*der Gegenstand*); their form is universality (*die Allgemeinheit*).'[1] In the introduction[2] he has told us that the form is 'the way in which we know the object', so that when he says that the form is universality he apparently means that we know the object, that is, the common character, in a certain way, not as it pertains to this or that phenomenal object, but as it pertains to many. He adds that the form is always *made* by the understanding even when the matter is given.[3] This would seem to mean that the observing of the universality of the character is an intellectual rather than a sensory activity; it cannot mean that the phenomena do not in fact have the common character, or that it is the intellect which makes the latter. What is intellectual is the recognition that they share a character in common. This seems the most sensible interpretation, though admittedly to say that the form is invariably made (*gemacht*) may be taken to mean more than this.

Nor is the *Logic* very helpful on the distinction between empirical and pure concepts. Empirical concepts come from the comparison of sensible objects. The pure concept on the other hand is purely intellectual. (He equates the pair *empirisch* and *rein* with the Latin pair *empiricus* and *intellectualis*.) It is intellectual in the sense that it is not derived from experience, though this does not rule out the possibility that a pure concept may order the manifold of experience. In this last

[1] *Logic*, section 2. [2] Ibid., section 5. [3] Ibid. i. 4, Anmerk.

respect the pure concept is contrasted with the Idea (*die Idee*) which is never met with in experience in any form.[1]

The matter of concepts may be given *a posteriori*, that is in experience, or *a priori*, but it may also be *made*; the form, as we have seen, is always made. How, then, is the concept made in respect to form? In other words, how is it that we universalize? What processes of the understanding are involved? Kant discusses the point in the *Logic*[2] and finds three processes to be present, namely, comparison, reflection, and abstraction. He takes the example of three trees, the pine, willow, and linden. 'Comparing' them we notice the differences—the stress on observing differences is interesting—in trunk, branch, and leaf; we then 'reflect' on what is common, at least all possess trunk, branch, and leaf; finally, we 'abstract' from the 'trees' particular sizes, shapes, colours, and so on, and thus gain the concept of tree. Kant here speaks of three processes, but they also may be conceived as one complicated process of noting differences and seizing what is common. Kant adds that the processes imply a 'unity of consciousness', though he does not here seek to explain the nature of this unity.

Such are the main points of Kant's discussion of the concept in the *Logic*. A comparative and abstractive process gives us the concept, which is also the universal. He appears to be thinking of empirical concepts, and his account so far as it goes is not very different from that of Locke and the empiricists. But even of empirical concepts the account does not go very far and must be adjudged inadequate. And though he maintains here that *a priori* concepts exist he gives no account of their origin. It would hardly seem likely that they also are produced by the threefold process. For from what original material could they be abstracted? Thus the account of concepts in *Logic* is on the whole disappointing and leaves much unexplained.

37. In the *Logic* concepts come into being through comparison, reflection, and abstraction, all of which involve a 'unity of

[1] Ibid., 3.

[2] Ibid., 6, and three notes.

consciousness'. In the *Critique* the account is less straightforward; for though judgement is still the use of concepts and so would seem to presuppose concepts, the conceiving of concepts through comparison, reflection, and abstraction now itself appears to be a judging. Concepts are presupposed in judgement and yet apparently only come into being in so far as we judge.

This difficulty emerges early in the *Analytic*. At one point[1] Kant is analysing the judgement and discussing the instance *All bodies are divisible*.

> In every judgment [he says] there is a concept which holds of many ideas, and among them of a given idea that is immediately related to an object. Thus in the judgment *All bodies are divisible* the concept of the divisible applies to various other concepts, but is here applied in particular to the concept of body, and this concept again to certain appearances that present themselves to us.

Now obviously this judgement would be impossible were we not already able to conceive divisibility and body. Consequently, the two concepts are presupposed. Invariably, the predicate of every judgement is a concept and so, supposing with Kant that all judgements are of the subject-predicate type, every judgement involves at least one concept and no judging is possible without the prior conceiving of concepts.

Yet in the same passage Kant proceeds to argue that 'we can reduce all acts of the understanding to judgements' and if conceiving is an act of understanding it would appear to be a judging and so the concept presupposes judgement. Nor is this a chance statement. Kant says in discussing the nature of the understanding that it can be defined as the 'faculty of concepts or again of judgments' and that 'these definitions, when they are adequately understood, are identical'.[2] Thus conceiving presumably would be one with judging. The word 'conceiving', however, is perhaps ambiguous here; it may mean bringing a concept into being or it may mean using a concept. And when Kant says that conceiving is one with judging he may merely be saying that using a concept is one with judging. Yet there are texts to disprove this interpretation. Thus in the passage in

[1] A 68–9 = B 93.

[2] A 126.

which Kant praises Locke for 'opening out a new line of enquiry' into the way we 'advance from particular perceptions to universal concepts' he excuses himself from this inquiry on the ground that his concern is with pure concepts not derived from experience. But he adds one sentence to explain, though the explanation is far too brief, how such universal concepts come into being.

> The impressions of the senses [he says] supplying the first stimulus, the whole faculty of knowledge opens out to them and experience is brought into existence. That experience contains two very dissimilar elements, namely, the *matter* of knowledge obtained from the senses, and a certain *form* for the ordering of this matter, obtained from the inner source of the pure intuition and thought which, on occasion of the sense-impressions, are first brought into action and yield concepts.[1]

Here concepts are brought into being only when the *matter* of the senses is ordered by the *form* of the understanding, an ordering of the manifold which is essentially what Kant means by an act of the understanding and a judging. Such an act appears essential if concepts are to be brought into being (*Begriffe hervorbringen*). But a further complication becomes apparent here. The ordering principles 'obtained from the inner source of the pure intuition and thought' are the *a priori* concepts or the pure concepts. These, therefore, are presupposed in the coming into being of empirical concepts, so that an explanation of how empirical concepts come into being cannot also be the explanation of pure concepts. Accordingly, when Kant says in the *Logic*[2] that the three logical operations of the understanding, comparing, reflecting, and abstracting, are 'the essential and general conditions for the production of any of these concepts', he must mean empirical concepts though he does not say so.

[1] A 86 = B 118, cf. further B 133–4 note. Conceiving involves analysis and synthesis. In analysing the content of a concept we must hold the content together. Again in thinking extensionally we think of many instances yet held together in the synthetic unity of apperception. 'An idea which is to be thought as common to *different* ideas is regarded as belonging to such as have, in addition to it, also something *different*. Consequently it must previously be thought in synthetic unity with other (though, it may be, only possible) ideas, before I can think in it the analytic unity of consciousness, which makes it a *conceptus communis*.'

[2] i. 6, Anmerk. 1.

The doctrine of the *Critique* is at any rate clear. Did the mind not already know how to formulate the given in terms of pure concepts, no empirical concepts would ever come into being.

It would seem correct to conclude from these passages, and from others which point in the same direction, that conceiving, in the sense of bringing concepts into being, is an activity of the understanding and a judging. But we have also seen that judgements use concepts, so that we are left with the circle that judgements presuppose concepts and concepts presuppose judgements. The difficulty is perhaps artificial, for as soon as we have concepts we may use them in those acts of judgement which yield further concepts. Thus it is only in the case of the very first concepts that we should appear to contradict ourselves in saying that they are brought into being by judging, whereas judging itself presupposes concepts. May it be that a solution of the difficulty lies in a theory of concepts which would account for some of them less in terms of explicit judgement than of custom-bred disposition?

38. Certainly no solution of this preliminary difficulty would do justice to Kant's position which failed to emphasize the importance of the concept in judgement—and consequently in inference. 'Besides intuition there is no other mode of knowledge except by means of concepts.'[1] And we must now ask how precisely the concept is used in judging and understanding. The answer which Kant gives is that it is used as a rule. This account of the concept's function is explicit in the celebrated threefold analysis of the judgement in the first edition of the *Critique*.[2] Judgement, it is there said, involves first a synthesis of apprehension in intuition, that is to say, the manifold now being experienced must be run through and held together; it involves, secondly, a synthesis of reproduction in imagination, that is, ideas which have just been experienced but which are no longer being experienced must be retained for reproductive imagination; but also, thirdly, it involves a synthesis of recognition in a concept. In experiencing the mind already has its concepts and

[1] A 68 = B 93.

[2] A 99–106.

recognizes an instance in the experience because it can think the concept. When, for instance, I judge that this is a triangle, then first I see the figure as one, apprehend its parts, the three lines, the three angles, and so on. I must also be able to reproduce in imagination the respective parts as I saw them. But, thirdly, I must recognize the whole as a triangle. I already have the concept in my mind and here in what is before me lies that which, as it were, fits the concept. Thus the concept has an important part to play in judging for, Kant holds, I should not be able to say *This is a triangle* did I not already possess the concept of triangle. The concept is a rule by which synthesis of recognition, an essential element of all judgement, becomes possible; or, in Kant's words: 'A concept is always, as regards its form, something universal which serves as a rule.'[1]

That concepts are rules is perhaps the most important thing Kant has to say about them, and he has in mind here empirical as well as pure concepts. Concepts generally, of whatever kind, are rules for recognition. He discusses the matter further in his chapter on schematization.[2] The opening paragraphs of this chapter might suggest that only pure concepts are to be considered and that nothing will be said about empirical concepts. For the schema is set forward as a necessary intermediary between pure concept and sensory intuition, whereas no intermediary seems to be needed between empirical concept and sensory intuition. Nevertheless, he does consider the empirical as well as the pure concept in this chapter and throws further light on the sense in which a concept is a rule.

Kant begins with a questionable statement that there must be likeness (*Gleichartigkeit*) between an idea of an object and the concept under which it is subsumed, between the idea of a particular table, for instance, and the concept table. This is questionable since it suggests two objects, the particular table and the conceptual or universal table, and that these two objects are like one another—surely a false account of the matter. But beginning in this way Kant finds a special problem in the case of the pure concept. It is not empirical and so

[1] A 106. [2] A 137 ff. = B 176 ff.

cannot be like the empirical intuition or appearance; we must accordingly search for 'a third thing', an intermediary homogeneous both with the pure concept and with the sensible appearance. This is obviously a difficult quest; for if the intermediary is sensible it would not be pure in Kant's sense, and if pure it would not be sensible. Kant, however, claims to find such an intermediary in the transcendental schema. If we think of a pure concept not so much in itself but as it orders the manifold under temporal conditions, the temporality, Kant thinks, would secure the sensible connexion. To determine whether in fact it does do so would lead us to an examination of Kant's view of time and take us too far afield for the purposes of this chapter. Our interest is in the examples of schemata he proceeds to give, and these can be understood without determining whether the schema is in truth an intermediary between the pure and the sensible.

The schema, like the pure concept, is an ordering and synthesizing principle, yet it belongs to the imagination. It is no particular image, for then it would not be an ordering principle; but it is a way or a method of imagining. Kant considers the schema of number, for instance, five, a thousand, a million. I see five dots set out on paper; this is a sensible representation of five. Now I can imagine a thousand or a million dots set out in this way. I do not in fact set them out, but just as when I think of five I can imagine the five dots so in thinking of a million I can imagine a million dots. This way of thinking imaginatively of a number is not a particular image, it is a schema, 'a method whereby a multiplicity may be represented in an image in conformity with a certain concept'.[1] Or consider the triangle. Berkeley had held that whenever I think of the triangle I must be thinking of a particular sensible or imagined triangle, but Kant thinks this view erroneous. 'No image could ever be adequate to the concept of a triangle in general. It would never attain that universality of the concept which renders it valid of all triangles, whether right-angled, obtuse-angled, or acute-angled; it would always be limited to a part only of this sphere.'[2]

[1] A 140 = B 179.

[2] A 141 = B 180.

In spite of Berekeley, therefore, we must say that there is a general idea of triangle. But what is this? Not a triangle laid up in heaven, nor a purely intellectual triangle wholly unrelated to the sensible and imaginable triangles. It is, says Kant, 'a rule of synthesis of the imagination, in respect to pure figures in space' and it can 'exist nowhere but in thought'. This does not tell us a great deal, but relating it to the previous example of number it would appear that the mind possesses a method of thinking the right-angled, the obtuse-angled, and the acute-angled triangles together in such a way that it can set out a right-angled, an obtuse-angled, and an acute-angled triangle on paper and be able to say: 'All these are triangles.'

Kant then proceeds to the empirical concept, for instance, dog. This concept, he says, is not a particular dog nor a particular image; rather it 'always stands in immediate relation to the schema of imagination, as a rule for the determination of of our intuition, in accordance with some specific universal concept'. We have the concept, but we can also think a series of particular creatures, differing in certain respects, and yet of all of which we know that they are dogs. The empirical concept would appear to be different from the 'rule for determination' (*Regel der Bestimmung*) which is the schema. Yet it becomes increasingly difficult for Kant to keep the two apart. For what is the empirical concept apart from the schema? In the very next sentence the concept itself becomes the rule. 'The concept dog signifies a rule' and its function is identical with that of the schema. It is 'a rule according to which my imagination can delineate the figure of a four-footed animal in a general manner, without limitation to any single determinate figure such as experience or any possible image that I can represent *in concreto*, actually presents'.[1] He terms this 'the schematism of our understanding' and it seems clear that empirical concept and schema have, for the moment, been identified in his mind. Thus, as in the threefold analysis of judgement, so here, the concept functions as a rule, but now it is more than a rule by which to test any particular object, it is also a rule according to which my

[1] A 141 = B 180.

imagination can so run over the particular images, for example, the different dogs, that recognition becomes possible. It is, he says, a sort of general monogram (in the old sense of an outline or sketch) although it must not be thought of as itself a particular sketch. The mind possesses that by which it is enabled to imagine the particular images whenever necessary and recognize particular instances. The nature of this power, Kant says, is a mystery; it is 'an art concealed in the depths of the human soul, whose real modes of activity nature is hardly likely ever to allow us to discover'.

Does this discussion of schematization throw any additional light on the empirical concept? It confirms the view that a concept is a rule, supposing we are correct in maintaining that concept and schema become identified in Kant's mind when considering the empirical concept—otherwise the schema becomes the rule. The concept dog is not a particular image of dog, nor is it the name, but it is something in the mind's possession—a something most difficult to explain—which enables us to say, 'That is a dog', when we meet one. It is in this sense that it is a rule. It would be dangerous to read more than this into what Kant says.

39. Yet Kant's primary interest in the passage on schematization is not in the empirical concept; the discussion of the latter is merely intended to illustrate and lead up to the schema of the pure concepts. A full examination of Kant's doctrine of pure concepts would require a very close study of the whole of the *Analytic*, to say the least. We shall confine ourselves to one or two points of considerable relevance to our present argument.

Kant's objection to the empiricists is that they ignore pure concepts; and in making this objection he appears to be making exactly the same stand as the rationalists did. Would he say that the pure concepts are known innately, and does he defend innate knowledge? It is difficult to answer; but he would certainly say that these concepts are known *a priori* and that they 'issue from the understanding itself'. Thus he uses the very language of Leibniz, though it would perhaps be erroneous to assume that he means the same thing by it. The *Critique* is clear on two points. First, pure concepts are essential for human knowledge. He sums up the position in the preface to the second edition: 'Experience is a species of knowledge which involves understanding, and understanding has rules which I must presuppose as being in me prior to objects being given to me, and therefore as being *a priori*.'[1] Pure concepts are necessary if we are to make sense of our experience. Secondly, they are not derived from experience. Kant's reason for saying this is the one he found in Wolff, Leibniz, and the rationalists, namely, that the empirical can never account for the necessary; it cannot tell us what must be. But we do know certain things necessarily and this knowledge, we find, is grounded on pure concepts as principles.

Kant terms these pure concepts *Grundbegriffe*;[2] they are the categories.[3] Perhaps the best description of them is that which he gives at the opening of the *Dialectic*, namely, 'keys to possible experiences'.[4] They make experience possible, even the experience of the natural world. They 'confer upon appearances their conformity to law. . . . The understanding is something more than a power of formulating rules through comparison of appearances; it is itself the lawgiver of nature. Save through it nature, that is, synthetic unity of the manifold of appearances according to rules, would not exist at all.'[5] But this passage also reveals the limitations of this knowledge; it is of the phenomenal only. In explaining what he means by calling the pure concepts 'keys to possible experience' he contrasts them with Plato's 'Ideas', which are 'archetypes of the things themselves'. The pure concepts are the principles of experience, they are not the laws of the noumenal, of things-in-themselves. Kant speaks of Ideas of Reason which regulate our reflections upon things-in-themselves though we cannot know whether they are valid or not; but the pure concepts of the understanding, or the categories, are principles of experience only. The phenomenal world is unified and determined by a necessary order, for otherwise the

[1] B xvii. [2] Cf. A 111. [3] Cf. A 97.
[4] A 313 = B 370. [5] A 126–7.

necessary and universal knowledge of it which is science would not be possible. This, however, presupposes a 'transcendental unity of apperception', and the principles of this apperception are the pure concepts of the understanding.

Yet these principles being pure cannot themselves be experienced. Hence the need for a schematism. The schema will be different from that of an empirical concept. We cannot here imagine instances; a pure synthesis is not instantiated in a particular image. On reflection it is difficult to see what the schema *can* be. 'It is', says Kant, 'a transcendental product of imagination, a product which concerns the determination of inner sense in general, according to conditions of its form (time), in respect of all ideas, so far as these ideas are to be connected *a priori* in one concept in conformity with the unity of apperception.'[1] It is a determination of inner sense, holding of all ideas or throughout experience, according to temporal conditions. Kant's examples may help us here. The schema of the pure concept of substance is permanence of the real in time; of cause the real upon which, whenever posited, something else follows, that is, regular succession of the manifold; of community or reciprocity the co-existence, according to universal rule, of the determinations of one substance with those of the other. In other words the schemata under consideration are, first, a real abiding through time, second, regular succession and, third, co-existence. These we understand. But what in that case are the pure concepts of which they are the schema? The point is discussed in the later chapter on phenomena and noumena.[2] In this chapter Kant says that the only idea we can have of the pure concepts themselves is as purely logical notions entirely empty of content. Substance is something which can exist only as subject and never as predicate. As to cause we 'find in the pure category nothing further than that it is something from which we can conclude to the existence of something else'. In other words, while the schema is regular sequence, the pure concept is the logical notion of ground-consequent. But to think of it as pure concept we should have to try to think of it apart

[1] A 142 = B 181. [2] A 235 ff. = B 294 ff.

from any of its empirical exemplifications which in fact, as Kant himself points out, we cannot do. The pure concepts are therefore empty of content unless we are prepared to admit that bare logical notions too vacuous to grasp in themselves make up content.[1]

40. We now appear to have reached this position: Kant criticizes the empiricists on the ground that they neglect pure concepts though such concepts provide the general underlying principles of knowledge and there is no explanation of human knowledge without them. Yet he himself does not explain how we gain these all-important concepts nor does he make their nature clear. All that he tells us of their origin is that they are not given in experience but are *a priori*. As to their nature, we should not expect to know much—if anything at all—since they transcend experience. We can know their schemata for these are nearer the sensible; but what is left when we seek to delete the time element from the schema and so reach the pure concept itself is not at all clear, and we cannot in this way determine the precise nature of the pure concept. Thus Kant can tell us little about pure concepts and his criticism of the empiricists as a consequence loses something of its force. Empiricists may have neglected an important feature in neglecting pure concepts, but we cannot be sure of this until we know what these concepts are.

Thus, any suggestion that Kant has said the final word which disposes of the empiricist case once and for all will not bear examination. After Kant's day it was still possible to argue that empiricism was correct in essentials even though it needed modification in certain directions. It is true that Locke had had difficulties with such notions as substance and cause, but ascribing them to the *a priori* did not solve these difficulties. It is true that we do not experience substance, cause, and the rest directly, certainly not in the course of our adult lives; it is true that we already have these notions as guiding principles in ordering our experience. But may they not, none the less, be

[1] Cf. A 243 = B 301 and A 147 = B 186.

derived from past experiences now forgotten? Since our experiencing began we have always experienced certain pervasive features, thinghood, causality, co-existence of qualities, and so on, and our minds are long since accustomed to them. We assume without question, and without realizing that we make the assumption, that our present experiences will also possess these features. They thus become principles operating in our minds, principles which are empirically derived, but yet 'part of our being'.

Now Kant, we may be sure, would have rejected this theory out of hand because, in his view, it could not possibly explain the necessity and universality of science. He even rejected, it is interesting to note, the dispositional but rationalist theory of Leibniz. In the *Critique* he considers the possibility that the categories are 'subjective dispositions of thought, implanted in us from the first moment of our existence, and so ordered by our Creator that their employment is in complete harmony with the laws of nature in accordance with which experience proceeds—a kind of *preformation-system* of pure reason'. He sees a 'decisive objection' to this possibility in 'that the necessity of the categories, which belongs to their very conception, would then have to be sacrificed. The concept of cause, for instance, which expresses the necessity of an event under a presupposed condition would be false if it rested only on an arbitrary subjective necessity, implanted in us, of connecting certain empirical ideas according to the rule of causal relation. I would not then be able to say that the effect is connected with the cause in the object, that is to say, necessarily, but only that I am so constituted that I cannot think this idea otherwise than as thus connected. This is exactly what the sceptic most desires.'[1] These principles are objective and necessary; they have nothing to do with my dispositions, for then they would be subjective. Kant would undoubtedly say the same of the empiricist theory outlined in the previous paragraph. I may be disposed to think in a certain way as the result of my past experience. This gives subjective necessity. But what I need is objective necessity and

[1] B 167–8.

this it does not give. So Kant would reject both forms of dispositional theory, the Leibnizian and the Humean.

Yet it also remains true that Kant has not succeeded in showing us the nature of this objectively necessary knowledge which he argues must be there. We are left in doubt whether such knowledge does in fact exist, whether, that is to say, the necessity of mathematics is known by *a priori* insight independently of experience and whether the other sciences do reveal objective necessity in Kant's sense. After examining his account of concepts both in the *Logic* and the *Critique* we are also left in doubt whether his analysis of the concept has been thorough enough. It is a notion of supreme importance in his philosophy. Is it wrong to suggest that it remains throughout a vague notion, vague even in the case of the empirical concept and considerably vaguer in that of the pure? A more adequate examination of the sciences, and a more exact analysis of the concept, might possibly have led him to a different theory of knowledge. He shared in the rationalist recoil from empiricism, but no more than the rationalists did he succeed in refuting the theory of universals which the empiricists had put forward.

41. Nevertheless Kant understood how central to the theory of knowledge is this question about the nature of concepts and of universals. The concept was the key to the analysis of thinking and discursive knowledge; it might even be argued that he over-emphasized its importance in claiming that all human knowledge was through concepts, that is to say, discursive, excepting only the sensory *Anschauung*. In view of this it is disappointing that his account of the concept is so incomplete. He did, it is true, see the complexity of the problem and tried to distinguish between various kinds of concepts, particularly the pure and the empirical. His main contribution was the thesis that the concept was best regarded as a rule; pure concepts were rules, that is, principles guiding thought in its ordering of the manifold, but empirical concepts, too, were rules used by the mind in recognition and assertion. In the chapter on schematism there are suggestive hints both psychological and

epistemological, though the relation of concept to schema is never clear. Yet there is nothing definitive in Kant's discussion of the concept; he leaves us with the main problems unsolved and with many of them untouched. Nor does he state the rationalist opposition to empiricism in such a way that we feel empiricism to be finally refuted.

We may conclude our historical inquiries with this examination of Kant's position. After his day the discussion of concepts and universals was carried forward by various writers, sometimes at considerable length.[1] But few of these discussions have any permanent value and it is unnecessary for us to study any of them here.

[1] Many of them are discussed by K. Marc-Wogau in *Inhalt und Umfang des Begriffs*, Uppsala, 1936. Cf. also N. Kemp Smith 'The Nature of Universals' in *Mind*, xxxvi. 142–5.

PART II

VI

THE APPROACH TO THE PROBLEM

42. The study of history is an antidote to parochialism and the narrow outlook. One advantage of knowing something of the history of our present problem is that we are saved from viewing it solely from one angle, the angle of our own predominant philosophical interests and concerns. Prominent in mid-twentieth-century thinking has been the upsurge of positivism and the interest in linguistic and logical analysis and it is natural that our thoughts about universals should have been coloured by this fact. Thus it is not surprising that statements that universals are real are viewed with suspicion, for there is little room for realities of this order in our positivist schemes. It is not surprising too that we tend to think of the problem as solely linguistic and that we seek to find a solution in purely linguistic terms.

But at other times other pressures have been evident. The question with which Greek philosophy began was whether there existed some common element in all things in terms of which the world could be explained, something, for instance water, out of which all things were made. This presupposed at least the possibility that there could be real common elements. And as long as this remained an urgent question for the Greeks, culminating in the problem of the One and the Many in its various forms, a fundamental condition of thought was the assumption that the existence of real common elements or universals could be discussed sensibly. When Socrates switched the interest of thinkers from natural philosophy to human values the language of universals was maintained, but it was now used primarily to meet the need for absolute and eternal standards and the universal was ultimately found in the Form. Since such universals were not realized on earth they tended to be viewed as 'separated', though things 'participated' to some measure in the Forms. Again as Aristotle, and to a lesser extent Plato, moved gradually towards logical problems, such as that of the formal nature of inference, of the primitive truths held to be pervasive in all inference, of the nature of proposition, and of the subject-predicate relation, the point of emphasis in the theory of universals changed too. For Aristotle the universal was still necessary and eternal; but it was the necessity in inference and the eternity of basic principles of thought that more and more engaged his attention, and when he spoke of the common quality it was the way in which the same quality could be attributed to different subjects that become uppermost in his thought. The universal is 'that which is of such a nature as to be predicated of many subjects'.

This same phenomenon can be found in later philosophy, in the medieval schools, in Locke, Leibniz, Kant, Frege, and others. The exigencies of the main philosophic interest colour the account given of universals. And I believe that this is equally true of the positivist philosophy of our own day. Needless to say, the view taken of universals will in turn influence the development of the philosophy in question.

It may be that we are very slowly moving away from positivism and out of the shadow of the Vienna Circle; it may be that we can now make a better estimate than our immediate predecessors could of the significance of this phase in the development of twentieth-century thought. It is certainly possible to do so in respect of the theory of universals. Positivism is a protest against transcendent entities. It regards affirmations of their existence as lacking in significance. Accordingly, its bias is strongly against certain theories of universals, that is to say certain realist theories. Questions about universals, it prefers to think, are not questions about real objects but about logical and even linguistic issues.

This comes out very clearly, I believe, in a thoughtful paper which Morris Lazerowitz contributed to *Mind* some years ago.[1]

[1] 'The Existence of Universals', *Mind*, no. 217, January 1946, pp. 1–24. Cf. further, 'Universals' by David Pears, *Phil. Quarterly*, April 1951, pp. 218–28, and 'Names and Universals', by D. J. O'Connor, *Proc. Arist. Soc.*, 1952–3.

He argues that if we examine modern theories of universals we find that there is little real disagreement about the basic facts. For instance, all agree that we begin with the observation of likenesses and not with the discovery of universals. But disagreement arises about a linguistic problem. How are we to classify such a word as 'red'? Some thinkers do not regard 'red' as a general word. Can we view it as a proper name? In that case it would help if the quality, red, were viewed as a universal, and the universal as an entity to which a proper name could be given. Lazerowitz suggests that the ultimate explanation of the continuance of the argument about the existence or non-existence of universals is not to be found in any desire to establish ontologies; it lies rather in this desire to classify words properly.

> By asserting that universals are entities, they [the philosophers] are not, in an indirect way, making the obviously false statement that abstract words, as a matter of ordinary classification of parts of speech, are proper names. Rather, to put the matter provisionally, they are making in concealed form the *linguistic proposal*, 'Let us classify such words with proper names'. The statement 'Universals are entities' hides the linguistic proposal to reclassify, formally, abstract words with proper names.[1]

Lazerowitz is throughout confident that the ontological issue is not the real issue; and when we ask 'Are there universals?' we are not really asking whether there are such and such entities amongst real existences. He takes it for granted that such a possibility is ruled out from the start and thinks most of the philosophers of the thirties and forties would have agreed with him. The issue is linguistic; it has to do with the way in which we speak of things and the conventions we then employ. Lazerowitz is here expressing the linguistic and nominalist view of universals and on this basis he puts forward an interesting and ingenious explanation of why the dispute about universals continues, in spite of general agreement, as he assumes, that ontological issues are not involved.

[1] Ibid., p. 20.

Now we today cannot begin with this assumption. The question is once again an open one, and whereas linguistic and conceptual issues are involved and must be looked into, we cannot rule out the possibility that we are dealing too with expressly ontological problems. This means that the existence of the universal, either as a 'separate' entity or as a common quality, is a genuine issue; it follows too that the debate between the identity theory and the resemblance theory is relevant. We cannot assume, therefore, without further inquiry, that Lazerowitz's remark is correct: 'The *fact* with regard to abstract words is that they are applicable to each of a number of things because the things resemble each other more or less, without there being anything common to all of them to set exact boundaries which would mark off correct from incorrect applications of the words.'[1] This is the resemblance theory which favoured the positivist and nominalist theory of universals. We have no right to begin by accepting its truth. We must look to the evidence, including naturally the sort of evidence which Lazerowitz brings forward in this article.

43. But where then are we to begin? What approach should be chosen in considering this problem? The danger is that in posing the problem we already beg the question. It might appear natural, for instance, to begin with the question, 'What is a universal?' But are we then assuming that universals are existent objects? Obviously we assume this if we ask, 'What sort of real entities are these universals?' We may be assuming it too if we ask, 'How does a universal differ from a particular?'

A useful comparison can be made here with the practice of postulating *sensa* in the study of sense-perception. The philosopher is faced with the demand for a consistent theory of sense-perception. Conflicting appearances and illusions create difficulties for him. He, therefore, tries out the hypothesis that the immediate object in sense-perception is unique in character, a *sensum*. He then asks such questions as the following: How is the *sensum* related to the physical object? How is *sensum*^{1},

[1] Ibid., p. 15.

seen at a place from point p^1, related to *sensum*[2], seen at the same place from point p^2? Are there unsensed *sensa*? The critics hold that he is here creating further difficulties for himself because he is now assuming that the *sensum*, a mere hypothesis of his, is a real entity like a physical object, and because he attempts to find a place for it in the real world and relate it to other objects in the real world.

Now universals too, like *sensa*, it can be argued, are possibly fabrications of the philosopher; they may be introduced by us in our attempts to explain thinking, just as *sensa* are introduced to explain perceiving. Having introduced them the philosopher then asks: How are universals related to particular things? What is the status of the universal? Which comes first, the universal or the particular? But these questions presuppose that universals are real entities. The philosopher begs the question.

Whether these criticisms can be sustained or not we need not now consider. The wise course to follow, as far as we can, is to make no assumptions in approaching this subject. If it is wrong to begin on the supposition that the nominalist theory is the correct theory, it is equally wrong to start with realist, conceptualist, or any other, assumptions. To begin by asking, 'What sort of real entities are universals?' or again, 'Is the universal a proper name or a general word?' is in both cases to take certain things for granted. We have to tread more warily. Our starting-point must be one which begs no questions vital to the argument.

44. My approach to the problem in this book is not that of the physicist seeking for the universal features of the physical universe, nor that of the moralist seeking universal standards; I approach it rather from the study of thinking. Now a characteristic of thinking is that it is carried forward in general terms. We need not digress to ask whether we ever 'infer from particular to particular', for it would be agreed by all that thinking for the most part is general. The thinking under consideration need not always be verbal thinking; this is a point to which I

shall return in the next section. When, however, it is verbal the thinking then is carried forward with the help of general words. Now this is the point from which I propose to start my inquiry, and the appropriate question to ask is, 'How do we use general words?'

This question needs to be approached from two angles. First, there is the more formal and methodological approach. What is the function of the general word in the sentence? What are the syntactical and semantic rules involved? Secondly, there is the psychological and genetic approach. How do we learn to operate with general words? How is our present use of general words linked with our past experiences? What sort of objects and what sort of arrangement of objects in the experienced world enable us to use general words successfully? If, then, we begin with the question 'How do we use general words?' both sets of questions have to be answered. We must expect to find syntactical, logical, psychological, and ontological issues arising in our discussion.

I begin then with the consideration of general words. Now a critic might argue that I have myself, in emphasizing the verbal, already forgotten my own solemn warnings and begged the question. By beginning with the question 'How do we use general words?' it may be said, I am assuming that the problem of universals is a linguistic problem. This is 'the spirit of the age' and I have succumbed to it. Brand Blanshard in his examination of universals in *Reason and Analysis* deprecates 'the tendency, now fashionable, to deal with the problem as if it were an issue of language'.[1] I agree that it is a grave error to assume that the problem of universals is a linguistic problem. But it seems to me none the less true that the best starting-point for a discussion of universals is the consideration of the general word, and my reason for starting here is that it appears to me to be the quickest way of getting to the heart of this problem. Further, as I have made clear, the question 'How do we use general words?' cannot be answered on linguistic grounds alone; it involves also psychological and ontological investi-

[1] *Reason and Analysis*, ch. 9, particularly p. 416 n.

gations. Consequently, it is certainly not the case that just to ask this question is itself to assume that the universal is a word. The outcome of these considerations, beginning with this question, may equally well be a realist theory as a nominalist; beginning in this way leaves the final issue entirely open. No one questions that we do use general words in thinking. Everyone would agree too that 'How do we use general words?' is a significant question and one that requires investigation. Finally, in starting here, if I am right, we beg no questions and make no assumptions about the theory of universals.

Thus the task we set ourselves is to examine the nature of universals, but to do so by first examining general words and by considering what is implied in their use.

45. One point should be emphasized before we begin this discussion. It is possible to think and to communicate with others without using words, whether general words or other words. Communication can be through non-verbal signs and some of these signs are used in ways not unlike the use of general words. The behaviour of animals on occasion suggests an acquaintance with certain rudimentary general signs, which are not verbal, and we have the more definite evidence of human beings who are unable to use words and yet use general signs. Interesting work on this topic was carried out by German and French psychologists at the beginning of the century, and their examination of untrained deaf mutes is particularly relevant. Ribot sums up the evidence in *The Evolution of General Ideas.*[1] It would seem that deaf mutes generalize successfully without the use of words. They have their general signs, but these are gestures rather than words. Ribot gives a 'vocabulary' of such signs and discusses the 'syntax' of this gesture-language. It is a 'natural' language, much the same the world over. Here are one or two instances from Ribot's vocabulary: '*Large*—Raise the hand and look up. *Bad*—Simulate tasting and make grimace. *Lose*—Pretend to drop an object and hunt for it in vain. *Love*—Hold the hand on the heart. *Bread*—Signs of being

[1] pp. 39 ff.

hungry, of cutting and of carrying to mouth.' Naturally the extent of this vocabulary as used by such deaf mutes is very limited; the value of a word-vocabulary is seen in the great extension which becomes possible once words are used. Ribot shows how effectively the lack of words limits the intellectual growth of these unfortunates. Yet they certainly use one gesture to signify at different times many different objects, for instance, the gesture for 'large' to signify any large thing. It could well be claimed that the fundamental questions which we have to face in discussing the problem of universals are already present.

Whilst, therefore, we take the question 'How do we use general words?' to be the most suitable starting-point in our quest for a solution to the problem of universals, we do not assume either that the problem is a verbal one only or that the sole symbol used in any thinking that is general is the general word.

VII
GENERAL WORDS

46. According to ancient tradition a word is 'a sound significant by convention'. This still remains a useful working definition though it is open to misinterpretation. Thus it would be false to interpret it to mean that the word is the unit of speech sound. The most promising account of a speech sound is that it is one speech utterance, an unbroken stream of sound, a continuum bounded by pauses. Now a word could be a speech sound in this sense. Suppose you ask what is on the table and I answer 'Bread', my answer is one speech utterance and it is a word. But most often a speech utterance contains many words. 'I'll come back to Aber tomorrow' is one unbroken stream of sound as I now utter it. In this sense it would be quite wrong to say that the word is the one and only unit of speech sound. Incidentally, it would be wrong to say too that the phoneme (*p*, *t*, *m*, etc.) is the unit of speech sound, if we are thinking of the concrete utterance. For one phoneme glides into the next and there is no break.

In the second place, the above definition may be taken to mean that a word is always significant, that is, always has a meaning. But what then of nonsense words? If we frame a nonsense word must we either at once ascribe a meaning to it or deny that it is a word? Again, words are used to express emotions, for instance, the word 'Ouch!' It might be said that such words have no meaning. Would they then cease to be words? And what of proper names? Some logicians deny that proper names have meaning. Would they then be words? If we persist in speaking of 'Boojum', 'Ouch', and 'John' as words, are we not then doing violence to our original definition that a word is a *significant* sound?

On the other hand, if we stress the point that a word is essentially a significant sound, we may be tempted to interpret the definition as signifying that the word is a morpheme, the smallest unit of meaningful content. But this will not do. No linguist would identify morpheme and word. Consider the distinction between the word 'cat' and the word 'cats'. The linguist explains the difference by saying that 'cat' is a morpheme but 'cats' is two morphemes, namely 'cat' and '-s', the '-s' being itself a unit of meaningful or semantic content. It follows that there are some morphemes which are not words. It is incorrect to say that the smallest unit of meaningful content is invariably a word. A morpheme cannot be further divided if it is to retain its meaning, but a word may contain many morphemes and so can be divided. The word 'cats' can be divided into 'cat' and '-s' and the word 'eatables' into 'eat' and 'able' and '-s'.

Thus in seeking to explain what we mean by a word we can neither say that it is the unit of speech sound, meaning by this that every single stretch of speech utterance is invariably a word (for a sentence may be such a stretch), nor can we say that it is the smallest unit of meaningful content. It is indeed difficult to find a characteristic or characteristics possessed exclusively by all words to provide the needed differentia for accurate description and definition. One characteristic which words have is a certain autonomy; they stand, as it were, on their own feet. Thus, in the above example, '-s' is a morpheme but it is not a word, for it leans on the morpheme 'cat', whereas 'cat' itself is, in comparison, independent. The autonomy of words is further illustrated by the fact that a word can stand alone. 'What is on the table?' 'Bread'. Here 'bread' is one word but it provides a complete answer to this question. In this sense of being autonomous it could be, and has been, described as 'a free form', and more as the minimum free form, and this might turn out to be a very useful description of a word. But unfortunately there are words that do not appear to be free forms, for instance the words 'the' or 'a' in English. These cannot provide complete answers to questions—unless we are willing to admit that 'the' is a complete answer in the following context: 'What is the definite article in English?' Answer 'The'.

Another characteristic possessed by words is a special sort of indivisibility. Though it is true that a word is in principle divisible, in the sense that it may contain more than one morpheme and can be divided into its morphemes, as a stretch of sound it is indivisible in the following sense. It cannot be so divided that another stretch of sound can be interposed between its parts. Thus the word 'elephant' as uttered is usually one stretch of sound, and though in principle one might pause after 'eleph-', what one cannot do is to introduce a speech utterance in between 'eleph' and 'ant', for instance 'eleph-big-ant'. This seems to hold true of all words as ordinarily used. Yet a modern poet might well experiment with just such an insertion.[1]

But to return to the definition, 'a sound significant by convention'. It is clearly difficult to explain precisely what is meant by saying that a word is a significant sound. What of the phrase 'significant *by convention*'? Certainly language is conventional, but the conventionality of language too may be misconstrued. For there is an over-academic statement of it which can be set out as follows: A speaker decides with his fellow speaker what sign to choose in order to convey a specific meaning; he is free to choose whatever sign he wishes so long as his listener accepts it and understands the convention. A word is a species of sign and the sign is chosen conventionally. If this account of the word were granted it would then be easy to see what a language is; it is simply a collection or a plurality of such signs. The conventionality of words is sometimes interpreted in this way.

Now words may in some uses play the role of signs, though they are to be differentiated from other signs (for instance, dark clouds as a sign of rain). Yet to say that language is a collection of conventional signs is most misleading in its suggestion. Language begins with the human need for communication with others; it is essential that the individual should state his wants, make his requests, express his emotions, and so on, if he is to survive. Children pick up language early, but they do not

[1] I am grateful to my colleague Arwyn Watkins for pointing out the importance of the characteristic discussed in this paragraph and for valuable comments on the rest of this section.

do so by learning that a word uttered by another is a sign and by learning precisely what this sign signifies.[1] A much more promising account of the matter is that children first imitate the sounds they hear and find that the utterance of some of these sounds is encouraged by those around them. The sounds are more often sentences than words, but, whether words or sentences, they are more properly conceived as points of contact in communication than as signs. Furthermore, along with the sounds the linguistic conventions guiding their use are also learnt. The children obviously do not create these conventions; they are the work of countless past generations of speakers who have used the language.

If then it is agreed that a word is a sound significant by convention this is not to be interpreted to mean that each individual decides for himself how to use certain signs and what conventions to apply, and then comes to an agreement with his listener on these points. A writer or a scientist, it is true, may decide to use such and such a term in such and such a manner and may successfully introduce new words into the language that he uses. Yet, in comparison with the total number of words in that language, such new words will very few; indeed the ordinary man in his hardly conscious quest for economy in speech is likely to affect and change the language more than does the writer or the scientist—though what needs to be stressed is that the changes that any one individual can bring about are minute.

None the less, it remains true that both the vocabulary and the syntax of a language are conventional. But this leads to a further point that must be made here. To say that a word is a sound significant by convention is not to say that each word has a fixed signification bestowed on it conventionally. It is a mistake to suppose that the dictionary, for instance, sets down the fixed, unchanging meanings of words. The most the dictionary can do is to illustrate various uses of the word; there *are* no fixed, unchanging meanings for it to set down. Words are

[1] H. H. Price deals fully with what he terms 'the Sign Theory' in *Thinking and Experience*, ch. 6.

understood as they are used, and their use changes with changing situations and contexts.

Admittedly the compiling of dictionaries works to a certain extent against change and for fixity, and so indeed does the practice of writing. As compared with speaking, writing is a late acquisition and there are still many spoken languages which have never been written. By the time men came to write they had become more conscious of the elements in the sentences they used. Words came to be separated from one another by inserting spaces between them, and this practice was significant. The separating arose partly no doubt from the consciousness of the existence of recurring minimum free forms in the sentence, that is to say, recurring elements or units able to stand alone, for instance, in answering questions. No doubt crude logical considerations helped in the work; for instance, the function of operational words such as 'or', 'not', and so on was becoming understood. This too would help forward the separation of words. But, whatever the full explanation, the separation of words in writing certainly made it easier to concentrate on the word and on its function in the sentence, and this helped to give it a limited fixity.

To conclude this section, we may accept the traditional definition of a word as a sound significant by convention, but much depends on how this is interpreted. Perhaps the most useful modern insight is that of the word as a free form. The conventionality of language must certainly be accepted, as long as it is understood that the conventions are created by the race rather than the individual who may now be using the language. Theories such as the Sign Theory are naïve.

47. Our special concern in this chapter is with general words. The distinction between general and particular purports to be a metaphysical distinction and is related to the logical distinction between general and singular terms, which, in its turn, is related to the grammatical distinction between common nouns and proper names. Thomas Hobbes in a succinct paragraph in the *Leviathan*[1]

[1] I. ch. 4. 'Of Speech.'

has this to say: 'Of names, some are *proper* and singular to one only thing, as *Peter*, *John*, *this man*, *this tree*; and some are *common* to many things, *man*, *horse*, *tree*; every of which, though but one name, is nevertheless the name of divers particular things.'

Hobbes in this section, *Of Speech*, tends to identify words with names, then divides names into two groups, proper or singular and common or general, any one of the former being the name of 'one only thing' and of the latter being the name 'of divers particular things'. This supports the common vague assumption that words can be conveniently divided into these two groups and that the general word can be thought of as any word which is not a proper name. At the same time Hobbes in this passage has in mind the grammatical distinction between two sorts of nouns, namely, proper names and common nouns. If his thought were ruled solely by this distinction his grouping would then relate to nouns only. Yet the fact that he groups 'this man' with 'Peter' as 'proper' shows that logical considerations are in his mind as well as grammatical.

It is, of course, obvious that the division of words into two groups, proper names and common nouns, will not do. First, singular expressions, such as 'this man', are not ordinarily held to be proper names. Secondly, if we think of the description given of the common name, as a name common to many different particular things, it is clear that not all words other than proper names and singular expressions are common names in this sense. Not to mention nonsense words, what of ejaculations such as 'Alas!'? What of conjunctives, such as 'and', and prepositions, such as 'in'? Does it make sense to speak of 'divers particular things' of which these are the common names? It would be possible, perhaps, to bring pronouns into Hobbes's scheme. What of adjectives and adverbs? Hobbes does not entirely omit all reference to them, but the reference is oblique; a thing 'may enter into account, or be considered, for some accident or quality which we conceive to be in it', for instance, it may be hot. We can then modify, say, the common noun 'body' and speak of 'hot body'. 'By a little change or wresting' too we 'make a name' for this quality or accident, namely 'heat'. Such names 'are called *names abstract*, because severed, not from matter, but from the account of matter'. Hobbes acknowledges also 'names of names', for instance 'general', 'equivocal', and 'universal', together with 'negative' names, for example, 'nothing', 'no men', and 'infinite'. In this way, somewhat grudgingly, Hobbes gathers abstract names and negative words under the umbrella of common or general words.

48. This distinction between the proper name which is the name of one unique individual and the general word which is a word common to many things is a good starting-point for any discussion of general words. The use of the proper name is a prominent feature in communication. In addressing another person, in thinking about him, and in referring to him, it is most fortunate that we are able to name him; to forget a name puts one at a social disadvantage. The function of the proper name is to designate the individual. The ideal would be that a word be used exclusively to designate an individual, this individual and this individual alone. But the ideal is rarely attained, since, if for no other reason, its attainment would be too expensive on phonemes. In a specific context one may approach the ideal; thus if one speaks today of Hitler or of Napoleon or again of Winston Churchill the unique designation is understood. Still, other individuals are named Hitler (though very few), Napoleon, and Winston Churchill. In a narrow context, say in a family, 'John' is used to designate one and one only, and everyone in the family knows who is so designated. Yet this same series of phonemes is used as the name of thousands of other individuals. In another sense too the ideal is not attained. Proper names, according to this ideal, designate only; they should not be meaningful words in themselves. But if someone introduces 'John' into his discourse, even though we do not know which John is being talked about, we do assume that he is a male, that he belongs to a predominantly English-speaking community, of Christian stock, and so on. The John in question may in fact be none of the things we assume, but that we expect him to be so shows that the name 'John' as we

use it does not merely designate. Proper names can be observed in the process of being transformed into something other than a proper name, as when one speaks of 'a Hitler' or 'a Judas'. So too if he is 'a John' he is likely to be of Christian stock, of English-speaking parents, etc.

These uses lead us away from the ideal, presumably because they threaten the uniqueness of the designation. This ideal is sometimes stated thus: one name, one thing named, *unum nomen unum nominatum*. The fact that many men are called 'John', together with the further fact that the word conveys a certain amount of vague information, tends to take away from the precision of the ideal. It is attained when a proper name designates the one individual and does no more. But if this ideal is accepted or assumed, it is likely to influence the view taken of the general word. The multiplicity of individual things in the world, together with the fewness of phonemes, makes it impossible to give each individual a proper name. Moreover, if each were given such a name it would be impossible for us to remember the names given them. Yet some sort of naming is held to be essential and so one is driven *faute de mieux* to use one and the same name for many things, *unum nomen multa nominata*. This name, it is said, is the general word. It falls away from the ideal in that it does not designate one object but many. Consequently, it cannot but be imprecise and vague; it tries to do what the proper name does, but the attempt must inevitably fail.

Such assumptions as these seem frequently to be involved in our thinking about general words. The main assumption is that the function of the general word is one and the same with that of the proper name, but that the general word does not function so effectively. Yet, is it the function of the general word to designate individuals? It is true that general words are used to describe individuals. Again, they are combined with other words, such as the definite or indefinite article or a demonstrative pronoun, to frame singular terms. But, in spite of what Hobbes says, a singular term is not a proper name. (Nor, for that matter, is it a general word, though general words are used in the framing of singular terms.) General words may be used to describe individual things, but this is not to say they name them.

49. The question then arises, Granted that general words do not name individual things, can they be said to name anything? Do they possibly name abstractions? Are general words the names of ideas or concepts? The general word 'man' is not John's name nor Tom's; it is not the name of the collection of men, of all men; it is not the name of some men. Could it be the name of the idea or concept of man? Conceptualists say that it can, and is. 'Words become general', says Locke, 'by being made the signs of general ideas'.[1] 'John' is the sign of John, it is said by Locke to 'stand for John'; and in the same way the general word 'man' is the sign of the idea of man. What differentiates the general word from the proper name is not that the latter names and the former does not name, for both name; but the proper name names the individual existence, whilst the general word names the general idea.

Locke's account of this matter is made additionally difficult by his ambiguous use of the term 'general idea'. He seems to be thinking primarily of a logical content, definable and objective; but it is also true that psychological and subjective elements enter. The ideas are 'in the mind'. Frege deals with the same theme in his essay, 'On Concept and Object', but he aims at being more precise than Locke. He expressly states that he wishes to deal with the idea or concept in a purely logical sense and does this by linking it with the logical predicate. He thinks of this predicate, it is important to add, as a function, and a special sort of function, namely, one whose values are truth-values. In a subject-predicate statement something, the 'object' in Frege's language, is being talked about and something is being said of it. In 'Tom is tall' '. . . is tall' is said of Tom. The logical form is $f\ a$, where 'a' is the sign for the subject and 'f. . .' is an expression for a concept. A predicative expression, for instance ' . . . is tall', he thinks of as a concept word,

[1] *Essay Concerning Human Understanding*, III. iii. 6.

whereas the subject term is for him a proper name (used in a wide sense to include, for instance, singular expressions not normally regarded as proper names).[1] The relation which he now has in mind is, he thinks, irreversible. 'The concept', he says,[2] 'is predicative. On the other hand a name of an object, a proper name, is quite incapable of being used as a grammatical predicate.' The name of an object is a proper name, and the name of a concept is a concept word. As he explains in his *Foundations of Arithmetic*, 'the business of a general concept word is precisely to signify a concept. . . . The name of a thing is a proper name.'[3]

Since Frege's concern is with the contrast between thing (or object) and concept, his analysis is in terms of the distinction between logical subject and predicate. His interest is in this logical relationship, that is, in the function, *f*. . . . It is this he has in mind when speaking of irreversibility. The charge has been made that he teaches that once an expression is used as a predicative-term it cannot be used as a subject term. If he does say this, he is clearly wrong. The same expressions in sentences can be used in one way on one occasion and in another on another occasion.[4] But is not Frege's final concern with the irreversibility of *f a*, that is with the contrast of the roles that the two elements play? A function cannot be an object and an object cannot be a function. Incidentally, this should not be interpreted to mean that we cannot think about the concept. But in any statement, e.g. 'The concept *horse* is not empty', the expression 'the concept *horse*' is now, Frege explains, the subject term and is not a concept term.[5]

But to return to the point in which we are particularly interested, namely, the contrast between the proper name and the general word, it is, in the first place, noticeable that Frege's thought is much influenced by the tradition that the chief function of language is naming. The business of 'the general

[1] Cf. *Philosophical Writings*, tr. Geach and Black, p. 47 n. 1: 'I call anything a proper name if it is a sign for an object.'

[2] *Philosophical Writings*, p. 43.

[3] § 51.

[4] Strawson brings out the point clearly in *Individuals*, ch. 5.

[5] Cf. *Philosophical Writings*, p. 46.

concept word', he thinks, as well as of the proper name, is to name; the difference lies solely in what is named. But he does not then proceed to say that, whereas the proper name names the one, the general word names the many. He does not reassert the *unum nomen multa nominata* doctrine. On Frege's view what the general word names is the concept.

Both the general concept word and the proper name have sense and reference. Frege uses the terms *Sinn* (sense) and *Bedeutung* (reference) in an unusual way, but the meaning of the terms is made clear in the paper 'On Sense and Reference'. The concept word has its sense, and it also refers to the concept. This latter is no private idea, but a thought that is public, that is to say, many can share it. On the other hand, 'a proper name (word, sign, sign combination, expression) *expresses* its *sense*, *stands for* or *designates* its reference.'[1] And the reference here is to an object, to something existing, though it may be an error on our part to suppose that there is such an object. (It does not follow because a proper name 'expresses its sense' that there exists an object to which it refers.[2] Yet that there is such an object is implied in our use of the proper name.)

Perhaps, at first view, the more surprising part of this analysis is the assertion that the proper name expresses its sense. Frege does not take the view that the proper name is designative only; but then he uses the term 'proper name' so widely that it is obvious that proper names cannot be merely designative. Included in his proper names are all singular expressions. He even suggests, for reasons which we need not consider, that sentences are proper names.[3] But he holds too that ordinary proper names, for instance, names of persons, also express 'sense'; thus the meaning of 'Aristotle' in some of its uses is said to be 'the pupil of Plato and the teacher of Alexander the Great.'[4]

So great is Frege's concern with the proper name that the hasty reader, particularly if unacquainted with 'Concept and Object', might sometimes think it is his only concern. But this

[1] *Philosophical Writings*, p. 61.
[2] Cf. ibid., p. 58.
[3] Ibid., p. 62 ff.
[4] Ibid., p. 58 n. 1.

is not so. What he is concerned with is the proper name in statement, and this means that he is concerned equally with the other factor in statement; that is to say, he is as concerned with functions as he is with proper names. And a function of necessity is a general element, for a function can in principle have many objects falling under it. The concept word is general. But the same word which is used as a concept word in one use of it, for instance, the word 'wise' in 'Socrates is wise', can be used to help frame a proper name (that is, a singular term) 'the wise philosopher who died through drinking hemlock'. So too we may have a predicate, '. . . is a tree', but the same general word 'tree' can be used to frame the proper name 'the tree near the window'.

This throws light on the common noun, for instance, 'tree', and on the thing-universal, or the substantival universal. What we should note now is that the general word used as a concept term can also be used to frame a proper name. Further, it can be used in quantifying expressions, for instance, we can speak of 'all trees', 'some trees', 'any tree', and 'no trees'. Frege was particularly concerned with these and in his celebrated *Begriffsschrift* (a very significant title) he sets out his theory of quantification, a theory basic to modern logic. Such expressions as the above, 'all trees' etc., contain no direct reference to individuals, to objects in Frege's sense of the term. Yet he still thinks that there is a referring, but that the reference is to concepts. This point is brought out very clearly in the *Foundations of Arithmetic* in a passage where he discusses the statement 'All whales are mammals'.[1]

> It is true [he says] that at first sight the proposition 'All whales are mammals' seems to be not about concepts but about animals; but if we ask which animal we are speaking of, we are unable to point to any one in particular . . . the word 'whale' is not the name of any individual creature. If it be replied that what we are speaking of is not, indeed, an individual definite object, but nevertheless an indefinite object, I suspect that 'indefinite object' is only another term for concept and a poor one at that, being self-contradictory.

[1] *Foundations of Arithmetic*, tr. J. L. Austin, § 47.

That is to say when we use the expression 'all whales' in this statement we are not speaking about all (or any) whales, just as when we use the expression 'no whales' we are not speaking about no whales. What we are speaking about, in Frege's opinion, is the concept. Admittedly, the question immediately arises whether we can speak about the concept *whale*, without 'the concept *whale*' becoming itself the object term. But I do not wish to discuss this and other difficulties now, since what is first necessary is a full discussion of the nature of the concept itself, and this will be attempted later,[1] when further items in Frege's account of the concept will have to be considered. But what emerges as of prime importance in Frege's discussion, in spite of his constant concern with naming and referring, is the contrast he makes between the proper name and the concept word, and the key to the understanding of the latter, and to our use of general words, is the function.

50. When we speak of general words we have in mind common nouns, abstract nouns, adjectives, pronouns, and verbs and it has become clear that these are used in ways fundamentally different from those in which proper names are used. The general word is not to be thought of as a pale imitation of a proper name, and the effectiveness of its use is not to be determined by the same criteria as determine the effectiveness of the proper name. The *unum nomen unum nominatum* ideal in the case of the proper name is not to be regarded as the ideal—though unattainable ideal—in the case of the general word. Precision in our use of general words does not lie in giving one and the same name to one and the same individual and in confining the use of this name to naming this individual. The general word is never used to name in the way in which the proper name names, and further, it is not used merely for referring to objects. Obsessive concern with proper name precision and with naming leads to too narrow an account of the general word.

We do use general words to refer to objects, for instance, they form part of our singular expressions when explicitly referring to

[1] Cf. §§ 72 and 84 below.

individuals. But we use them too in other ways, for instance, we use them to characterize. This is the use Frege has in mind when he speaks of concepts, although it is true that he still thinks of '*f*...' as a name, in this case the name of the concept. Yet characterizing is a different activity from naming and from referring. Furthermore, we may describe without referring; we may do so using singular statements or again general statements involving quantification. In these contexts general words may be used without any intention to refer, and where referring is part of the intention it is not the whole of it. Quantifying, too, presupposes grouping or classifying; and the importance of the use of general words in grouping is obvious.

General words are used then to refer, to describe, to characterize, and to group; it is entirely misleading to speak of them as if their only use was for referring. These uses are interrelated, for instance, characterizing and grouping are needed for describing. What of the relations between characterizing and grouping? It is generally supposed that the limits of a class are determined by the character, or characters, that can be predicated of each and every item included in the class. But this notion of a common character is ambiguous and needs examination. Moreover, the question arises whether a distinction can be made between a mere enumeration and a class. The logician W. E. Johnson thinks the distinction can be made; 'there is involved in the notion of a class an element entirely absent from that of enumeration.'[1] This element is the determining of the limits of the class by a character or characters. But the point then arises whether there exists any group or enumeration not so determined. Even if an enumeration were made at random, in the sense that it was not determined by a character or characters, would not all the items after the enumeration possess at least this common character, namely, that they were selected for enumeration by the enumerator? But this, perhaps, is a trivial point. The important point is the assumption that normally the group has its limits determined by a character or characters. Or, to put it in grammatical terms,

[1] *Logic*, Part I, p. 122.

our use of the common noun, itself substantival, has adjectival implications.

51. The above may be stated in the traditional logical terms of extension and intension or denotation and connotation. 'In the language of Mill', says Johnson, in the passage to which I have just referred, 'the denotation of a class may be said to be determined by connotation, i.e. by a certain conjunction of adjectives.'

The doctrine of denotation or extension and connotation or intension was put forward to help illuminate our use of general words, but it is questionable whether it has done so. It was supposed to provide the completely reliable criterion for distinguishing between the general word and the proper name. The proper name is denotative or extensional only, whereas the general word is both denotative and connotative, extensional and intensional.[1] But that no such criterion is provided by the doctrine is clear once we recall what has been said above about the function of the proper name. The function of the proper name, in the strict sense of the term, is purely and solely to designate. We may talk of the designating as a denoting but only if we then stress that denoting in this sense is different from denoting in the sense in which the general word denotes. The general word 'man' does not designate all men. It does not designate at all. It denotes John, Peter, Paul, and the rest, all of which are instances of men. 'Hitler', on the other hand, does designate, but does not denote in the sense of denoting the instances; in this sense it does not denote Hitler. Thus the proposed ground of distinction between the general word and the proper name turns out to be a muddle; the word 'denote' is being used in two quite different senses.

This does not mean that the distinction between denotation or extension and connotation or intension has no value in the discussion of the general word. It points to the latter's characterizing use on the one hand and to its grouping (and

[1] Cf. J. S. Mill, *System of Logic*, I. ii, 'Of Names', but note too the qualifications which Mill makes in this chapter, which are all too frequently ignored.

so instantiating) use on the other. To say that the general word has denotation or extension and connotation or intension is to say that its use enables us to speak of many rather than of one, and this because the many objects are linked together, for instance, by the possession of common characteristics. And, if we were to reject the theory of mere enumeration, it would then make sense to say that all general substantival words have extension and intension in this sense. It would follow that no purely extensional account of our use of general words could be adequate, for that would be to ignore the role of Frege's concept word. In these respects then the distinction may have some value; on the other hand, the doctrine that the general word has denotation and connotation whereas the proper name, in contrast, has denotation only is, because of the double meaning of the term 'denotation' in this context, highly misleading and to be rejected.

52. We use general words successfully in making statements—and these are not all subject-predicate statements. In addition to making statements we use general words too in questioning, commanding, expressing our emotions, and so on. The problem that arises is, How do we do this? What is involved in the successful use of the general word? We shall seek to answer this question in the chapters which follow and in doing so shall be obliged to discuss the following topics.

We speak of individuals being related through having common characters. To what have we committed ourselves in speaking in this way? Do we say that these individuals share one and the same character or quality? If we do, what then is involved? Have we, for instance, committed ourselves to the so-called *Ante Rem* theory of universals, that there must exist ultimate Forms to explain the being of individual things having common characteristics? It will be useful to look briefly at this theory before passing to consider theories of another kind.

Secondly, when we speak of 'a common character' how do we interpret the term 'common'? Do we mean that characters of qualities can be identical? Or do we merely mean that qualities resemble one another? The philosophy recently fashionable, as we have seen, rested on the resemblance theory and for a time it became the acceptable theory almost without question. Today, however, the question is again open and this involves us in a reconsideration of the issue.

Thirdly, the suggestion made by Hume needs further examination. Our responses to various situations are frequently guided by habit and custom, and we must ask what part custom plays in the ordering of thought and the organization of language. In particular, to what extent is our use of general words guided by empirically induced habits? Will the study of dispositions throw any light on our use of general words and on the character of the universal?

Fourthly, we shall take up the point that the general word is the name of the concept. But the term 'concept' is ambiguous, and it is essential that we should try to clarify our minds in relation to it. What do people mean when they speak of a concept, and what when they put forward a conceptualist theory of universals? How true is the theory that the universal is the concept?

When these matters have been considered we shall be in a position to seek a solution of the problem of universals. This will involve a final assessment of realist, conceptualist, and nominalist solutions of the problem, together with a statement of the theory which, in the light of the previous argument, appears then most acceptable to us.

VIII
ULTIMATE FORMS

53. Does the fact that we successfully use general words imply that we are already acquainted with the general structure of the real world? And is such an acquaintance to be interpreted as *a priori* knowledge, independent of any information we acquire through experience? This is the first question that has to be faced, and I propose to begin by looking at the *a priori* solution in its most extreme form, namely the traditional *Ante Rem* or Ideal theory.

Our use of general words, on this theory, depends upon a knowledge of Ideas or Forms which are the reality behind the classes of natural objects and artefacts. We know the ultimate Form and so are able to recognize its incomplete manifestations in sensible things. Knowing the Form of Man we can recognize a man when we see one and use the general word 'man' significantly. This is the so-called Platonic Theory of Ideas or Forms, though whether Plato was always as convinced a supporter of the theory as is sometimes held is a matter in dispute which we need not consider here.[1]

Our use of general words such as 'dog' and 'table' is possible because, first, Forms exist eternally in the world of Being and have their shadowy manifestations in the world of Becoming and because, secondly, we know these Forms *a priori* and innately so that we do not cognize but *re*-cognize the manifestations. Now this theory has its difficulties. It is difficult to believe that the minds of babes are stocked with the innumerable Ideas which the theory would require. It is difficult to believe that before ever seeing a bed the child already conceived the Form of a Bed; and it is still more difficult to believe that it knew the Form of Blue all along and then re-cognized it when for the first time it came across a blue object. We need very strong evidence in favour of this view if we are to accept it.

But such evidence is not forthcoming. There is the evidence in Plato's *Meno*: a boy, ignorant of geometry, answers Socrates's

[1] On this point compare Sir David Ross's *Plato's Theory of Ideas*, Oxford, 1951.

questions about certain geometrical truths in such a way as to satisfy the hearers that he had known these truths all along. But this evidence is of doubtful value. Socrates's questions, which are immediately about empirical rather than *a priori* relations, appear to be leading ones hinting at the right answers, and even if Meno's slave was so precocious as to think out the correct answers this would not prove that he was recalling them.

In the case of the general words 'dog' or 'table' the theory seems almost perverse. It is so obvious that we first see many dogs and observe how they resemble one another before we acquire the use of the word; a previous knowledge of an alleged Form of the Dog is in no way necessary. But to this it might be replied that we use the general words 'unicorn' and 'dragon' successfully before seeing unicorns and dragons. Why should we not know how to use the general word 'dog' before seeing any dogs? Yet this argument is specious. The use of the general word 'unicorn' is in fact as much grounded on the observation of recurrences in nature, the recurrence of teeth, eyes, horns, and so on, as is the use of the word 'dog', and this is so though it is true that we observe no unicorns. Is it not natural to suppose that we first observed horned animals before we acquired the ability to use the general word 'unicorn' significantly? It is true that we 'combine' the qualities that go to make up the unicorn in ways which are not to be found in nature, but we 'combine' qualities too in thinking of dogs, although this combination *is* to be found in nature. At least such a theory has been put forward, and if we accepted it we could claim that we acquire the ability to use the general word 'unicorn' in very much the same way as we acquire the ability to use the word 'dog'. It is not necessary to suppose that we know the Idea of Unicorn innately and prior to all experience.

54. But, in fairness to it, this philosophy is not solely or primarily interested in such general words as 'dog' and 'unicorn', but rather in those regulative general words, the use of which, so we usually suppose, helps us to order our experience and gives us our criteria by which to measure experience. Experience as a whole is significant because such general words as 'cause', 'substance', 'goodness', 'beauty', 'unity', and 'triangularity' are

significant to us. And these can only be significant because we possess innate *a priori* knowledge of the Ideas in each case. Thus, on this theory, such general words as 'cause' and 'substance' have an important ontological reference. We know what they stand for prior to all experience and in knowing this know the principles by which the world of nature is ordered. It is essential, therefore, if we are to think of our experiences in an orderly fashion that we should first know the Forms of Cause and Substance.

Such is the argument, but it is clearly open to criticism. For there are at least two alternative explanations of how we know such principles. We may know them by rational insight, that is, discover them in the course of experience, though not by the senses. Or, secondly, we may find them given in experience or derive them from it. Granting the point that if they are used to order the experiences of any moment they themselves must have been known previous to that experience, they may still have been *given* in prior experiences or derived from earlier experience. It is important to distinguish between knowing the categories prior to *all* experience and knowing them prior to the present experience. In the latter case they may still be empirically given or empirically derived. And indeed there is considerable evidence for the theory that the categories are themselves gained empirically, that our present experience is ordered in terms of general principles learnt in the course of past experience. Perhaps the principal evidence lies in the very vagueness of these categories. If cause and substance were known innately in the way suggested would they not be known precisely and infallibly? The fact that our knowledge of them is so uncertain makes it more likely that they are suggested by experience. In the case of substance, at least, there are many who think that the suggestion of experience is here false and that we are attempting to order our experiences in terms of an erroneous principle. This possibility could not be admitted for a moment if substance were in truth known innately as an eternal principle of the real —if, that is to say, we knew the Form of Substance.

It is not self-evident, therefore, that we have *a priori*

knowledge of categories, nor that our use of such words as 'substance' and 'cause' necessitates the theory that we know innately the Forms of Substance and Cause. But what of the remaining words, 'goodness', 'beauty', 'unity' and 'triangularity'? Is it a condition of their use that we should know before all experience certain ideals which experience could never give us? The answer to this question about the words 'goodness' and 'beauty' would necessitate comprehensive ethical and aesthetic disquisitions, which cannot be undertaken here. For instance, involved in it is the problem whether the moral and the beautiful can be explained in naturalistic terms or whether they demand a non-naturalistic explanation. This is perhaps the fundamental problem in these inquiries.

In the case of mathematical knowledge one or two obvious comments may be made. In the first place, if we suppose that mathematical truth is conventional then what is taken to be the necessary element in mathematics is certainly no justification of the theory of Forms. Of necessity there cannot be an integer between 3 and 4, for the conventionally framed arithmetical series does not permit it. Suppose, however, we reject the conventional theory and consider mathematical knowledge as essentially rational, it could still be argued that such knowledge in no way justifies our theory. For mathematics would then be discovery, not the discovery of sense-perception but rational or intellectual discovery, and it would remain discovery even though we needed certain conventions by which to express it. Reference might be made here to some of Poincaré's works, but I may illustrate the point by quoting from Professor G. H. Hardy's *A Mathematician's Apology*. Speaking of 'mathematical reality' he remarks:

> Some hold that it is 'mental' and that in some sense we construct it, others that it is outside and independent of us. . . . I will state my own position dogmatically in order to avoid minor misapprehensions. I believe that mathematical reality lies outside us, that our function is to discover or *observe* it, and that the theorems which we prove and which we describe grandiloquently as our 'creations' are simply our notes of our observations. [pp. 63–64.]

And a little later:

> A chair or a star is not in the least like what it seems to be; the more we think of it the fuzzier its outlines become in the haze of sensation which surrounds it; but '2' or '317' has nothing to do with sensation and its properties stand out the more clearly the more closely we scrutinise it. . . . 317 is a prime, not because we think so, or because our minds are shaped in one way rather than another, but *because it is so*, because mathematical reality is built that way [p. 70].

I have taken these interesting quotations from Professor Hardy's work to illustrate this line of speculation about mathematics. At first reading, he might appear to be advocating a theory of mathematical Forms. There exists a 'mathematical reality' furnished with such entities as '2' and '317'. But this is not his point of view. For Professor Hardy insists that he is speaking throughout of the one world which *appears* to us in sense-perception (though it is not *as* it appears), and claiming that it has a mathematical structure which we can discover. Thus his view of mathematics does not imply that there is a distinct world of mathematical Forms. Nor—for he stresses the fact of discovery—does he assert that we have always known these mathematical truths. His, therefore, is a rationalist, non-conventionalist theory of mathematics which involves no theory of Forms.[1]

Thus neither the conventional account of mathematics nor the rationalist necessitates the theory of Forms, and it goes without saying that an empiricist account that derived all the principles of mathematics from experience would be still farther removed from this theory.

The same argument would hold of the 'ideal' in mathematics. The theory of Forms asserts that we come into the world knowing what pure circularity is, what absolute straightness is, what the One and the Two are. Yet it is clear that other accounts of such ideals are possible. We may suppose them to be nothing

[1] I here repeat that I use the word 'Form' in this context as meaning a real, eternal object known innately. No doubt Plato's doctrine of Forms, particularly in the works of his middle and later years, is different enough from this and nearer Hardy's views. But it will be understood that I am not expounding Plato's doctrine.

other than conventional contrivances arbitrarily agreed upon. Or, secondly, we may think of them as rationally apprehended, discovered (though not by sense-perception) and acquired. Such ideals are not confined to mathematics; Husserl, for instance, finds them in logic as well as in mathematics. Husserl is particularly interesting in this connexion since he expressly affirms that his position, though anti-empiricist, is not to be interpreted in terms of the theory of Forms.

Thirdly, there is always the empiricist interpretation. These ideals, on this interpretation, are at least suggested by, even if we deny that they are given in, experience. For instance, I see that this line is straighter than that line, and that a third line is straighter than either. This is sufficient to suggest the notion of an absolutely straight line to which the visible straight lines approximate. Thus even if it were true that I never see an absolutely straight line, as supporters of the theory of Forms argue, experience might still suggest such a line as an ideal limit to the increasing straightness of the lines which I do see. But is it true that I never see a straight line? The edge of this paper upon which I write *looks* to me perfectly straight; the central object in this design before me *appears* perfectly circular. But, it will be said, you can never know that the line is really straight and the circle truly circular. Even so, if they *look* absolutely straight and absolutely circular that is enough to enable me to talk sensibly of absolute straightness and absolute circularity. It may be true that I can never know for certain that this line which appears straight is 'in reality' straight. I might look at a length of it under more and more powerful microscopes and find that it is not straight. But it now looks straight and that is enough. The line looks absolutely straight and so experience, it would appear, *gives* the ideal and does not merely suggest it.

We may leave it to the mathematicians and the mathematical philosophers to decide finally between these and, no doubt, other theories. The point we can safely make is the following: the existence of such alternative theories at once proves that the claims of the theory of Forms in respect of mathematics can at least be questioned. It is not true that reflection upon mathematics inevitably leads us to adopt this theory. And in particular, it is not true that knowledge of the ideal, for instance perfect straightness or perfect circularity, must inevitably have been gained prior to all experience.

We may conclude this section, then, by asserting fairly confidently that while it still may be true that our use of the words 'good' and 'beautiful' necessitates the theory of Forms—and this is a matter which cannot be decided here—yet no such theory is necessary to explain our use of other general words. Rival theories have, to say the least, equal plausibility.

55. But are we justified in talking of equal plausibility? Is the theory of Forms as here interpreted plausible at all? Is it a genuine alternative? Granting for the moment that our use of general words is founded on our knowledge of the real, does the account of the real given in the theory of Forms provide a satisfactory foundation for that usage? In its cruder, and possibly non-Platonic, expressions it certainly does not. Each Form in the eternal world of Forms is viewed as an entity, having a detached, individual existence of its own. Here is the real Bed, the one Bed of which all other beds are but shadows. But surely the Form is now itself a particular individual, and how could such particulars ever explain our use of general words? 'Bed' has become a proper name. The problem of the general word re-emerges unsolved in the form of the traditional Third Man argument.[1] If Man in the world of Forms is an individual, he has something in common with the mortal Socrates. This common element points to a Form. So there is a further Form, a Third Man, and if this again is an individual the argument is repeated *ad infinitum*. Our use of general words cannot be founded on a real world of this kind.

Furthermore, if these Forms are conceived as isolated entities, how could they provide the basis for the infinite interrelations

[1] It is noteworthy that one of the earliest statements of this argument was made by Plato himself in the *Parmenides*, 132–4. In the opinion of some commentators Plato, however, failed to see the full implications of the argument. Cf. Vlastos, 'The Third Man Argument in the *Parmenides*', *Phil. Rev.* 1954, republished in *Studies in Plato's Metaphysics*, ed. Allen, 1965.

involved in the use of a language such as ours? Consider two sentences. First, 'The man is tall'. On this theory the words 'man' and 'tall' presuppose Forms of Man and Tallness. (Presumably the verb 'is' presupposes a Form also, not to mention the word 'the', but we had better ignore this additional complication.) How then can the two Forms, Man and Tallness, each an isolated individual, provide any sort of basis for the sentence 'The man is tall'? Secondly, 'Man is an animal'. If there is the Form Animal and we say that man is an animal, can there still be a Form Man? Or does it become superfluous? There can hardly be the two Forms Man and Animal in isolation. Would asserting the Form Animal mean denying the Form Man?

And why stop at Animal? We say animals are living beings. Is there a Form Living Being? Then delete the Form Animal. But we also say that living beings are beings. The outcome seems to be that the world of Forms would in fact contain one Form and one Form only, the Form of Being, since all other Forms would have collapsed into it. Perhaps there might also be Forms of an entirely different order, for instance value Forms, such as the Form of the Good, and there would always be the Form of Form. But in so far as we speak about existence there could be but one foundation, the Form of Being, and in that case it is not clear how we could speak of dogs, tables, and chairs, which all exist. Our ontological monism would give us a one-word language, the Being of Parmenides and Reality of Spinoza. Of course it will not do to restrict the Forms of Being to one Form in this way, as the supporters of the Ideal theory realize. But are they, then, consistent when they speak of Forms of Man, Animal, Dog, Table, *and* Being? We may at least conclude that the foundation presupposed by human language is one in which there is real difference as well as real recurrence; it must be a world in which dog and cat are really different though both are animals. In other words, the general word 'dog', even though it be an incomplete symbol and even though the rest of the sentence is necessary to show how it is being used at present, refers in itself to a certain difference in the real and so makes an essential contribution to the sentence. But this is a difference which cannot be expressed in the theory of Forms without, apparently, contradicting oneself.

The theory of Forms which we have outlined lacks plausibility. We cannot believe that to explain our successful use of general words it is necessary to posit a Real behind the veil of appearances, a Heaven where are laid up the Forms of Table, Tree, Mud, Beauty, and a host of other Forms; just as we cannot believe that a child knows the Form of Red before it has experience of colours. A more plausible interpretation of the theory stresses the 'mixture of Forms'. An individual is the consequence of the 'mixing of Forms' within one piece of matter (ὕλη). This theory has one outstanding difficulty in that a new element enters, namely, matter, of which there is apparently no Form, so that if we claim a knowledge of the material individual, some part of that knowledge must be other than a 'reminiscence' of Forms. We need not devote very serious attention to this theory, however, for what is important in it is the doctrine that things have qualities in common, and this is a doctrine which can, and had best, be considered apart from the theory of Forms.

56. If, then, we postpone the consideration of common qualities till the next chapter, we can conclude that the doctrine of Forms as set out above is assuredly not a necessary presupposition of our use of general words in speech. It is almost fantastic to suggest that we can use the general word 'red' significantly only when we know *a priori* the eternal existence, the Form Red. Possibly, our use even of the general word 'red' will take quite a considerable amount of explaining, more than we may at first think; but we can safely say that the above explanation of it is not the true one and is not necessary.

On the other hand, the theory that we can speak in general terms of the real world because we know innately its general structure is not fantastic. It is not fantastic to argue that we have *a priori* knowledge of such categories as substance–attribute and cause–effect and that we order the given in experience in terms of them. The denial of the *Ante Rem* theory does not necessarily carry with it a denial of innate knowledge in this sense. But neither are we compelled to suppose that innate knowledge of this kind is in fact necessarily presupposed. As we have seen, there are at least two other alternatives. For, first, we may independently of experience have acquired rational knowledge of these categories which is certain and necessary, and in that sense *a priori*, but yet not innate. The immediate objection to this view is that if our knowledge of, for example, substance–attribute and cause–effect were the fruit of such rational insight it would not be the vague thing it undoubtedly is. We should have a clearer rational perception of these categories which rule our thought. Consequently, we find ourselves tempted to look to experience itself as a third alternative. Can we explain our knowledge of such categorial principles in empirical terms without introducing innate or even necessary rational knowledge? This question is vague until we make clearer what is meant by categorial principles and what by experience. The discussion of common qualities, dispositions, concepts, and universals in the chapters which follow should help to formulate the problem more clearly. In the meantime the purpose of the present chapter has been to show the inadequacy and lack of plausibility of the *Ante Rem* theory as an explanation of what is presupposed in our successful use of general words.

IX
COMMON QUALITIES

57. We reject the view that our successful use of general words presupposes a world of Ideas together with an *a priori* knowledge of that world. We have now to consider a second theory, namely, that it presupposes the existence of common qualities and a knowledge of them. It is only because we know common qualities that we can use general words significantly.

But this theory need not be interpreted in extreme realist terms. It need not be asserted that whenever one uses a general word one is consciously and explicitly referring to an identical quality (or set of qualities) shared by many individuals. In view of what has been already learnt about the use of general words it would be difficult to maintain this position. But it is not the one that needs to be defended. The only doctrine which can be seriously considered in this context, and it is the one which I propose to examine in this chapter, is a minimum thesis which may be stated thus: In nature there are common qualities and we become acquainted with them. On the strength of this knowledge we are able to use certain words signifying these qualities in a general way. This provides an explanation of the significant use of some general words on some occasions—though not of all on all occasions. We should not expect to find here a full explanation of the use of general words, but we may find in it a partial explanation. Can we justify this minimum thesis?

58. We cannot assume that even this minimum will be universally accepted. It is usual to suppose that the Resemblance or Similarity theory rejects it, and this is certainly true of the Resemblance theory in one of its forms. I shall argue, however, that the theory in this form, if worked out fully in all its consequences, ends in absurdities and cannot possibly be true. In another form the theory is less objectionable, and in this form

it permits of common qualities. The distinction between the two interpretations of the Resemblance theory can be set out thus: On the first, each and every quality is particular; there are no common qualities in the sense of identical qualities, for each quality is as particular as the thing to which it belongs. Nevertheless, qualities resemble one another and on the basis of this resemblance we generalize. On the second interpretation, some generalizations, though not all, are the outcome of observing resemblances, that is to say, generalization does not rest solely upon the observation of identical qualities. In its second form the Resemblance theory permits of common qualities.

In its first form the Resemblance theory is in conflict with what is usually known as the Identity theory. According to the latter, if we have two objects, *A* and *B*, with a common quality *q*, then identically the same quality belongs to *A* and *B*. Supporters of the Resemblance theory in the first form insist that no two objects can share identically the same quality, and so reject such identical qualities. One finds the first suggestion of this argument in the celebrated footnote in Hume's *Treatise*, to which I have already referred, but the dispute between the Resemblance and Identity theories belongs essentially to the twentieth century. In spite of the fact that in some of its parts it tends to be arid we cannot entirely ignore it. For if we wish to hold that common qualities exist we must find some means of refuting the Resemblance theory in this first form. At the same time, rejection of the Resemblance theory, as we shall see, does not necessarily involve acceptance of the Identity theory.

It has been argued that the Resemblance theory is not consistent with itself since it presupposes one identity. The argument runs as follows: even if no common *qualities* exist, there is at least one instance of a common *relation* which is identical. For the Resemblance theory itself presupposes that resemblance is an identical relation. Thus we observe that *a*, *b*, *c* resemble each other and on this basis we generalize; we also observe that *x*, *y*, *z* resemble each other and again generalize. Now the relation of resemblance must itself be one and the same in the two cases. Here, therefore, is a relation identical in the two situations, and the Resemblance theory has been shown to rest upon an identical relation of the very kind which it sets out to deny.

To this argument it may be answered that even in this instance the two resemblances merely resemble one another. Just as *a* and *b* resemble each other and so enable us to group them together, so resemblances may resemble each other. In such a case resemblance would not be identically the same relation as between *a b c* and *x y z*. This reply, however, it has been argued, would involve an infinite regress. The resemblance between *a* and *b* resembles, but is not identical with, the resemblance between *x* and *y*, thus introducing a third resemblance, that between the two resemblances. This third resemblance would in turn resemble any one of the first resemblances, and so introduce a fourth resemblance, and so on *ad infinitum.*

This has been assumed to be a fatal objection to the above argument, but I should like to question the assumption. For admitting the infinite regress, does it make the argument invalid? What the Resemblance theory needs by way of presupposition is that we should be able to recognize a resemblance when we see one. Now we do see that the resemblance between *a* and *b* resembles the resemblance between *x* and *y*. And we see this without first having to attempt the impossible task of observing an infinite series of resemblances. Supposing we have a case where *a* is true if *b* is true, and *b* is true if *c* is true, and *c* is true if *d* is true, and so on *ad infinitum.* Then admittedly we could not know that *a* was true. But our present case is a different one. The regress is there, but we *can* know the resemblance in question without observing the infinity of resemblances. Consequently the argument does not refute the Resemblance theory.

59. The Resemblance theory is not refuted, but the reader may already feel that the argument is to some extent unreal. The disputants are arguing about the existence or non-existence of absolute identities, absolutely identical qualities, and absolutely identical relations. But what is an absolute identity? It will be

useful to bear this question in mind as we follow the debate farther.

Supporters of the Resemblance theory say that a quality can be at one place, but at one place only, at any one time; their opponents reply that whilst this is true of a thing it is not true of a quality or relation, for these can be at two places at the same time. Supporters of the Resemblance theory then challenge the other side to produce a single satisfactory instance of an absolutely identical quality being in two places at the same time. And their opponents find it difficult to meet the challenge. They admit at once that if we think of sounds, smells, and tastes it is unusual to find that precision which would enable us to say that sound s^1 is identically the same in tone, pitch, and intensity as sound s^2 heard a moment later, or that this smell is precisely the same as the smell we smelt a moment ago. With distinctive smells, for instance ammonia or coffee, it may be possible to say something of the kind, and so with tastes, for instance that of orange. But the supporters of the Identity theory are unlikely to look to such experiences for their examples. They are more likely to turn to the most precise of our senses, seeing.

But even here they find it difficult to meet the challenge of their opponents. We say that three pieces of material now before us have the same colour, namely, blue. But to say that the three pieces are blue is not to say that they are absolutely identical in colour, and we do not ordinarily wish the listener to assume this. It is necessary to distinguish between 'blue' as signifying blue in general, a word covering *all* shades of blue, and 'blue' as signifying one shade of blue. Suppose we first interpret 'blue' to mean blue in general. What, then, is the blueness which, on the Identity theory, is the identity known whenever we observe blue things to resemble each other in colour? This is certainly a difficult question to answer. For blue cannot be some common element in the shades of blue since the particular shades ultramarine, royal blue, navy blue, and so on, seem to be simples and not complexes consisting of x plus blue and y plus blue respectively, where x and y are the *differentiae.*

There is nothing in the shades over and above the colour. What, then, is the identical element present, supposing such an element to be present?

The suggestion has been made that a scale of colours may exist, from the lightest to the darkest blue. This would be the blue scale, and what would be shared by all blues would be the characteristic of being within the scale. The shades ultramarine and royal blue in such a case would not have an additional common element over and above the colour, but to be ultramarine or royal blue would be to be in the scale. But this surely is not the kind of identical quality which the Identity theory requires. Being within a vaguely delimited scale of colours can hardly be the 'absolute identity' of which it speaks. We do not know precisely where the scale begins or where it ends. At what precise point does a colour cease to be blue and become some other colour, or cease to be some other colour and become blue? Moreover, this notion of the one blue scale is a gross oversimplification. In fact we have to do not with one series of shades beginning with a very light blue and passing to a dark blue, but rather with a complication of series of blues radiating out of a central standard blue. One series beginning with the central blue radiates out to a whitish blue, another to a greenish blue, a third to a blue-black, and so on. This seems a more adequate picture of blue in general than that presented by the one blue scale, though it also may need modification. But what is clear in all this is that blue in general cannot possibly be regarded as an identical, common quality in nature. Blue in general cannot be the answer to the challenge of the Resemblance theory.

The supporter of the Identity theory, however, may change his ground. He will not claim that blue in general is an absolute identity in his sense of the term. But what of the specific shades of blue? Here are three pieces of material before me, all present in my field of vision. I observe that the three have one and the same colour, let us say ultramarine. Or I might even take one piece of material and divide it into three parts and observe that the three parts have one and the same colour. Let us suppose the colour to be the same shade in intensity and saturation. Would not this, then, be truly an identical quality?

The supporters of the Resemblance theory would still answer in the negative. They would argue in this way: The only ground for supposing that the pieces of material share the same colour is that we cannot see any difference between them in respect to their colour. The evidence is wholly empirical. But empirical evidence is notoriously fallible; our eyes are not sharp enough to discern minute differences. Yet is it not conceivable that in reality the three colours are different? May not ultramarine itself turn out to be a range of colours like blue, but the range be shorter and the differences between the shades within the range so minute that we human beings cannot perceive them? Yet they may be there though we fail to perceive them. Supporters of the Identity theory find an instance of an absolutely identical quality here only because they mistake identity for indistinguishability. Once these are distinguished we shall no longer be able to say that ultramarine is an absolutely identical quality of the three pieces of material.

But the critics themselves are now on most dangerous ground. They are assuming a distinction between what appears and what is real. They assume that there are real colours other than those which appear and that the real colour of this piece of material is not the same as the real colour of that piece of material, although they now appear to me to be the same. Direct disproof of their assumption is impossible, yet their position is fundamentally weak. For, first, just as it is conceivable that the three colours are different in reality, so it is conceivable that they are identical. In the second place, the empirical evidence points to the existence of identical qualities. To deny their existence would appear to be closing one's eyes to the facts for the sake of the theory. Moreover, implicit in their position would be the belief that there are as many shades of blue as there are blue things. No shades are identical, the colour of every object is unique; so that in respect to colour nature never repeats herself. Indeed we should have to go farther. If we took one coloured surface, say the petal of a flower, then no two segments of that petal, however minute, could be of the same colour, but every segment would have a distinct colour. So there would certainly have to be as many colours as there are *minima visibilia* (to revive an ancient term). Furthermore, this same argument would apply not only to colours but to other qualities and to relations. To be consistent we should have to defend the view that nature never repeats herself either in quality or relation, and this seems an absurdity which it would be very foolish to attempt to defend.

60. Such consequences appear to be involved in the Resemblance theory, interpreted in this way, and they are such as to make the theory appear absurd. Yet the argument cannot be said to justify the opposing theory, for it certainly does not establish the existence of absolutely identical qualities and relations. If it shows anything at all, it shows that such identities are not experienceable objects since they apparently transcend our experience and knowledge, so that we are not in a position to assert or deny them. Thus the victory does not lie with the Identity theory. A debate which at the beginning was one about experienceable qualities has now become one about entities which cannot be experienced. Obviously the common quality with which we began is not the identical quality that the Identity theory affirms and the Resemblance theory denies. But we followed this debate in order to gain greater insight into the common quality. What, then, has happened to it? We must retrace our steps to find an answer.

Both theories begin with a point of agreement. Consider the three pieces of material. Both sides agree that the colour of the three pieces looks one and the same. This means absolute identity, say the supporters of the Identity theory; no, it merely means that for us the colours are indistinguishable, says the other side. But both are prepared to grant that the colour of the three pieces is one and the same in the sense that we can see no difference between them. Now this is the important point. It seems to me that in admitting this the supporters of Resemblance and Identity theories alike are admitting the existence of just those common qualities which we need as bases for our use of general words. For whether there are absolute identities in a non-experienceable world, or whether in that world the colours of the three pieces of cloth are really distinct though *we* cannot distinguish between them, are irrelevant questions from our point of view and we need not even ask whether they are real questions. What we wish to know is whether there are common qualities which can provide a foundation for our generalizations, and the two schools admit that there are.

For the rest it may be the case that both schools have been driven into false positions by the arguments of their opponents. What supporters of the Identity theory really want to defend is the position that sometimes our use of general words rests on the observation that one and the same quality pertains to two or more objects. They are driven, however, into defending the existence of non-experienceable, absolute identities. In the same manner, the strength of the Resemblance theory lies in the assertion that sometimes our use of general words rests on the observation of resembling qualities and in the denial that we can only generalize when we have observed one and the same quality. But it can take up this position without at all denying that we do frequently experience one and the same quality to pertain to different things—for instance, that the three pieces of material have one and the same colour. The strength of the Resemblance theory, if I am right, does not lie in its denial of absolutely identical qualities; indeed it is here at its weakest in view of the absurd consequences which are involved.

But whether this is the true solution of the dispute between the Identity and Resemblance theories or not, the sense in which we can rightly speak of a common quality in this chapter is becoming clearer. It is the sense in which both of these theories admit that we do experience two or more things as having one and the same quality. Ultramarine is a common quality of these three pieces of material.

61. The common quality is no absolute identity lying beyond experience; but neither is it a mere abstraction, something sub-

jective, less concrete than the rest of our experience. It is necessary to insist on its concreteness; it is common yet it is concrete. And here we touch upon another point in dispute in contemporary philosophy. Can a quality remain a quality and yet be common or universal? Does it not lose in concreteness as it gains in universality? For, how can it remain a concrete quality and be here *and* there at one and the same time? Philosophers have felt that there is something self-contradictory in the notion of a *common* quality. As a consequence some have held that qualities are universal, and, so, essentially different from tables and chairs, which are concrete; others have held that they are concrete and therefore particular, never common, so that when we talk of common qualities we cannot really be meaning qualities in the ordinary sense.

Those who set up a dichotomy between the concrete thing and the universal quality were influenced by Russell, who assumed such a dichotomy in his early writings and who was in turn influenced by Frege's insistence on the absoluteness of the distinction between the 'object'-term and the predicate-term in the subject-predicate proposition. It should be added, however, that Frege's distinction was one in logic, as he expressly stated, and its development into a metaphysical doctrine asserting a dichotomy of nature into particular things and universal qualities was not inevitable. It is one thing to say that the functions of subject-term (Frege's 'object'-term) and predicate-term are essentially different, and another that a quality and the thing which it qualifies must belong to different realms of being, such that a quality cannot be as concrete as the thing which it qualifies. It is dangerous to confuse the ontological with the logical. In 'The book is blue' the subject-term and the predicate-term have different functions, but it does not follow that we must deny the evidence of our eyes that the blue of the book is where the book is, nor must we deny that the blue of the book is as concrete as the book itself is.

Not unnaturally the dichotomy theory produced a reaction. One group set forward the Resemblance theory and explicitly denied that any quality could be common or universal. They thus came into conflict with supporters of the Identity theory, a conflict we have just examined. Others who were equally emphatic in their rejection of the dichotomy and who insisted upon the particularity of the quality, nevertheless found it impossible to deny common qualities. A quality, they said, is particular and cannot be universal; but a quality may none the less be an instance of a natural kind or class. Just as there is a class of men so there is a class of ultramarines. When we talk of 'a common quality' we are referring to a class of this kind. *This* shade of blue pertaining to this piece of material is particular, as particular as the material itself. But this shade is only one instance of a shade of which we find many other instances in nature, so that we recognize here a natural kind, which is the common quality. The common quality in this sense is 'a distributive unity'.[1]

This theory appears attractive at first sight in that it secures the concreteness of the quality as against the dichotomists, without compelling us to deny common qualities altogether, as does the false type of Resemblance theory. But it has very great difficulties of its own and I shall at once mention its main difficulty. We can think of a class of men; each member is different from every other, but together they make a natural class because, so we suppose, each of them shares certain qualities in common, or possibly has qualities which resemble qualities in other men. Now whether this account is satisfactory in the case of man or not, it is obviously not satisfactory in the case of the common quality. These books belong to the class of royal blue objects; the common quality is being royal blue. We are now, however, asked to suppose that each occurrence of royal blue in each particular book is particular, but that it is an instance of the class or the distributive unity royal blue, just as each book is particular but is an instance of the class royal blue objects. Yet the ground of classification in the case of the books is the fact that they are all royal blue. What is the ground in the

[1] Cf. G. F. Stout, *The Nature of Universals and Proposiitons*, British Academy Lecture, O.U.P., 1921, and 'Are the Characteristics of Particular Things Universal or Particular? *Proc. Arist. Soc.*, supp. vol. 3, 1923.

case of the class royal blue? It must be royal blue itself. But this suggests that it is pervasive and not wholly particular. Can we, that is to say, hold the particular royal blue and the universal apart? Does there exist along with this royal blue and that royal blue a universal, royal blue? The theory of Forms would grant us such a universal; we should have the Form of Royal Blue. But if, for the reasons mentioned in the previous chapter, we reject that theory, it is then not possible to find the universal over and above the particulars. On the distributive unity theory the universal is not the concrete particular, but neither is it something over and above the particular. To make sense of the theory we seem to be driven to saying that the universal is simply the collection of instances. Yet is a universal a collection? And, anyway, why do just these particulars form a collection? The truth clearly is that this royal blue which is here before me is also elsewhere; it is a common quality.

The common quality, we must conclude, is (1) a quality, and (2) common or universal. We cannot accept the view that it is merely particular or that it is merely universal; it is the meeting point of particularity and universality. As such it provides a foundation for our use of general words.

62. We have now examined the arguments of those who, for one reason or another, would deny that there are common qualities, and we find them unconvincing. We affirm the existence of common qualities, though not as absolute identities nor as distributive unities, but as qualities observed to belong to two or more objects. Some further comments may help to make their nature clearer.

In the first place, not all claimants to this title of a 'common quality' have a right to it. A common quality may be a distinct shade of colour or again a distinct smell, taste, or sound. But, for instance, the colour blue in general, though it may be assumed to be a common quality, is not in fact 'observed to belong to two or more objects'. What are observed are the various shades of blue; these are observed to resemble and on this basis we speak of blue in general.[1]

Secondly, just as there are common qualities so there exist common relations. If *a* is spatially inside *b* and *c* spatially inside *d*, then the relation of being spatially inside is common to the two situations. Further instances would be being above, being before, being to the left of, being equal to. And if we admit common relationships it is natural to think of resemblance, too, as such a relation; though supporters of the Resemblance theory, as we have seen, could argue without inconsistency that different instances of resemblances may themselves be supposed to resemble one another. But if we grant common relations there is no point in refusing to recognize resemblance as a common relation.

Thirdly, I have spoken of *observing* the common quality. What I wish to stress in using this verb is the element of discovery or givenness present when I observe that the three pieces of material are one and the same colour. I am avoiding here questions about the ultimate nature of sense-perception, and I do not wish to say that observing that the colour of this piece of material is ultramarine and observing that the three pieces are one and the same colour is precisely the same process. Moreover, I do not deny that dispositional elements are present, both in the recognition of the colour and in the observation that two or more objects have the same colour. But, in either case, none of this makes the discovery less of a discovery. Here at this moment

[1] Commenting on this point in *Philosophy*, April 1955, p. 186, D. F. Pears says: 'Can it really be right to deny that blue is a common quality and to confine the title to determinates like ultramarine? Admittedly it would be very odd to say that two pieces of ultramarine silk were similar in colour: but the statement that two merely blue pieces had something in common would not be at all odd.' Pears is here using the phrase 'something in common' in a loose sense. The two pieces of blue, not of identical shade, resemble one another, and in that sense have something in common. I do not object to this, but indeed acknowledge its importance in § 63. But it is necessary to distinguish 'having something in common' in this sense from 'having a common quality' in the precise sense, the sense in which the two pieces of silk have a common quality. The question at issue in this chapter is whether there are qualities or characters or properties in the precise sense, and Pears seems to me to be acknowledging that there are in admitting that it would be 'odd to say that two pieces of ultramarine silk are similar in colour'.

I see the colour of this material and see, too, that the pieces of material before me have one and the same colour.

Finally, I return to the question about abstraction. Is not abstraction necessary to the knowledge of the common quality, and if so, does it not follow that it cannot be a discovery or a finding? In answer, it is necessary to recall that the word 'abstracting' is an ambiguous word. In Berkeley's sense of 'singling', abstraction is necessarily present in the discovery of a common quality. I concentrate upon the colour in noticing that the three objects have the same colour. In this sense of 'abstracting', it is true, I abstract even in seeing the colour, for I single it out for observation. Thus if observing that the objects have one and the same colour involves abstraction, so does the observing that this object is royal blue. But observing that the objects have one and the same colour does not involve abstraction in another sense, namely, framing an abstract complex idea. The common quality I speak of in this chapter is no abstract construction of mine. I find and discover it.

63. That we thus find common qualities in nature is obviously a fact of the greatest significance for our understanding of how we use general words. It begins to explain the applicability of certain general words on certain occasions. The general word 'ultramarine' can be used to refer to the colour of many objects, because many objects have one and the same colour, ultramarine. This does not wholly explain its use as a general word, for we recall that it might still be used even if there were no objects coloured ultramarine. Moreover, certain general words are used by us, even when speaking of colours, which do not refer to common qualities in the present sense of the term—for instance, we speak significantly of blue in general. Consequently it would be erroneous to suppose that we have said all there is to say about the use of general words when we point out that the applicability of some of them depends upon the experience of common qualities. Nevertheless, here is part explanation: we use general words correctly and successfully in referring to things because we experience common qualities in nature.

But that we observe common qualities is of still greater significance. Not only does it explain the applicability of certain general words in certain contexts, but it also helps to explain the tendency to generalize. Our generalizations have been conceived from time to time as economies, as aids to communication, and as conveniences in the technique of human thinking. They may be all of these, but it is also true that nature invites us to generalize and suggests the generalization. The world experienced by us is a world in which one and the same quality and one and the same relation are constantly recurring. In generalizing, that is to say, we are not moulding nature in accordance with our wish; on the contrary, we take nature's mould and are ourselves guided by nature. As we shall see, we do not follow nature blindly. None the less generalization is grounded in our experience of nature, that is, in our experience of common qualities.

We must, however, make two qualifications here. In the first place, recurrences in nature are to be defined more widely than in terms of common qualities alone. For not only do we find one and the same qualities recurring but *like* qualities recur. Resembling qualities, relations, objects, and situations are to be found in the world we experience and they appear again and again in that world. These, too, invite a grouping and a generalizing, so that the basis for generalizing in the experienced world of nature is not merely the common qualities but also the resemblances. The upholder of the Resemblance theory is right in saying that we group and classify on the basis of resemblances; he is in error only when he denies that we can classify on the basis of common qualities. On the other hand, the advocate of common qualities errs if he denies that resemblances can be the bases of our classifications.

It should be emphasized too that when we speak of resemblances here we do not refer to resembling qualities and relations only but also to resembling objects, resembling occurrences, and situations. And when, for instance, objects resemble one another they sometimes do so because they share identical qualities or again because some of their qualities clearly resemble one another. On the other hand, objects sometimes have merely an overall resemblance; they are alike although we cannot pick out identical qualities or even markedly resembling qualities. The stock example of such a resemblance has been the family face and Wittgenstein has provided a further instance in games. It is erroneous, however, to say that Wittgenstein's discussion of this point in *Philosophical Investigations* (§ 66–67) presents us with a new theory of universals. It is a restatement of the Resemblance theory, stressing something which has been part of that theory throughout, namely that resemblances or similarities may be 'overall' rather than 'detailed'.

The second qualification to be made is the following: Nothing in the above should be taken to mean that a person can only use general words to refer to common or resembling qualities. He may use them to describe or to group and not then be explicitly referring to qualities. Or he may use them to influence an audience or just because he likes their sound. He may be speaking of them purely as words, as when one says, 'The word "ultramarine" comes towards the end of the dictionary'. Moreover, when he does refer to the quality the reference may be vague. He may speak of 'ultramarine' and yet not be quite sure of the shade and perhaps fail to recognize it when he sees it. It is obvious that it would be entirely false to say that whenever we use general words we always have in mind, and are referring to, specific common qualities.

Our conclusion is that common qualities exist in the world experienced by us and that we also find resemblances there. These facts help to explain how through using general words we refer in certain contexts to natural qualities and things. But they in no way justify the view that general words are never used except when referring to common qualities or resemblances in nature. Clearly, the realists who spoke of the general word as invariably the name of a real common quality were committing a gross error. On the other hand, the minimum thesis set out at the opening of this chapter has been justified, and so a foundation has been set down for a theory.

X
DISPOSITIONS

64. We are attempting to make clear what is involved in our use of general words and how it is that we succeed in using them, and a partial explanation has already emerged. In nature certain qualities are being repeated constantly. I am used to a world in which this shade of blue frequently reappears so that it is natural for me to speak and think of it as something which is not merely here but elsewhere, not merely present now but has been present in the past and will be present in the future. I have learnt that the word for this shade of blue in the English language is 'ultramarine' and part of the explanation why I use it successfully as a general word in speaking of the world around me lies in the fact that the shade recurs in that world.

Yet this is only part of the explanation even in the case of the word 'ultramarine'; the whole explanation would involve additional considerations. And in the case of many other general words it is not even part of the explanation. Further, we do not count such words as 'if', 'or', 'but', 'yes', 'no', as general words and there is no suggestion that these words can be even partially explained by reference to recurring qualities. It might be more to the point in their case to link our use of them with our observation of recurring relations. And yet on what relation could we ground our use of the word 'but'? There may be such a relationship, but its connexion with our use of 'but' is not so clear as is the connexion, say, between our seeing the recurring shade ultramarine and our use of the word 'ultramarine'. Even in our use of adjectives, which we do regard as general words, not all are as precisely used as 'ultramarine' is usually used; such adjectives as 'busy', 'bald', 'fat', are used more loosely. So, too, are the adjectives 'blue', 'red', 'green'. In these cases it would be difficult to discover the precise common qualities. But the most interesting group of general words to discuss in this context are common nouns. How account for our successful use of the common noun 'house'? What is the basis of its use, as the recurrence of ultramarine may be said to be the basis of our successful use of the adjective 'ultramarine'?

I am speaking of the ordinary use of the word 'house'. I may attempt to speak more carefully. I may say that I mean by the word 'house' a combination of qualities *a*, *b*, *c*, *d*, and *e*, each one of which is perceived precisely, and the combination itself rests on the apprehension of the constant co-existence of these qualities. But normally I do not use the word in this way, I use it vaguely, that is to say, I do not fix the qualities as I did in the above analysis. One important consequence of this is that I am not at all clear as to the range of the class of houses, that is, I am not sure where to draw the line of inclusion and exclusion. And yet in my daily thinking and in practical intercourse with other men I use this word quite successfully. Obviously the use in this case is not based on any conscious concentration upon a fixed number of recurring qualities and relations. This kind of explanation will not work.

A more promising suggestion is that the use of such words rests on a familiarity with an undifferentiated whole met with frequently in experience, a pattern or *Gestalt* whose parts have not been analysed. When I do discriminate between the various parts I find that these objects differ more from one another than I had at first thought. But at first I do not differentiate, but fall into the habit of grouping together objects which roughly resemble one another and associating a name with the group. I hear the word 'houses' used sometimes in the presence and sometimes in the absence of houses and I come to understand from the context what the word 'houses' means. I do not remember consciously grouping the *Gestalten* together, I do not remember learning how to use the word. But I find myself now possessed of certain habits, habits of expectation, habits of behaviour and of speech. Such habits or dispositions are gained by me not by my observing the recurrence of precise qualities identical with one another or closely resembling one another, but as a consequence of a long familiarity with recurring *Gestalten* between whose detailed features I do not differentiate.

As the result of these experiences I know how to use the word 'house' successfully and I am also ready to recognize an instance of a house when I see one and to deny that something wrongly called a 'house' is in fact a house.

65. Now this account of what lies behind our ordinary use of such a general word as 'house' seems more promising than any attempt to rest it on our experience of precise common qualities and relations. Prominent in the account is the theory that we are guided in using these words by dispositions, of whose presence we are ignorant, but which nevertheless must be there. In this chapter I should like to consider this theory. Recently no term has been more freely used in philosophical writings than the term 'disposition'; perhaps it has been too freely used. It would be interesting to consider why it has been found useful and what it helps us to explain in the present context.

Dispositions, we suppose, are closely related to recurrences. We distinguish between occurrences and continuants; an occurrence takes place at a certain time, is instantaneous, or takes up a relatively short time and then ceases; but the continuant goes on existing and lasts through time. Occurrences make up the life-history of continuants; and if we examine this life-history we frequently find that the behaviour of the continuant generally follows a pattern, and that many of the occurrences become *re*-currences. Thus a particular human being will be found to dress and shave and to go about his work in much the same way each morning. He tends to walk, gesticulate, and speak in the same manner, so that we say we know him by his walk or gestures. Harry no sooner gets into his bathroom than he begins to sing, 'For I'm off to Philadelphia in the morning'. Each craftsman has acquired the skills of his craft and each professional man the etiquettes of his profession. Thus men regularly follow certain patterns of behaviour and this, it appears, is what we mean when we describe them as having dispositions.

But patterns of behaviour are of many kinds and it will already be clear that the term 'disposition' is an umbrella term covering, for instance, reflexes, whether conditioned or unconditioned, habits, whether acquired automatically or through learning, skills, etiquettes, tendencies, capacities, and so on. Its use, therefore, will need great care lest we get muddled between its various meanings, but, given the necessary care, umbrella terms are valuable and this word 'disposition' need be no exception.

How are dispositions related to continuants and occurrences? It is clear that the disposition is not to be identified with the occurrence. Harry's disposition to sing in the bath is not to be identified with any instance or occurrence of the singing. Perhaps, for some reason or other, Harry will not sing in his bath this morning, but the disposition, we say, is still there. So the disposition cannot be identified with the occurrence. Nor can it be identified with the continuant. A disposition is something which a continuant may be said to have or not to have, to have now and not to have later. But here it must be noted that if we define a continuant as that which lasts through time, then dispositions too are continuants. It is clear, however, that we think of a continuant, rightly or wrongly, as something substantival which lasts through time. Harry is a person who *has* dispositions, he is not merely a continuant but a continuant of this particular kind, a substantival continuant; and in that sense of the term, we usually suppose, a disposition is not a continuant.

Certain adjectives that we use signify dispositional qualities of such continuants. For instance, 'soluble' signifies a dispositional quality of salt. The difference between continuant, occurrence and disposition is illustrated by the fact that 'soluble' can be predicated of the continuant, the salt, but cannot be predicated of the occurrence, namely, salt-dissolving-in-water. It is absurd to say that the latter is soluble (or insoluble).[1]

[1] 'Dispositional' adjectives are not confined to those ending in -uble, -able, and -ible. Obviously 'brittle', 'poisonous', and 'hard' are dispositional. Nelson Goodman in *Fact, Fiction and Forecast*, Univ. of London Press, 1954, has remarked: 'Indeed, almost every predicate commonly thought of as describing a lasting objective characteristic of a thing is as much a dispositional predicate as any other' (pp. 44–45).

Dispositions, we next note, can be grouped according to their genus and species—or possibly we should say according to whether they are determinables or determinates. A man may be disposed to sing; he may be disposed to sing in his bath; he may be disposed to sing, 'For I'm off to Philadelphia in the morning' in his bath. Moreover, there are earlier and more primitive dispositions than the disposition to sing. Primitive to a man would be, possibly, the disposition to move the parts of his body, including his tongue and larynx. Such a disposition has been called 'a disposition of the first order' and it is sometimes said to be innate; the disposition to move tongue and larynx so as to utter words or to sing would be a disposition of a second order; tending to recite a particular poem or sing a particular song would presumably be a disposition of a third order.

As we have seen, dispositions pertain not only to living beings but also to things. It is neither unnatural nor strained, for instance, to say that a rubber band when extended will, if released, tend to return to its previous shape. Perhaps it is less natural to call this tendency a 'disposition' but the term would not appear to be erroneously used in this connexion. In like manner it is permissible to speak of the quality of stimulating the nerves as a dispositional quality of tea, or the quality of attracting iron filings as a dispositional quality of a magnet.

But if we speak of inorganic things as having dispositions we should not ignore certain differences of meaning in such a use of the word as compared with its use in the case of organic things. Human beings and animals are for ever acquiring new dispositions; they appear to start with a few dispositions of a primary order and then develop them in constantly new ways with dispositions of a second order. For instance, we are able to move our limbs and acquire the ability to walk, run, swim, cycle, and so on. So, too, we are able to remember, and acquire the ability to speak, to repeat poetry by rote, to learn French, and so on. But this apparently is not the case usually with dispositions of things; at any rate we most often think of them as having dispositions which are not in this way changed into dispositions of a second order. This is an important first difference in the meaning of the term as applied to inorganic things.

A second difference arises from the fact that organisms appear to possess a certain measure of spontaneity. While, for instance, much of the behaviour of human beings is explicable by reference to their dispositions we do not normally think that it is wholly explicable in this way. A man, so we suppose, can resist and break a habit; but a thing must behave according to its dispositions. In this respect Harry's disposition to sing in his bath is very different from the magnet's capacity to draw iron filings. Harry might not sing in his bath though he has the disposition, but the magnet would cease to be a magnet if on the next occasion it did not draw the iron filings. This distinction, perhaps, does not hold absolutely. We might find a disposition which inevitably determines Harry's behaviour if he is to continue to be; for instance, the disposition to breathe. But the point is that most, if not all, of the dispositions of inorganic things seem to be of this kind, whereas the most interesting human dispositions are of another kind.

While, therefore, people do speak of inorganic things as having dispositional qualities, we should note that the word 'disposition' is then given a slightly different meaning. The dispositions of inorganic things are most like the so-called primary dispositions of organisms.

66. But there remains a more serious problem which we can no longer ignore. Should we speak of dispositions as existing? I hear Harry go into the bathroom, turn on the water and begin to sing. I see the salt being dropped into the liquid and watch it steadily diminishing in size till it disappears. But in neither case do I hear or see the disposition, and I should think it absurd if I were asked to try to listen more intently in the hope of hearing Harry's disposition or to strain my eyes in order to see the salt's tendency to dissolve in water. Is the disposition then something inferred, an x, which I do not observe but which I suppose to be present to explain my experience? If it is an

inferred existence of this kind it exists as a transcendent entity, necessary to explain my observations but itself unobservable. For it is not the sort of hypothetical entity which might later be observed, as was the case when astronomers, observing unexpected variations in the movement of the planet Uranus, inferred that another planet existed and later discovered Neptune. Neptune was always observable in principle; but a disposition, it would seem, is not the sort of thing which can ever be observed.

But why speak of it as an existence, whether observable or not observable? Possibly, these nouns 'disposition', 'habit', and 'tendency' mislead us; answering to the word 'disposition' we expect a substantival continuant to exist. Possibly, we assume that every statement about dispositions is a statement about substantival entities comparable to statements, say, about bricks and houses. But it is not only of things that we can speak or of particular occurrences in the history of these things; we can also speak of tendencies, and these, it will be said, are not to be taken to be existences. Thus to say that salt has the dispositional quality of solubility is merely to say that when salt is put into water, granted certain conditions, it dissolves; it is not to say that in salt there is an existent, the disposition. To say that I have the habit of muttering 'countrymen' if anyone says 'Friends, Romans' is only to say that whenever these two words are repeated in my hearing I say the third; it is not to say that a habit exists in me. Putting it generally, to say that x has a disposition to behave in manner y is to say this and this alone, that x has regularly behaved in manner y and is likely to behave in manner y on the next occasion. All we have is the regular sequence.

Now this may be the true philosophic account, particularly from the strict empiricist standpoint, yet it is noteworthy that it is not the ordinary way in which people speak of dispositions. When people speak of a habit, for instance, they do not normally mean a certain regularity of succession in experience, an x followed by a y; they mean rather a certain power or pressure which belongs to the structure of one's mental life, so that x

brings about *y*. Even Hume, the critic of the popular theory of causation, refrains from explaining custom and habits in terms of observed regularities solely, they are 'gentle forces which commonly prevail'. We talk of '*force* of habit'. To say that Harry has a disposition to sing in his bath is, we ordinarily think, more than to say he sings every time he is in his bath. We also suppose that a certain pressure is being put upon him. Not that he is compelled to sing; he is a free agent. But if he doesn't sing it will be through resisting the habit, and the word 'resisting' suggests bringing up a counter-force. To say that Harry has a habit is to say that a certain force will be working in a certain direction in certain situations. Or, to take another example, we say that tea tends to stimulate the nerves. More is meant then, rightly or wrongly, than that after drinking tea we are refreshed and revivified. We ordinarily assume that the tea has a certain power to refresh and revive us.

On this view the disposition is a continuant not in the sense of being an observable regularity but as being the abiding force which accounts for the regularity, and it is undoubtedly true that normally when we speak of dispositions, habits, skills, reflexes, or tendencies we speak in this way. Yet admittedly even in ordinary speech we find ourselves frequently distinguishing between the two. Speaking of some phenomenon or other I may say, 'I don't know how to explain it but the tendency is obvious'. I seem to mean in this context simply that the regularity is observable. And there are sorts of dispositions, for example, inefficiencies, weaknesses, and inabilities, which we clearly do not think of as powers. We think of the boy's inability to bat in terms of the fact that he regularly scores no runs at the wicket, though even in this case we tend to turn the inability into a positive habit, for instance, the habit of holding the bat in a certain way, a practice in which the boy may continue even after he has been told that it is wrong, simply out of 'force of habit'.

Even in the more careful, philosophic use of the word 'disposition' we find the tendency to introduce an extra surreptitiously, over and above the observed regularity. Thus I doubt whether the important distinction between innate and acquired dispositions could be made on the regularity theory solely. We notice in the case of the person *A* that *y* regularly follows *x* and we speak of a disposition. We know that twenty years ago this sequence was not a regular part of his behaviour and we are therefore justified in saying that he has acquired the disposition in the intervening period. But how could we ever know that he possessed a disposition innately? We might say that we find the sequence however early we begin, but this would be no proof of its innateness. It would still, so far as we know, be acquired, for *ex hypothesi* we can only know of it in observing regular sequences in the individual's life-history. Clearly, the notion of an innate disposition is of a certain power or ability existing prior to birth, and no account of our knowledge of this, if we have such a knowledge, can be given in terms of observed regularities. If, accordingly, we say that scientifically and exactly we can only mean by an innate disposition a regular sequence which is observed to be present from our earliest experiences of that which has the disposition, we should then in fact be giving up the distinction between innate and acquired dispositions. If the regular-sequence language is the sole permissible language of philosophers and scientists, then the psychologist who distinguishes between innate and acquired dispositions is neither philosophical nor scientific.

We do seem to assume that some at least of these dispositions are powers. We assume even that the dispositions of inorganic things are powers, that tea has the power of stimulating, the magnet the power of drawing the iron filings and so on. In the case of organic things we think of dispositions such as habits, skills, learnings, as at least temporary modifications of the structure of their being which somehow influence their behaviour and which facilitate behaviour of a certain pattern. We even claim to experience the force of our own habits, especially when we seek to resist them and to break them. The chain-smoker who is attempting to give up smoking would not be amused if told that his smoking habit was merely a regular pattern of behaviour consisting of putting cigarettes to his mouth and smoking them.

While, therefore, on a strict empiricism to say that something has a disposition is merely to say that in its case *y* regularly follows *x*, yet when ordinary men and some scientists and philosophers speak of dispositions they clearly mean more; rightly or wrongly they mean drives, forces, or powers. This point should be borne in mind in the discussions which follow.

67. Having examined the nature of dispositions at some length, and with a growing consciousness that much remains dark, we may now consider the theory that the use of some general words is best explained in terms of dispositions. Hume, as we have seen, by implication rejects the traditional theory that we abstract common qualities and frame out of them a general idea for which the general word is the name. He holds that having long been familiar with recurrences of the same or like experiences and having learnt to associate a name with one such recurrence, the mind is disposed to react in certain ways whenever the name is seen or heard. For instance, if the word 'apple' is mentioned we are disposed to imagine a particular apple (so Hume thought with Berkeley) which stands for all the others we have seen. In the same way, if someone presents us with a pear and says, 'This is an apple', we are disposed to deny the statement. We tend to approve one application of the word and reject another. These dispositions have come into being in the course of our experience, but how they have come we do not know. They are certainly not the product of any conscious activity of ours but are involuntary.

Thus Hume's suggestion is that we should look for the explanation of our use of general words and of generalizing in the way in which we are conditioned by experience. Our dispositions are the key to the situation. Now if we do look in this direction it does appear to be true that we can rid ourselves at once of some of the difficulties which beset the traditional theory. I may give three instances of this. First, on the traditional theory generalizing is inevitably a difficult technique requiring considerable skill in abstracting and synthesizing, a skill that a child, for instance, could certainly not be expected to possess. And yet children do generalize and know how to use general words. How is this possible? Hume provides the answer. Children in fact make little if any use of the above technique, but they are old enough to have acquired dispositions and their grouping and generalizing is to be explained in terms of dispositions. They do not consciously set out to generalize; they find themselves generalizing.

Secondly, the traditionalists had great difficulties with the common quality. Are we sure that *a* is a quality common to each and every apple? If we have first to prove that this quality *a* is indeed common to every apple, we are likely to be a very long time in abstracting sufficient common qualities to frame our general idea. Hume, on the other hand, does not need a common quality in this sense. It is recurrences in experience, and they need not necessarily be recurrences of identical qualities, that condition us, and these are all that his theory requires.

Thirdly, the general idea on the traditional theory consists of a sum of so many common qualities, and yet the general words 'apple', 'table', and 'house' signify things and not sums of qualities. How this is so remains a mystery on the traditional theory, but the problem does not arise if we begin with Hume's. For we are acquainted in experience with things having qualities and not merely with qualities as such. We become familiar with these things and with their recurring pattern. Consequently, what we expect when the word 'apple' is mentioned is more than a sum of qualities; we expect the apples which have the qualities.

68. In this way the acceptance of Hume's suggestion would rid us of some of the principal difficulties confronting the traditional theory of generalization. I shall now seek to develop and elaborate this suggestion, beginning with an incursion into child psychology. It has frequently been pointed out that advance in intellectual prowess is an advance towards increased discrimination and that the experience of very young children is largely undifferentiated. Certain objects stand out from the mass they experience and these are distinguished, though their

detail is not observed. Very young children find it difficult to distinguish between objects which resemble one another fairly closely; for instance, they may call all the men they see 'Dad' and all moving vehicles 'Choo-choo'. Only gradually do they come to differentiate between, say, the kinds of trees or the species of birds. Children's first experiences appear to be of undifferentiated wholes. Now many of these wholes constantly recur in the child's experience and as a consequence a disposition is formed. A name is associated with the recurrence, with the help possibly of parental reinforcement, and the child is then, as it were, ready with his 'There it is' of recognition or his 'That isn't it' of rejection, whenever the name is mentioned in his hearing. What he expects on hearing the name is not the concrete particular of the philosopher with all its details precisely known, but the undifferentiated whole. Experience and language begin with vague syntheses; analysis comes later; and the use of the general word is facilitated by the early failure to differentiate. At this stage what the mind is disposed to recognize when the word is uttered is the whole which is general, not the specific and certainly not the concrete particular. Or, to speak more accurately perhaps, these primitive experiences precede the recognition of the distinction between general, specific, and particular. In the same way our first words are, strictly speaking, neither general words nor proper names, for this distinction too comes later, though it emerges soon.[1]

What I have just said, however, should not be taken to mean that the child is able to generalize in this primitive way without first being aware of objects. The present theory involves no such thesis; it merely denies that it is necessary first to be aware of a precisely determined object. Awareness of objects is presupposed, though the objects remain unanalysed; what is not presupposed is an awareness, for instance, of a precise particular quality which can be abstracted from the present context. A full examination of the awareness presupposed on this theory

[1] Grammarians have drawn our attention to a class of words, usually called 'mass words', which even in adult usage are neither strictly singular nor strictly general. Such words are 'water', 'iron', etc.

is unnecessary here but one comment may be made which seems relevant to our present discussion. We are apt to think of it in terms of seeing and sense-perception, but seeing, hearing, and touching all help us in using, and we are aware of objects in using them. To the child it is not merely the *looks* of an object that matter, there are its uses also and its abuses. The words 'house', 'table', 'knife', for instance, in the case of the English child, awaken expectations not merely of an object that looks so and so, but of one that can be useful in such and such ways, or can be misused possibly in dangerous ways. A house is a place to live in, with a door to enable us to enter, with windows to receive the sun's rays, with a chimney through which the smoke may pass out, and so on. It is interesting that young children when they draw a house rarely attempt to represent a particular house they have seen; their purpose rather seems to be to get into the picture all the necessary features, and these are mostly utility features. There must be a door, windows, chimney, a roof overhead and a path leading up to the door—for without the path how could one get to the house? The drawing reveals the meaning of the word 'house' for the child at the time, namely, a vague *Gestalt* having certain salient features. This is what children are disposed to think when the word is mentioned in their hearing, and they are so disposed simply because their past awareness of houses has conditioned them in this way.

So far I have been developing the doctrine implicit in Hume, but it is necessary to modify that teaching in one respect in order to present a true account of the matter. Children are conditioned by their early experiences of a world containing recurrences, and this natural conditioning seems a most important element in any account of how children come to use general words. But, of course, children are not automata. If this conditioning is a necessary factor in their coming to group things together and in their using general words, conscious learning is another factor which is not to be ignored. In coming to use general words successfully more than one sort of disposition is involved. The child has been seeing houses, living in them, going in and out of them, he has been hearing the word 'house' used and his mind is conditioned by these experiences. An abiding change has been made in his life, as his behaviour testifies, the disposition has been formed and it is not incorrect to say that in that respect he is conditioned by the world around him. But he is also active and intelligent, he soon begins to note things and to distinguish between them, he learns to distinguish between words. Certain new habits emerge which are permanent or semi-permanent modifications of his being, but which are now more accurately described as the outcome of his own effort to learn rather than of the way in which his environment conditions him. Thus a child's behaviour reveals habits of the second as well as of the first kind, or perhaps it would be more correct to say that his present habits are the outcome both of learning and conditioning. But the latter feature cannot be omitted, especially if we recall that the environment includes other animate beings who also condition the child's growth by, for instance, drilling and training, a process which is soon facilitated by the child's own intelligent participation. Thus learning in the widest sense of the word must be taken to include the conditioning of the environment, the training by others, together with the child's own noting, distinguishing, observing, and conscious classifying. In this section we have been discussing mainly the conditioning of the child by the early environment. No account of the way the child comes to generalize and of his use of general words is complete which ignores this. He uses general words successfully not only because he consciously observes the recurrences that are in his environment and classifies them, but because also that environment conditions his mental life from the start.

69. Now this account of children's generalizing throws light, too, on adult generalizing. In the ordinary employment of such words as 'house', 'man', 'tree' there is no conscious construction out of discovered common qualities. The hearing of the word stimulates certain reactions which are what they are because of the system of expectations which habit has ingrained within us.

To borrow a technical term from the psychologists, the mind is 'set'; we are prepared beforehand for certain things and not prepared for others. Consider the use of the word 'houses' in the following sentences. If someone says: 'Houses in this neighbourhood are built of local stone' this is a use of the word 'houses' for which we are prepared. In our experience houses are objects that are built and they may well be built of local stone. The sentence is in accordance with what we expect. But if someone says: 'The houses walked together in earnest conversation' we are surprised. We are not prepared for such a use of the term; it is not how we tend to use it.

The dispositional system has its emotional counterpart. In the instance given a child might well be angry at hearing of houses walking and talking together. And the adult, though he may not feel anger, may yet feel a certain uneasiness when faced with what does not conform to his experience. But frequently this uneasiness and tension are themselves transmuted into something pleasant, so that the emotions aroused are those of curiosity and wonder. An examination of these matters could not fail to prove useful to students of art and aesthetics.

Dispositions clearly are an important factor in the governance of a man's life and this is particularly true if we include in the meaning of the word skills, capabilities, and techniques, and not merely the early dispositions in which little if any conscious learning is involved. Man's dispositions in this wide sense account for those abiding assumptions and expectations in terms of which his behaviour can be understood. These, rather than any conclusions arrived at after due deliberation, are the probabilities which most often guide his life. Having the disposition is having the plan of action ready to meet the familiar ever-recurring situation. Associated with these dispositions are general words, so that hearing a general word he is ready to behave and respond in the appropriate way. Moreover, the use of general words is itself part of the technique acquired to enable him to respond successfully to his environment.

70. To develop this last point let us return to the world of the child. I have been speaking of the way in which his experience of his physical and social environment engenders dispositions part of whose realization consists in uttering words. To complete the picture it is necessary to point out that when a child does come to learn the use of such a general word as 'house' he uses it as an item in a sentence. Now he speaks in sentences only when he has acquired dispositions of another kind, namely, the syntactical and grammatical skills possessed by persons able to converse and think in that language. The child acquires these by listening to others use the language, and by being taught by others. The English-speaking child learns to put the verb in a certain place in the sentence; the German child learns to put it elsewhere. For those who can read, the grammar books set out the rules of the language, but the child does not wait till he is old enough to read the grammar book. Indeed, unless he had first learnt most of the rules mentioned in the grammar book he could not read the book. The grammarian merely points out to the child what he already knows, if he is using the language properly. He has picked these things up long ago, and for the most part he has picked them up without realizing what he is doing. Henceforward he uses the language according to the rules; the English-speaking child would be most uneasy when faced with a sentence such as, 'Tom Mary loves'.

The grammatical structure of the language we use has much to do with the logic of our thinking. There can be no doubt that part of the explanation of why we think as we do is to be found in the fact that we use English in thinking and we should be thinking differently if we were using another language, particularly if the grammatical structure of the language differed greatly from English. The logician cannot wholly ignore linguistic habits. Yet it is an error to suppose that grammar and logic are one. Linguistic habits are not the only ones that matter. When a child says, 'There are big houses in our street', the habits involved in the use of the word 'houses' are not solely linguistic in the sense in which we have now been using the term. We have seen that the child's constant experience of houses counts too. Semantical considerations are not entirely linguistic, and the logician's concern is with the semantical. It would therefore be erroneous to identify grammar with logic, but equally erroneous to ignore linguistic habits in attempting a theory of thinking.

71. In concluding this chapter I return to the main problem; How do we use general words successfully? We are now in a position to give a fuller answer though still an incomplete one. The existence of common qualities and relations, as we saw in the previous chapter, provides a basis for our use of general words. But the general word is rarely, if ever, the name I consciously choose for and give to an observed common quality. Almost invariably I learn the word from others. I may be told explicitly that the name of this quality is such and such, or I may hear people use the word and realize from the context that they are using it to refer to this quality, or, thirdly, without ever having consciously linked word and quality together I find myself using the word successfully, having picked it up from others, though I do not now remember ever having done so. Children's learning appears to be mostly of this third kind. Such learning can occur only when the child is accustomed to seeing the quality and to hearing the word, so that two sets of habits are involved and are being blended together, the one concerned with qualities perceived and the other with words heard.

But we should not confine ourselves to adjectives. How do we use common nouns successfully? We do so, it is now clear, first, as the consequence of our possessing certain linguistic habits resulting from our familiarity with the language, from hearing it being used and using it ourselves; but, secondly, as the consequence too of possessing habits of a non-linguistic kind, which are equally necessary, namely, those which result from our long familiarity with objects which closely resemble one another and are observed to be different from other objects, so that at a subconscious level we have grouped them together and are now disposed to think of them and behave in relation to them in certain ways. The strength of our linguistic habits is frequently not realized by us until, for instance, we hear a foreigner speak our tongue. He may perhaps be able to repeat the grammatical rules more accurately than we can ourselves, yet he hesitates, flounders, and makes slips that we should never make. He is consciously learning the language, whereas it has become part of us; from our mother's knee we are disposed to use words and sentences in just these ways and in no other. In the same way the pressure of our environment upon us brings into being habits of response. In particular, the constant recurrence in our experience of qualities, relationships, situations, and those undifferentiated wholes which we refer to as things, moulds our behaviour. The result of all this is that we know how to respond correctly to a general word when we hear it, we are able to recognize instances of the common noun used and reject what are falsely claimed to be instances. We are not conscious of the moulding which has taken place, but our behaviour and our speech bear testimony to its effectiveness.

Now to be disposed in this way is to have in one's possession a useful principle of classification. We recognize instances and have a standard by which to judge whether, for instance, the object before us is or is not an apple. The principle, no doubt, is crude at this stage; to make it precise we should need to reflect upon it and define it. Yet we possess it and are already using it. Moreover, since my neighbour's experiences seem to be roughly the same as my own, he understands my use of the general word 'apple' and seems himself to use it in very much the same way as I do. He, too, apparently possesses the same principle of classification. But when sometimes we fail to understand one another, when I find him using the word 'apple' for an object that I should not call an apple, I begin to realize how indefinite my own principle is and so I set about to define it. But use of the principle precedes the clarification of it.

Thus these dispositions provide us from an early stage with principles for classifying and ordering our world. They are not merely linguistic, for speech is only part of the behaviour which they determine; they arise also from an acquaintance with the recurrences and regularities in our environment. They thus provide a second foundation for a theory of universals.

XI
CONCEPTS

72. Having considered common qualities and dispositions, we must now turn to concepts. For as we have seen there are philosophers who hold that the universal is a concept and we must try to understand what they mean. This will be difficult, for the term 'concept' is used in a wide variety of senses both in daily life and in philosophical reflection. Today it is almost as much of a rag-bag as was the term 'idea' in the eighteenth century.

In philosophy three interpretations stand out. Most precise is Frege's that the concept is the reference of the logical predicate term; in contrast to it is the traditional view that the concept is 'whatever is before the mind' excepting only all particulars perceived and all memory images of particulars as particulars; thirdly, the concept is presented not as an object before the mind, there to be thought, but as itself part of the thinking, a capacity, a disposition, or possibly an attitude. In studying these various interpretations we shall meet the main problems connected with concepts, first, that of their formation and, secondly, that of the relation of concept with image, with the general word and with the group or class.

73. Suppose, with Frege, we think of a concept as a logical predicate, not the linguistic predicate term but the predicate itself. It is what is predicated of an object, and is never itself an object. Platonists may think of the concept as a real entity, indeed the most real entity, and so may Idealists who find the greatest reality in ideal or conceptual existence. But, for those who think of the world as a plurality of individual things, concepts lack reality. This does not necessarily mean that they are subjective. They are not subjective in the opinion of the traditional rationalists; and for Kant too, pure concepts, though they are essentially concepts of the understanding, are none the less objective.[1] Frege, distinguishing between an image

[1] Cf. § 35 ff. above.

and a thought (*Gedanke*), identifies the concept with a thought and thinks of it as objective, for 'one and the same thought can be grasped by many men'.[1] Thus the concept though it is not, in Frege's terminology, an object is yet objective.

In another sense, however, the concept is subjective. It depends for its being on being conceived and does not exist independently of the thinker thinking it. Some concepts, it is true, have been held to be *a priori* and known innately, so that they cannot be said to depend upon the thinker thinking them. But Frege in speaking of concepts does not appear to be thinking in particular of these. His examples are frequently of *green*, *man*, *planet*, and so on, that is to say of empirical concepts.

74. How are these concepts formed? This is not a question which Frege sought to answer, but certainly, to understand what the philosopher means when he says that the universal is the concept, it is essential to ask about the formation of concepts. About empirical concepts, such as those instanced above, the traditional answer is clear. In the first place, they are acquired by abstraction from sensory experience. We may admittedly acquire some of them in other ways. For instance, having seen cats and ducks, I may frame the concept of a cat with webbed feet. Or, if I come across, say, the word 'dromond', and inquire as to its meaning, I am told that a dromond was a medieval ship used both in war and commerce. By understanding this description I acquire the concept of *dromond*. No one would want to say that abstracting from experience was the sole way of acquiring concepts, but none the less it is generally held that, so long as we speak of empirical concepts, the primary source of such concepts is abstraction from the empirical.

Such is the general view, but, as we have seen, it has been criticized from time to time. For instance Berkeley held that Locke's account of abstraction through 'singling' was psychologically false.[2] Criticism of 'abstractionism' on somewhat the same lines has been made recently by P. T. Geach in his *Mental*

[1] *Philosophical Writings*, p. 79.
[2] Cf. Ch. III above, particularly § 19.

Acts. In this book he remarks[1]: 'I shall use "abstractionism" as a name for the doctrine that a concept is acquired by a process of singling out in attention some one feature given in direct experience—*abstracting* it—and ignoring the other features simultaneously given—*abstracting from* them.' He holds that such abstractionism 'is wholly mistaken; that no concept at all is acquired by the supposed process of abstraction'.

Now if Geach's point were that we sometimes gain concepts by concentrating on resemblances between objects rather than by singling out 'some one feature', then his criticism would be sound. It might be argued too that the usual empiricist account, outlined in the last paragraph, is inadequate. But Geach goes much further than this. He thinks it obvious that 'logical concepts, like those of *some*, *or*, and *not*' are not gained in this way,[2] neither are arithmetical and relational concepts. But he also denies that 'abstractionism' is the correct doctrine even in the case of 'concepts of simple sensible qualities' such as *red* and *round*.[3] 'No concept at all is acquired by the supposed process.'

We ordinarily believe that for a man to have the concept of, say, *ultramarine* he has first to see the colour and attend to it. In doing this he singles it out from other qualities and particularly from other colours. But Geach rejects this explanation. A man born blind, he argues, may have a concept of *ultramarine*. He may acquire it by listening to the descriptions of others. For instance, it may be said in his hearing that just as a surface can be hot all over, so it can be ultramarine all over, or again that ultramarine is a cold colour. He may thus begin to gain a concept of *ultramarine* in spite of the fact that, having always been blind, he cannot possibly gain it by abstraction from experience. Now presumably it would be agreed that the blind man has acquired a concept, or the beginnings of a concept, of *ultramarine*. But the abstractionist too would surely not deny this. If he were to say that blind men are incapable of acquiring any concept whatsoever of *ultramarine* then he would be talking nonsense. He could, however, fairly affirm that Geach's argument is irrelevant to his own thesis. It would be more relevant to his

[1] *Mental Acts*, p. 18. [2] Ibid., p. 22. [3] Ibid., p. 34.

thesis to ask how the blind man has acquired the concepts of *hot* and *cold*, for it would be highly probable that he has acquired them by 'singling' certain touch sensations and abstracting them. It may well be the case, too, that a man *able* to see may yet never have seen an ultramarine object, but that he none the less has acquired some concept of the colour, having been told, say, that it is a shade of blue. On the other hand, he may see ultramarine objects and make special note of the colour, and he may gain the concept of *ultramarine* in this way. Geach is wrong, I believe, in saying that 'no concept at all' is acquired by a process, part of which consists in abstracting from sense-experience.

Not that this is the whole of the process. If Geach were protesting against the view that this was the whole of the process few would dispute with him. Clearly if we are talking of concepts in verbal thinking (Geach admits that some thinking is not verbal[1]) then part of the process involved in acquiring the concept of ultramarine is coming to know how to use the word 'ultramarine' in the English language. In reference to verbal conceptual thinking I accept the point made by Rush Rhees: 'No one can get the concept of colour just by looking at colours, or of red just by looking at red things. If I have the concept I know how the word "red" is used.'[2] Or again: 'I cannot learn the colour unless I can see it; but I cannot learn it without language either.'[3] The second clause in this latter statement is true in the case of verbal thinking, but the first clause too is true. At any rate it is usually true, though we admit that in principle we may learn something, say, about ultramarine without having seen it. But, generally speaking, part of acquiring the concept is seeing the colour, attending to it, and 'singling' it.

Geach says: 'The ability to express a judgement in words thus presupposes a number of capacities, previously acquired, for intelligently using the several words and phrases that make up the sentence. I shall apply the old term "concepts" to these

[1] Ibid., pp. 11–13.
[2] *Proc. Arist. Soc.*, supp. vol., 1954, p. 80.
[3] Ibid., p. 81.

special capacities.'[1] I should argue that the intelligent use of the word 'ultramarine', generally speaking, presupposes that one has seen the colour and attended to it, so singling it out and abstracting it. When this does occur it is then an essential part of the whole process of acquiring the concept, and an essential part of the analysis of 'a capacity for intelligently using' in this context. This is an important point that needs emphasizing. Extreme statements about the empiricist position are made from time to time which one can well reject. But we are confronted here with a minimum statement and if we reject it we reject the whole of the empiricist doctrine; I do not believe that the evidence permits us to reject it.

I shall later express some doubts about the view, fashionable at the moment, that a concept is, as Geach says above, a capacity.[2] Geach argues too that we *make* our concepts and this seems appropriate language in some cases, as we shall see. But then if concepts are capacities, is it sensible to speak of our making our mental capacities? This is an obvious difficulty to which I shall return later; at the moment it is to another related question that I wish to refer. 'Having a concept', says Geach, 'never means being able to recognize some feature we have found in direct experience; the mind *makes* concepts, and this concept-formation and the subsequent use of the concepts formed never is a mere recognition or finding; but this does not in the least prevent us from applying concepts in our sense-experience and knowing sometimes that we apply them rightly.'[3] This suggests that the mind *makes* the concept of *ultramarine*, but how precisely it does make it is not explained by Geach. What he tells us is that it is not made by 'singling' or abstracting, on our seeing objects coloured ultramarine. However, once we have made it we may then come across objects coloured ultramarine and find the concept fits and so apply it. How this works is a mystery. Is there a pre-established harmony between the concept we make and the colour? Without having Geach's

[1] Ibid., p. 12.

[2] Cf. also p. 13: 'A concept, as I am using the term, is subjective—it is a mental capacity belonging to a particular person.'

[3] Ibid., p. 40.

positive account of how we do make the concept of *ultramarine* it is impossible to pass judgement on this theory.

75. I take the view then that we who can see and who know how to use the word 'ultramarine' intelligently have generally acquired the concept of *ultramarine* by seeing ultramarine objects, noting the colour, differentiating it from other colours, and so singling it out in attention, that is, abstracting (in this sense of a term which has other senses); further, we have learnt how to use this word in speaking or writing and how to understand it when it is used by others. This is not the full analysis of the process but these are essential elements in it in the present context. I admit at the same time that a person blind from birth may, in spite of his disabilities, have some concept of *ultramarine*, but he will not have acquired it in the way which I have just described.

But now, to go deeper into this matter of concept-formation, the question may be asked whether we are ever justified in speaking of the concept *ultramarine*? For should we not rather be speaking of the percept? Or again of the image? In this context certainly conceiving, perceiving, and imagining are all closely related. Yet the concept of a quality or a relation is never to be identified with a mere percept or a mere image. Not that the colour we *con*ceive in the case of ultramarine is any different from the colour we *per*ceive; it is obviously one and the same colour. But in conceiving the colour I am conscious of it as possibly belonging to more than one object—this perhaps because I now perceive it to belong to at least two objects. This is a further feature in acquiring the concept of *ultramarine*. Conceiving is different from perceiving and also from imagining. If I recall in memory an image of what I have previously seen, imagining it in the particular context in which I saw it, I should not call such an image a concept. But I can imagine ultramarine as a colour belonging to more than one object, that is to say, as a common quality, and this I should call conceiving.

The characteristic feature of such concepts as these is that the whole of the content is present in each instance. In this respect the concept *ultramarine* may be contrasted with the concept *man*. In the case of ultramarine as now conceived there can be nothing more in my concept, in its ultramarineness, than is already present in what I perceive. But though I conceive man as a rational, two-legged creature, I am not surprised if, for instance, a particular man is not rational or has lost a leg, or if he has qualities which I do not include in my concept of *man*. These concepts, clearly, are very different in character.

Since they have this characteristic, concepts such as those of *ultramarine* are exceptionally useful in classification. For when we group objects into those which are coloured ultramarine and those which are not, the boundary between the two classes is clear and precise. Here is a sure principle of classification and discrimination. It is obvious that the conceiving of such concepts helps us greatly in the task of grouping our materials and so ordering our world.

The philosophers of the seventeenth and eighteenth centuries thought of them, too, as simple units out of which to compound more complex concepts or ideas; they were the primary concepts with all others as secondary. But this language is dangerous, for it involves the assumptions, first, that all concepts other than the primary are constructions, and secondly, that the elements in these constructions are all primary concepts. And this soon becomes an indefensible position. Nor are these concepts necessarily primary in the sense of being chronologically prior to all other concepts. The concept of *man* might well be conceived earlier in the individual's development than that of *ultramarine*.

If then we speak of primary concepts in this context we should do so guardedly. But whether we describe them as primary or not, it seems legitimate to refer to them as concepts. More must be said in what follows about the nature of these concepts but we can note now that they satisfy Frege's logical criterion, for the word 'ultramarine' could be a predicate term in a proposition; in that sense it is a general word.

76. These are concepts which we are assumed to acquire consciously in the course of our experience. We discover that ultra-

marine is a common quality and acquire the concept of *ultramarine*, possibly on perceiving two ultramarine patches. Having acquired the concept we then have it for use, for instance, we may use the concept of ultramarine in classifying objects.

But it is not only by consciously acquiring them that we gain concepts, for even that of *ultramarine* may be gained in another way. I may not first see ultramarine and consciously realize that this is a quality which I see, or have seen, or could possibly see elsewhere. I may rather have become used to recurring ultramarines. I have the concept, but I cannot say precisely how I gained it. This sort of explanation of how we acquire concepts is the one that best seems to fit many of the concepts of our daily life, before we begin to think precisely and scientifically. What we should refer to as our concepts of blue, sweet, table, house, and so on, have been gained empirically through our familiarity with qualities and objects in the way described in the previous chapter. The characteristic of such concepts as these is their vagueness, their boundaries are only sketchily drawn. In ordinary life this is more often an advantage than a disadvantage; for the practical purposes of daily life we do not need extreme accuracy in classification and should find the demand for it irksome if not stultifying.

In this sense of the term, 'having concepts' seems to mean having those dispositions, some of which are empirical and some verbal, which enable one to classify houses, to say whether this is or is not a house and to talk significantly of houses. It is a form of mental retention and clearly a very important form. But it is not consciously remembering the past, for I do not remember the scores of experiences which result in my tending to speak, think, and behave now in the way I do. Nor is the retaining in this case an imagining of the past. In using the concept of *house* I may frequently, perhaps usually, be imagining a house, but this is not the essential part of the conceiving. It would be wrong, too, to think of the concept in this case as a sort of generic image. Psychologists sometimes speak of generic images as resulting from the experiencing of many resembling objects, neglecting differences, and as it were superimposing one resembling object upon another, just as photographs of human faces may be imposed one upon another to give a generic or composite human face. Such images would not be unlike Spinoza's universals of *Imaginatio*. The concept we speak of now, however, is not a generic image of this kind.

Very relevant in this context is Kant's discussion of the 'empirical concept'. It will be recalled that Kant defines the schema of the empirical concept (I am not thinking of the schemata of number and triangle) as a rule for determining experience, determining, for instance, that the object now before me is a dog. For Kant the schemata of empirical concepts belong to the imagination. But the schema of dog, for instance, is not a particular image of one dog; for if it were it could not be a rule for determining all dogs. Kant does speak of it, it is true, in a passage we considered earlier, as a sort of outline or sketch, 'a delineation of the figure of a four-footed animal in a general manner'. Yet it is no ordinary sketch since it is expressly stated that it is not a particular image. Kant is clear as to its function, it makes recognition possible; but he admits that its nature is a mystery.

Some part of the mystery may possibly be removed if the Kantian schema is thought of in terms of dispositions and tendencies. But Kant is right in the suggestion that having a concept of this kind means being able to group, to recognize, to differentiate. Thus there is a legitimate sense of the word 'concept' for which the question, 'Does this child possess the concept of *cat*?' is equivalent to the further two questions, 'Can the child recognize a cat when he sees one?' and 'Can he understand and use the general word 'cat' (or any of its linguistic equivalents) significantly?' If an affirmative answer is given to both these latter questions, then the first can also be answered in the affirmative. To have the concept, that is to say, is not necessarily to be able to imagine a particular cat; all that is necessary is to be able to recognize a cat as a cat (or to be able to say, 'That is not a cat' when some animal other than a cat is held to be a cat), and to be able to use the word 'cat' significantly in verbal communication, which includes understanding what is meant when the word 'cat' is used. If I describe a scene and use the word 'cat' in the description and this is significant to a child, or if with Lewis Carroll I talk nonsense about cats and the child shows that he understands that I am talking nonsense, if he himself uses the term 'cat' significantly in describing a scene, then he may be said to have the concept and to know how to use it.

77. But while it would be foolish to deny that we gain some concepts in the way just described, it would be wrong to find here the source of all concepts. As we have seen, this account will not always explain how we come to gain the concept *ultramarine*. If we consciously realize that a quality or relation is common we have come to conceive a concept in another manner. Further, the indefiniteness of the concepts gained in the way described in the last section will itself in time make us reflect and search for more precise concepts. I know what a house is until someone asks me whether the Eskimo's igloo is a house, and then I begin to think. To answer I find I have to conjure up in imagination the elements essential to houses, or possibly state these elements in so many words, defining the word 'house'; or I may use both methods.

Consider first these imaginative constructions. It is clear that we do construct in imagination in order to clarify concepts which we find we already possess, though we have not up to this time reflected upon them. And undoubtedly when people speak of concepts they frequently mean conscious, imaginative constructions or fabrications of this kind. Such constructions would then be used as principles of classification, just as having imagined the essentials of a house I am then in a position to answer whether an igloo is a house. In the past, admittedly, philosophers have been too ready to suppose that there are two sorts of concepts and two only, namely, the primary concepts, that is, common qualities and relations which are simple, and secondly, the imaginative constructions we are now speaking about, which may or may not be regarded as compounds of primary concepts. In this the philosophers were at fault, for no full account of conceiving can be given in these terms. But it would be equally fallacious to deny the possibility of imaginative construction or to deny that when people speak of conceiving they very frequently have in mind just such construction.

We have spoken of imaginative constructing as clarificatory in purpose; its function is to clarify the principle of classification. But we should be limiting our imaginative powers unduly if we confined them to this task of clarifying concepts already in our possession. A certain spontaneity and free play belong to imagination, and the imaginative synthesizing of elements need not always be in accordance with experience. We can, for instance, by omitting certain features of experienced objects or adding new features, conceive new species of animals never experienced by us. We may think of a cat with webbed feet or of a horse with an elephant's trunk; we can imagine mermaids, centaurs, and unicorns. Sometimes we speak of these as imaginations or imaginative creations, but it is also quite natural to speak of them as concepts.

It is an interesting question whether such creative imagining is ever more than 'a new ordering of old material'. Are we limited to the content given in experience though free to change its order, or can we imaginatively create new content? It would appear that in certain conditions entirely new material can be imagined. For instance, given two semi-tones we could surely imagine the quarter-tone between them, even though we had never heard it previously. So also with shades of colour. The reader will recall Hume's illustration at the beginning of the *Treatise*. A series of shades of blue is set out before us from a very light to a very dark shade, but one shade is missing and the gap is obvious. Could we fill it imaginatively supposing we had not seen the shade before? Hume thinks we could, though he admits this contradicts the general thesis he is seeking to prove. If this is the case, it means that we are able to imagine fresh content and not merely to rearrange in imagination content already given in experience. However, the situation is unusual in both the above instances, and the new material is certainly suggested by experience, even if it is not given in experience; the tones on both sides of the quarter-tone and the shades on both sides of the missing shade are given. Hence the content imagined is not entirely independent of the content experienced.

But this approach to the problem may be objected to on the ground of its unreality and artificiality. Is it not foolish to say that a symphony is not new because it is made up of sounds each one of which has been heard before, or to say that it is new in its ordering but not in its material? Or that a painting is not a new creation because it is merely a new ordering of colours seen before? What needs to be stressed is the fact of imaginative creation. The mind uses the old but thereby brings the new into being. So too with the imagining of centaurs and mermaids, and the child's imagining of ghosts with which it frightens itself at night; and so with the construction of concepts. They are all new creations. Perhaps the word 'constructing' is itself misleading as suggesting too mechanical a process, setting brick upon brick, and not bringing out sufficiently the creativeness of the imagination—though a building for that matter may, as artistic creation, be as genuinely new as is any symphony or painting. But perhaps we should talk of the 'creating' of new concepts rather than of their 'constructing'.

But whatever term we decide upon, the important thing is to recognize that in addition to the imaginative conceiving which is purposively clarificatory, there is that other which is essentially creative. In most cases, it is true, this creative imagining also clarifies, though it may also increase the vagueness, as when, for instance, it greatly extends the range of the concept. Thus it might be contended that the concept of the unconscious was clearer before Freud framed his new notion of it, though before Freud it was restricted and lacked the wide extension and significance which his imaginative genius bestowed upon it. Yet there is no reason in principle why the creative and the clarificatory should not go hand in hand.

78. The concepts we have been considering, closely related as they are to percept and image, have none the less as much right to the title of 'concept' as have any other concepts. Yet concep-

tualists might prefer to think of more intellectual and less empirical forms of conceiving. They speak of the pure intellectual concept, and find in it the concept *par excellence* which most deserves our attention. We must now consider concepts in this sense.

It would be well to make one reservation in turning to this field. It might be assumed that we are now crossing over into entirely new territory and that a hard and fast boundary is set up between the imaginative and the intellectual. This is an assumption we have no right to make. It may well prove to be the case that no thinking, however intellectual, entirely lacks imaginative elements. The thinker may find the use of imagery, usually visual, not only a help but a necessity. The advancement of geometry is held to be an essentially intellectual activity, but geometrical thinking is helped by the drawing or imagining of visual figures and is to that extent imaginative in character. Moreover this element may be essential to the thinking. Ernst Cassirer in discussing this point[1] aptly quotes the mathematician Klein: 'To pursue a geometrical train of thought by pure logic without seeing constantly before my eyes the figure to which it refers is impossible, at any rate for me.' And no doubt most geometricians would say the same thing. It might, however, be argued that geometry was not as intellectual an inquiry as some other sciences, for instance, algebra or logic, which would appear to make no use whatsoever of visual imagery. Yet even in these sciences the symbolization, so very necessary to the thinking, might be held to be imaginative, and anyway imagination is present in another form. It is not my purpose to present in this book a full theory of imagination, but I may be permitted to make here one point which would seem to be vital to any such theory. It is mistaken to think of imagination wholly in terms of having images whether these be visual, auditory, or any other. Our very handling of theories in thinking may be imaginative even if no recourse is had to images and pictures. If a thinker is being guided by his love of beauty, order, and simplicity, if, for instance, a scientist decides between hypotheses on

[1] *The Problem of Knowledge*, Yale, 1950, p. 36.

these criteria, then his thinking surely must be held to be as imaginative as it is intellectual. Accordingly, if in the pages which follow less will be heard of imagining, it must not be assumed that imaginative elements are entirely absent from the thinking under consideration.

79. With this reservation in mind we may now turn to examine the less imaginative and more intellectual forms of conceiving. We may begin with the traditional theory that the concept is what is before the mind, the object of conceiving. The concept, however, on the traditional theory, is not objective (in the sense of being an object outside the mind); it is subjective. It is not a physical object, nor again is it a Platonic Form or Idea. The conceptualist expressly and emphatically rejects the doctrine of Forms and has no sympathy with the *Ante Rem* theory. The concept or idea is an object of conceiving which is dependent on the mind; it has been described as an 'internal accusative'. As has been seen, too, the conceptualist holds that the general word is the name of the accusative. For instance, the word 'democracy' is the name of the concept *democracy*. Finally, the concept, as thus conceived, is said to be the universal. On such a theory, the universal is not part of the real objective world, nor is it merely a name as the nominalists say. It is a concept, that is, an internal accusative.

In discussing this matter I find an initial difficulty which others may share. I am supposed to be aware of these concepts as accusatives yet, however carefully I examine my thinking, I never come across them. Whether I introspect or retrospect I find no trace of them. But surely, it will be said, you can conceive democracy, surely the word 'democracy' has meaning for you. Of course it has, but for me 'conceiving democracy' is not being aware of an internal accusative, and the 'meaning' which the word has is not to be identified with any such entity. Admittedly, when I see a tree there is an object, the tree, which I am seeing, and when I imagine the tree I saw yesterday there is still an object imagined, whether it is the same tree, as some philosophers hold, or an image other than the physical object. Now when I use the word 'democracy' my use of it may possibly involve having an image or images and these may be taken to be objects of awareness and accusatives. I may have an image of people at polling booths, or of the people's representatives meeting in parliament. But the conceptualist is thinking of those occasions upon which no such images are present, and he holds there exists then an object of awareness, namely, the concept or thought of *democracy*. It is this pure conceptualist object which I fail to find.

But now even if it were agreed that intellectual concepts such as *democracy*, *beauty*, *truth*, and so on are not introspectible entities, it might still be argued that the internal objects we call 'concepts' exist and must logically exist, and that we can infer their necessary existence. Consider, for example, the following arguments in favour of this new contention:

1. Intellectual concepts are necessary to account for translation from one language into another. There must be, for instance, a concept of liberty for this is what the several words 'liberty', 'Freiheit', 'liberté' stand for; three words in the three languages, but one concept or one meaning. Moreover, in one and the same language, two words may be synonyms. If 'liberty' and 'freedom', for instance, are synonyms in English then there must be something, some one thought, which both these words express. One may imagine a man thinking of this concept and hesitating momentarily, not knowing whether he should speak of it as 'liberty' or 'freedom'; or of a good linguist waiting to know whether his auditors were English or German before using the appropriate word to express his thoughts. 'Good linguists', we are told,[1] 'who not only speak several tongues, but think in them as well, confidently assert that they often have a wordless idea before they can make up their minds as to the language in which they should express it. And indeed the detachment of thought from its verbal expression seems to be necessarily involved in translation from one language to another. When a Latin sentence is translated into English there must be

[1] P. B. Ballard, *Thought and Language*, 1934, pp. 40–41.

a moment when it is neither Latin nor English—when it has ceased to be one and has not yet become the other. What is the state of the thought in the interval? If it is not pure thought, what is it?'

2. We frequently find ourselves, as we say, 'having a thought (or idea or concept) in mind' but failing to put it into words. But if this is so these thoughts or concepts must be other than the words; they are entities in the mind which can be there even if we fail to express them in words.

3. It is a characteristic of a living language that new words are being constantly introduced into it. New phenomena are discovered and these are given names. Or new thoughts are thought out, and new words are found to express these thoughts. Some scientist or other thought of studying the habits and modes of life of living organisms and later the name 'ecology' was given to this study. The thought came first and existed when the word did not exist.

4. We must admit 'pure concepts' or 'pure thoughts', for only then can we deal satisfactorily with the problem of non-existents. What am I thinking of, for instance, when I say, 'There are no unicorns'? I am not thinking of existing animals as is the case when I say, 'There are lions'. I am not thinking of the picture or image of a unicorn, for these do exist and are not unicorns. All that I am thinking of, if I am to speak sensibly and not give the non-existent unicorn a sort of shadowy existence, is the thought or concept of *unicorn*. So there must be such concepts.[1]

5. Every one would agree that we think. Not all thinking is imagining, some of it is 'pure thinking'. But pure thinking must be about something or other, so there must be concepts, that is, pure intellectual objects, for otherwise there would be nothing to think about. Moreover, we speak of transcendent objects, that is, objects which we know cannot be perceived or imagined. These, too, must be pure concepts.

[1] Cf. the passage from Russell quoted above, p. 34.

80. These are some of the arguments that will be used to show that pure concepts as internal accusatives must exist. It will be noticed that they have to do with language and the use of words. It is clear that the intellectual thinking we are now concerned with is verbal thinking and that the problem of the concept in this context is bound up with that of how words are used successfully. We have seen that there is a tendency to think of all conceptual thinking as verbal and to refuse the description to any thinking in which no use is made of one or the other of the historical languages, English, French, and so on. If this criterion were strictly applied it might appear necessary to rule out mathematics from conceptual thinking on the ground that its symbols were not words in any of these languages, yet it is generally assumed that mathematics must be included in conceptual thinking. Certainly non-verbal thinking in images would not be classed as conceptual thinking, nor the thinking of the craftsman at his job—using no words and yet solving his problem—of the football player on the field, the chess player at his game of chess, the architect at his plans, the military commander on the field of battle, and the map-reader poring over his maps.[1] They do not (or at any rate need not) use words and so their thinking is not, in the present sense of the word, conceptual.

To digress for a moment—the thinking which is most unlike conceptual thinking as now set forward is musical thinking. A critic recently, discussing the cases for and against the introduction of words and choral singing into symphonies, such as Beethoven's *Ninth* and Mahler's *Resurrection*, remarked: 'Words are a legitimate way of enlarging a symphony in that they add conceptual to non-conceptual thought on the subject in hand.' It is interesting to observe that the writer assumed that what differentiates conceptual thinking is the use of words and that there is non-conceptual thinking of which musical thinking is an instance. The latter is of course as significant as the former. Great composers must surely be ranked amongst the greatest

[1] H. H. Price in *Thinking and Experience*, particularly in ch. 10, shows the important part played by non-verbal thinking in our lives.

of thinkers, even though they do not think 'conceptually'. No one would deny the intellectual eminence of a Bach or a Beethoven. Theirs pre-eminently is free creation, but their thought is none the less highly disciplined; it is a structure whose logic we can study. Such a logic differs in one important aspect from the logic of conceptual thinking as the latter is usually set forth. 'True' and 'false' are not the regulative values of musical logic. Further, if the end of 'valid' thought is the attainment of truth, then musical thinking cannot properly be described as 'valid'. Nevertheless, it has its structural rules and its 'correct' procedure, as a reference to the complications of the fugue at once makes clear. It would be interesting to inquire into the common features of verbal and musical thinking. Presumably it is only in so far as there are such common features that we can hope to set out in words the logic of music. But since there are also distinguishing features it may never be possible to give in words an adequate logic of musical thought.

81. But, to return, if we wish to hold that inner accusatives do not exist we must find some alternative theory to meet the arguments which the critics have brought forward in defence of such entities. The theory will be concerned with verbal thinking only—with a sufficiently wide use of the term 'verbal' to cover the mathematical symbol as well as the word. In confining ourselves to verbal thinking, however, there is no suggestion that all thinking or even all intellectual thinking is of this kind.

The alternative theory may be put forward in the following terms. If I say I know the meaning of the word or sentence '*x*' it need not be assumed that I am then grasping an internal accusative. I know the meaning of '*x*' if, for instance, I can do any of the following. I may be able to point to an object or to an occurrence and say 'This is *x*', as when I point to a table or to an accident in the street. Or I may be able to draw it or find a photograph of it, or explain in other words what I mean by '*x*'. It is not always possible to point; it would be difficult to do so in the case of the word 'freedom'. Yet, even in this case, the conceptualist's concept is not necessary. Everyone will agree that I know the meaning of the word if I can explain it in other words. By 'freedom', I may say, I mean being able within certain limits, imposed by my own nature and by the community to which I belong, to do what I choose, 'not to be subject to the inconstant, uncertain, unknown, arbitrary will of another man'. If you are satisfied that I am not repeating these words parrot-wise, you will admit that I am using the word 'freedom' significantly and you would not normally demand proof that there exists in my mind a 'pure concept' of freedom.

If '*x*' is not a word but a sentence the position is not greatly changed. Again I may be able to explain my sentence in other words and so show that I am understanding it and using it significantly, or I can point or picture or do various other things. Ostensive definition in this case is usually not so simple as in the case, for instance, of the word 'table'. I can't point to 'The King is in Paris', but I can point to a photograph in a newspaper and you will understand that I am using the sentence significantly. Or if I say 'Primroses are out', and you ask what I mean, I can take you to a clump of newly opened primroses in a hedge and say, 'This is what I mean'. With many sentences, however, my best means of showing that I use them significantly is explaining them in other words, though I may also deduce true consequences from them or reject suggested paraphrases of them and so on.

On this theory we are not obliged to suppose that conceiving or conceptual thought is an apprehending of a concept; we think of it rather in terms of the successful and significant use of language. One may think aloud, for instance, in conversation with a friend, though this is more likely to be called conversing than thinking. But 'one's conversation with oneself'—an ancient but useful definition of thinking—is of the same nature as conversation with a friend, the art involved is the art of using language significantly.

The art of using language significantly is a difficult one to acquire; it has been said that learning to speak is still the greatest of human achievements. One observes the difficulties of small children with vocabulary and with the formation rules of the language. Learning in this case, as generally, is differentiating; at the beginning the child's language is, as G. J. Romanes once described it, 'the undifferentiated protoplasm of speech'. Few words are uttered and these have to serve many purposes; they are helped out by gestures, another way of expressing oneself much favoured at this primitive stage. The word 'Ball' may be uttered and the ball pointed to with an imploring look; the meaning obviously is 'Fetch me the ball'. With other gestures the utterance of the same word may mean 'There is the ball' or 'I don't like the ball' and so on. It is only gradually that the parts of speech are learnt, and though the child speaks in sentences from the first (for 'Ball' in the instances given is a one-word sentence) it takes time for him to learn the sentence-structure of his language.

In later childhood and early adolescence, as our mastery of the language grows, delight is taken in finding verbal equivalences, sometimes unexpected equivalences—this is largely the fun of verbal puzzles. But not only do we find verbal equivalences in the same language; we learn also equivalences in more than one language and realize that things can be said in many different languages. At the same time there is a growth in our power of description which culminates in that accurate and precise description which is definition. The art will be learnt, too, of transforming sentences into other sentences. The exact rules of this transformation, so very important in the adult's conversation with himself, become explicit, perhaps, only to a few. They are the bare bones of logic. But in so far as we carry on that process which is usually known as reasoning, we are already using these rules of transformation. And once we arrive at this stage our conversation with ourselves may develop in remarkable ways; vast and complicated structures of ratiocination become possible. We are controlled by the rules of the language and yet are free within these limits to carry on our conversation as we choose. Just as there is free play in imagination, creating new imaginative concepts, so there is free play in reasoning, creating new systems of thought in the various branches of learning which interest the human mind.

82. Here is an alternative theory of conceptual thinking. To us at the present stage of our argument its chief merit lies in the fact that it provides a description of thinking which does not necessitate belief in concepts as mental objects or internal accusatives. But does it provide a description of thinking which is adequate?

It will not do so unless one fundamental point is duly recognized and stressed. No adequate analysis even of verbal thinking is possible on a narrow verbal basis, merely in terms of the utterance of words. We must recall all that we have learnt in the course of the argument of this book. Using words in significant speech involves far more than uttering them. It may involve being disposed in certain ways as the consequence of long-forgotten experiences, or possibly consciously recalling something of the past, or testing by present perception, or explaining to oneself in other words what one takes this word to mean. It involves, too, being guided by experience, in so far as the formation and transformation rules of language are themselves products of the pressure of our environment, physical and social, upon us. Moreover, we have a measure of freedom in thinking, and though habit and custom are potent factors in our significant use of language, we can and do steer the inner conversation in certain directions, as we choose. All this is involved in conceptual thinking, so that though we hold that it can best be analysed in terms of carrying on a conversation with oneself we should not be taken to mean that the analysis of thinking will ever be a mere verbal analysis.

Bearing these provisos in mind, it seems to me that the hint contained in Plato's dictum that thinking is the soul's conversation with itself may prove valuable at this point. It provides us with an alternative theory to the conceptualist's. I believe that we are more likely to find an adequate theory of 'conceptual' thinking if we speak of it in terms of our use of significant language than if we think of it as the apprehension of entities in the mind.

Let us now return to the argument for concepts as internal accusatives and consider whether this alternative theory provides us with a safe platform upon which to face them. Thus, if we again consider the argument from translation, we may translate, on the alternative theory, without necessarily having in mind and apprehending a concept. Conceptual thinking is a conversation with oneself which one may carry forward in more than one language. If we know two languages we know how to state in the one language what we are stating in the other; this it is to know the linguistic equivalence.[1] Imagining may be an accompaniment of our conversing in the two languages, though it need not be; but since, on our present theory, apprehending a concept or an internal accusative is no part of the thinking in either language, the translating from the one language to the other proceeds without the apprehension of such concepts.

In the second place, when we say, as we frequently do, that we have 'failed to express our thoughts', do we then mean that intellectual concepts exist in our mind and that we have no words for them? I think we sometimes mean that we are imagining something and are conscious that we have not described it accurately, just as we realize that we sometimes fail to describe accurately something we are seeing. Or we may fail to express adequately in words what we now feel. The poet wishes that his words could utter 'the thoughts that arise in me', and knows that they cannot. But his 'thoughts' seem to be feelings, of grief or of nostalgia, which are too deep for utterance. Clearly such a failure is not failure to find words for pure intellectual concepts. Again, when trying to state a case, we are only too frequently aware that we are not stating it in the best possible way, and we may describe this as 'failing to express our thoughts'. But this sort of failure is surely a failure to think. For it does not seem possible to be in the state of having our

[1] To know the equivalent of an English sentence in another language is not to know word to word correlations determined by exact synonymy. There is a way of saying something in one language and a way of saying it in another, and this, rather than determinate word to word correlation, is the linguistic equivalence in question here.

thoughts clear in our mind but yet failing to express them; and the more abstract and 'intellectual' the thinking the less this seems possible. For instance, can we in thinking a mathematical theorem divorce the thought from the use of the symbols to such an extent that we can think the theorem while yet failing to find symbols to state it? When we talk of 'failing to express our thoughts' can we ever justifiably mean that we have intellectual concepts or notions in mind but lack the words or symbols to express them? We may mean that we are searching for a word and failing to find it and this searching is part of what we mean by thinking. But it would be wrong to say that in such searching we are throughout conscious of an intellectual concept, an internal entity for which the word is to stand, since the truth seems to be that we are never conscious of such a concept.

In the same way, we can talk significantly of a non-existent object without necessarily having a concept in mind. In the case of such non-existent objects as unicorns we are likely to recall pictures of them and to imagine them. But where this is not possible, we simply describe them in other words. No meaning or concept over and above this description is requisite.

Then, as to new words, it is obviously true that such words are being constantly introduced into languages; but this does not necessitate the prior existence of 'thoughts' in the sense of intellectual concepts in the mind, though it does necessitate prior thinking. The latter may or may not involve the use of imagery. In thinking about the study of the habits of living organisms I may possibly picture a biologist at work. But I need not do this; the words are significant for me without the image. And when the image is absent I do not think an intellectual concept in addition to using the words.

Again, the argument that intellectual non-imaginative thinking must have some object, and that the only possible object is the pure concept, I reject as false on the ground that the premiss is false. It is not true that thinking must have an accusative. If thinking is conversation with oneself it is admittedly conversation about something, but the something is talked about and described, not apprehended as an object. It is true that I may be carrying on a conversation with myself about something I have apprehended, for instance an object perceived, but this does not make the conversation an apprehension. And when the conversation is about non-imaginative things, abstractions, formulae, and hypothetico-deductive systems, it is not necessary for me to suppose that in each case there is a concept apprehended as the table is apprehended in perception.

Finally, 'transcendent objects' exist, if they do exist, in themselves and not in our minds. If we claim that we know them intellectually through 'pure conception' this means either that we apprehend them, and not concepts of them, by pure rational insight or, failing this, that we try to describe them to ourselves in our conversation with ourselves. In neither case is the supposition of 'pure concepts' necessary. Thus none of the five arguments necessitates the view that pure, non-imaginative concepts exist in the mind.

83. I conclude that to think of conceiving or conceptual thinking as the apprehension by pure intelligence of a special object in the mind, namely, the concept, is erroneous. Talk of concepts or notions or ideas in the mind should not deceive us nor should talk of general words as names of concepts or general ideas. The traditional conceptualists (with whom in this context we should have to include Frege and even Russell in some of his utterances) whilst distinguishing firmly between general word and proper name yet assumed that the general word still named something. It did not name any individual thing, as 'Fido' is the name of the dog, but it named the concept or general idea.

We reject this assumption. We need not suppose that whenever a general word is being used it is used to name something or to refer to something. As has been seen general words can be used in expressions, such as 'the tree in the middle of the lawn', which are used to refer to individual objects, but general words have other uses, such as in characterizing, describing, and grouping. We err if we begin to talk of the general word as being used always to refer to something, for instance, the word 'tree' to the concept *tree*, and the word 'democracy' to the concept *democracy*.

Since today we are very conscious of this pitfall we tend to speak less of 'concepts' and more of 'having concepts', less of what is conceived and more of the conceiving. This tendency is strengthened by the view we take of how we come to conceive colours, houses, dogs, and such creatures of the imagination as unicorns and cats with webbed feet. Having such concepts, we think, is the outcome of experience and memory, both active memory and that other form of memory which is dispositional retention. That we have the concept is revealed by our behaviour and particularly by what we say. These empirical and imaginative factors count far less in the more intellectual forms of conceiving (although a case might be made for the view that they are never entirely absent), for in these forms what predominates is the use of language in the conversation and argument with oneself which is intellectual thinking. But this conversation with oneself presupposes those dispositions or habits without which the thinking could not take place. It presupposes, on the one hand, prior experiences of the physical world and of the social world around us; and, on the other, habits which have to do with language itself. We have to learn the syntax, we must know how to use operators such as 'if, then', 'and', 'not', and so on.

This is using language, but this too is verbal thinking. They are not two separate processes. Further, though such thinking leans heavily on habit both in our expectations of physical and social occurrence, and in our use of language to express and think about these expectations, such habits, and the schematic standards they provide almost without our knowing, cannot of themselves explain the whole of the thinking. For each thinker guides and steers his thought; he is free to evolve new methods of procedure and to follow new inquiries and as he moves forward to the more abstract and hypothetical sciences so the dominance of experience and custom is lessened and the presence of the controlling, advancing, speculating, and deducing mind is everywhere more obvious.

84. Such a view of conceptual thinking is to be preferred to the traditional conceptualist view of it as an apprehension of internal accusatives and of the relations between them. Its accents are Humean; they re-echo that brilliant analysis of the abstract idea which one finds in the *Treatise*.[1] Granting that the concept is not to be regarded as an internal accusative, how then, on the new theory, are we to think of it? It is best thought of, we are told, as a mental tendency or an attitude or again as a capacity. Not that we are ever directly conscious of this capacity itself; we know it only through observing its manifestations, through hearing a child, for instance, say correctly 'This is a grass-snake', or observing a person's use of the word 'democracy'. In such a case we are not confronted directly with the tendency or the capacity, for it is hidden from us, but we take it to be there to account for the observable behaviour. Nor do we introspect our own attitudes, tendencies, or capacities; all we can do is to infer their existence.

But though the new theory is to be preferred to the old it is not, in my opinion, without its difficulties. The concept is a capacity or a tendency or an attitude (not that these words are synonyms but they have been used from time to time in setting forth the theory along with other words such as disposition or propensity). But can we in fact identify concept with capacity? Now if a concept is a capacity in any sense, it is clear that it is not a capacity in that sense that would permit us to infer that any and every capacity is a concept. No one presumably would want to say that a physical capacity is a concept. Obviously the capacity in question must be a mental capacity. But can we identify concept with *mental* capacity without qualification? For instance, would anyone wish to say that the mental capacity to feel anger is a concept? The concept, it would seem, must be a special kind of mental capacity. But what kind? Should we say that it is a cognitive capacity as contrasted with a capacity to feel an emotion? But again, is every cognitive capacity a concept? A person has the capacity to see a point in an argument. Is this cognitive capacity to be identified with a concept?

[1] Cf. Ch. IV above.

We want to avoid saying that the concept is an object that we grasp, either an objective entity subsisting in a Meinong world or a subjective internal accusative. To avoid saying this we seek to view the concept not as a *cognoscendum* but as part of the mind's own activity. The concept is a pattern of thinking rather than an object thought. Yet we also say that the mind makes concepts, and we seem thereby to distinguish between the concept made and the capacity to make it. Does this contradict the theory that a concept is a mental capacity? In any case, if we say that a concept is a capacity can we sensibly say that a person makes concepts which are his capacities? We might try to think of him as consciously bringing into being new patterns of behaviour. But would he not then be conscious of the pattern which he is bringing into being, with the pattern, it might be argued, simply another internal accusative?

The new theory that a concept is a capacity or a disposition or, again, an attitude requires considerable further clarification. My own view is that the theory of concepts still needs, as it always has needed, the notion of what used to be called 'a cognitive content'. The question is whether we can retain the notion without thinking of this 'content' as an internal accusative. Can we retain it but think of it in terms of the new theory? This seems to me possible. Consider the concept of *ultramarine*. To have the concept is to be able to recognize ultramarine objects as ultramarine, to classify objects according as they are or are not ultramarine, and so on. It is not to grasp an internal object which is the concept. None the less it is legitimate to argue that there is a core or a nucleus here, namely, the abstracted colour, and that the conceiving develops around it. The colour image itself (whatever account we give of it) is not the concept. And even if the image were thought of as some sort of entity in the mind, the concept would not be an entity. Around this image have gathered, in the course of our mental development, those capacities and tendencies which enable us to 'have the concept of *ultramarine*'. So too around the fuzzier image of the grass-snake have gathered those propensities of the mind which enable us to recognize grass-snakes when we see them.

The same solution, it seems to me, could apply to the problem of the concept in verbal thinking, but here instead of looking to images we must look to words, to general words, either single words or phrases, that is to say to general locutions. Not that the word is a concept, any more than an image is a concept, but what has gathered around a word or phrase in our experience is such that we can think successfully using the word. To illuminate the role of the word in conceiving we may recall the manner in which the general word is used as predicate term. We may view it with Frege in terms of the mathematical function, unsaturated, in need of argument. With the help of these analogies of saturation and being in need of (which must not be pressed too far) the difference between the open and the closed sentence can be made clear; in the open sentence '. . . is tall' the predicate term needs completion. Now the way in which we can use a general locution such as '. . . is tall' as an open sentence seems to me to provide a clue for understanding the role of the concept in verbal thinking. The general locution '. . . is a democracy' is not itself the concept of *democracy*, but one has the concept if one can use this locution successfully. The general locution or open sentence is the core corresponding to the image in imaginative thinking. The successful use of general words involves the ability to describe and define, and behind this ability lie the empirical and the linguistic dispositions talked of earlier. What the mind has retained is being brought into the service of the conceiving present in using the locution '. . . is a democracy'. The concept, that is to say, in this context is not the general locution or the open sentence; it is rather the general locution *plus* all that is essential to enable us to use this locution successfully.

Such a view of the concept is far removed from the theory that it is an entity in the mind, an idea that we apprehend. But it goes further too than the assertion that the concept is either a disposition or a capacity. Nor can we identify a concept with a logical predicate. To understand what a concept is we should rather look to the accretions around images in our imagist thinking and around general words or open sentences in the more verbal kinds of thinking.

XII

A THEORY OF UNIVERSALS

85. After the examination of common quality, disposition, and concept we now find ourselves in a position to offer a theory of universals. It will be one resting on the discussions of the previous chapters, discussions which have ranged over a wide field. We may thus hope to be saved from basing the theory on too narrow a foundation. Often when some one fact or a few facts seem to point in the direction of one of the traditional theories, this is at once assumed to be the true theory. And this procedure is particularly dangerous if, as is usually the case, one's theory of knowledge and one's philosophy in general rest on this assumption from that point forward. Thus the conviction that the common quality is concrete may cause a philosopher to jump at realism; a feeling that we are guided in thinking by elements not given in perception may lead to conceptualism. Recently the drift has been towards nominalism. But it does not appear to be a nominalism conscious of itself in any positive sense; indeed, it is most difficult to find any positive statement of contemporary nominalism. What is attractive in it is its denials, its criticisms of other theories of universals. Yet it is dangerous to assume that nominalism is true because realism and conceptualism are false. If we are to accept it we must accept it in itself as a positive theory which we have considered and understood.

After taking as broad a view as possible of all the issues involved I find at the end of this study that I cannot accept any one of the traditional theories and I must explain first why I think it necessary to reject them. In speaking of the traditional theories I mean Aristotelian realism, conceptualism, and nominalism, omitting realism of the *ante rem* kind. The latter has been discussed already and, except possibly in the moral field where it may be contended that it alone does justice to the facts, the theory is hardly relevant to present discussions and need not be re-examined here.

86. The case against Aristotelian realism is a strong one. On this theory a universal is something we discover; it is part of the objective world of nature. Not that it is an object in nature, one amongst other objects, as is the chair or table; it is rather a common quality *in rebus*, a quality of this table, for instance, which is also a quality of that table and of other tables, and is as real as the tables themselves. Common relations, too, may be said to be universals in this sense. Many of these universals may be discovered to go together; for instance, the qualities *a*, *b*, and *c* go together in the object *O*, and we may discover this combination of universal qualities. Knowledge of universals in this sense gives us a basis for classification. Things which have certain qualities or relations in common are perceived to form a class which we may know, and we may further discover wider classes of which this class is a member, as when we find many species in one genus.

Such is the position of the Aristotelian realist; but it is at once disturbing to find that though the realist ought on this account to limit his universals to qualities and relations, he never does so. Man, it appears, is a universal, as well as white or triangular; and yet man is neither a common quality nor a common relation. This apparent inconsistency arouses suspicion; it suggests that the realists' original position is not one that can be sustained, and this is indeed the case.

Two major criticisms of realism can be made, and I shall limit myself to these. In the first place, the realist holds, and holds rightly if our previous argument is correct, that there are discoverable common qualities and relations; but he then concludes that all universals are either such common qualities or common relations. Yet, for instance, the quality human is not discovered as ultramarine is discovered. It is simply not true that all men have this quality, human, in common, so that we can observe it and discover it in observing them. Nor is it the case that we discover qualities *a*, *b*, and *c*, combined together to make up the complex quality human, in all men. Most men are two-legged, but some have lost a leg. Most men are rational, but some are idiots. If we say that to be human is to be two-legged and rational we are stating a standard or an ideal, what ought to be the case; we certainly do not discover two-leggedness and rationality as a common quality or combination of common qualities in all men. The realist account of these matters is misleading.

Logically it is not impossible for all men to share a quality by virtue of which they could be classified as men, an *x* which would belong to them all as the colour ultramarine is shared by these objects now before me. But it is clear that we do not discover this quality in experience. Yet we do speak of human as a quality, and the sentence '*A* is human' is quite significant. It is also a universal, at least in this sense that we can say '*B*, *C*, *D* . . . are human'. It would thus appear that some universals are not discovered. The quality human or being human is apparently a quality for which we ourselves are partly responsible. We frame it out of material derived from experience and on the suggestion of experience; nevertheless it is *post rem* and, to a certain degree, 'the workmanship of the mind'. Consequently, we must deny the realist position that all universals are discovered, for if human is a universal then it certainly is not discovered. This will hold too of the universal man. There can be no objection to this universal on a *post rem* theory, but it is palpably neither a discovered common quality nor a common relation. The universal man is certainly suggested by experience but yet it is determined finally in respect both to its content and to its limits by the thinker himself who uses the universal.

The second main objection to the realist thesis is the following. Realism assumes that classification is only possible on the basis of discoverable, identical qualities or relations *in rebus*. In fact, this is not the case. If we were confined to identical qualities and relations as bases for classification, classification even of natural objects into species and genera would have been impossible. For instance, it is this characteristic of being human, which is not a discoverable common quality or relation, which determines the class man. The classification is suggested by experience and is in this sense founded on the real, but it is not based on the discovery of identical qualities. Our primitive classifications and much adult classification, as we have seen, rest not on the conscious observation of identical qualities, but on a familiarity with the recurring elements of experience which leaves us disposed to group in certain ways. On the other hand, a Linnaeus will take greater care in classifying than the ordinary man and he will state explicitly the characteristics which he uses as bases for his classification, but these characteristics again are frequently not the common, identical qualities of the realist. For resemblances guide us in classifying as much as identities, and they bring in a more extensive field of objects. Obviously, in the practical affairs of life a loose classification of objects that resemble one another without, possibly, resembling one another closely, is frequently very useful. The demand for close resemblance, not to say identity, may prove a hindrance.

If the realist replies that all observation of resemblance presupposes awareness of identical qualities, since things resemble only in so far as they have qualities in common, this reply, as we have seen, is of doubtful validity. In some cases we do discover identical qualities which provide a foundation for the resemblance; in others we entirely fail to do so, and we have no right to assume that they must be there. Moreover, it is not things only which resemble one another but qualities themselves resemble, and resemble in circumstances which make it absurd to speak of an identity as the basis of the resemblances. We certainly cannot admit that we observe resemblances, and so frame our universals, only in so far as we discover identical qualities.

Thus the realist is at fault both in holding that all universals are discovered identical qualities and in supposing that classification is only possible when the characteristics determining the class are such identical qualities. This criticism, in my opinion, finally refutes Aristotelian realism and makes any rehabilitation of this theory impossible. Certainly no rehabilitation will be attempted here. Nevertheless, two points should be made. First, the criticism, while it refutes the traditional Aristotelian realism, in no way establishes either conceptualism or nominalism. Secondly, granted that the arguments prove that certain universals are not identical qualities nor complexes of such qualities, it yet does not follow that there are no universals of this kind. On the contrary, the evidence is plain, as we have seen in discussing common qualities, that identical qualities can be discovered by us, and it may well be the case that these are sometimes what we mean when we speak of universals.

87. In turning to conceptualism we recall the argument of the previous chapter. There we sought to feel our way towards a more satisfactory theory of concepts than the one provided by the traditional or classical conceptualists. The latter, the conceptualism for instance of Locke, is hardly a living theory and there are few philosophers who would subscribe to it. As we have seen, it leads to scepticism about human knowledge. It also leads to a deep suspicion of abstraction and a growing emphasis on the value of 'the bare, naked particular'. We begin, however, with this traditional theory and ask what these conceptualists meant to convey by their doctrine that the universal was the concept.

The answer they gave is clear—up to a point. The concept (or idea) was what was 'before the mind', that of which the mind was aware; at the same time it was not an object independent of the mind. In saying, therefore, that the universal was the concept they were saying, in the first place, that the universal was not part of the concrete, real world. Concrete particular things alone existed and there was no universal amongst them. But, in the second place, though the concept was dependent on the mind, it was none the less an entity, that is to say, an abstract entity. It was a cognized object. Thus the theory that the universal was the concept was for them definite and precise, since the concept itself was precisely conceived.

But it was precise so long as one did not probe too deeply. As has been seen, the empiricists themselves were uneasy about one or two points in the theory. First, if all things are particulars, are not ideas particular too? For consistency's sake, should not one say that what one was aware of was a particular idea? Could one then think of this particular idea as in some way representative of many and so give it a sort of universality? But this suggestion considerably clouds the previously clear theory. Secondly, the conceptual entity has not quite the same objectivity as a particular, concrete object. It is mind's creation. It is abstracted, possibly compounded, a complex construction of the mind. This makes it very different from the concrete object independent of mind. Is it then proper that we should speak of it as an entity? Yet if the concept is not an entity the traditional theory ceases to be clear and precise and becomes something vague instead.

But, if difficulties of this sort arose, the traditional conceptualists were still in a better position to make sense of the theory that universals were concepts than later conceptualists have been. At least, a case could be made that it makes sense to speak of ideal objects of awareness as *universalia post rem*. But suppose we adopt the view that concepts are mental capacities, can we then sensibly talk of these capacities as *universalia post rem*? To defend the view that a universal is a mental faculty would be a formidable task. If, on the other hand, we think of conceiving in terms of the use of general words, we might be tempted to say that the universal was the general word, but in that case conceptualism would be no different from nominalism, whereas the conceptualist has always insisted that it is different.

The conceptualist of course does not say that the concept is the general word. I have suggested that the safest way to state the theory of verbal concepts today is the following: the concept is the general word plus all the accretions necessary for its successful use. Now where, on such a theory, are we to find the universal? If the accretions are thought of as mental dispositions or mental capacities they scarcely provide us with the universals we are searching for, if as internal accusatives we are back with the traditional theory. Perhaps we should conclude that contemporary conceptualism, critical of the traditional doctrine, cannot provide us with a theory of universals and that it is misguided to seek for any such theory in it. And if we are speaking of a precise, clear theory this seems to me to be the case. On the other hand, it is true that we do use the general word successfully and that through its use we know how to apply a predicate which can characterize more than one object. Our successful use of general words too presupposes—as does our use of imagery in thinking—that we possess principles or rules of grouping and are applying them. Reflection on these phenomena may help to provide us with a theory of universals, but the one definite theory that conceptualism has put forward, namely, that the universal is the internal accusative, is to be rejected.

88. Now traditionally the only theory which remains is nominalism. But we should not be justified in assuming that since realism and conceptualism have both been shown to be false, nominalism must be true. We must examine the nominalist case in itself.

Yet, as has been seen, it is not easy to find a positive statement of nominalism; it is easy enough to trace 'nominalist' tendencies in contemporary thought, and it is not difficult to find out what is denied. Yet the doctrine is rarely set forward positively. One of the earliest attempts to do so in modern philosophy, that of Hobbes, is also one of the neatest: 'there being nothing in the world universal but names'. This means presumably that, for instance, each cat is an individual creature; it has individual, particular qualities. The universal is neither a common quality in cats, not a natural class, nor a concept. It is the 'name' or general word 'cat', and we should not seek beyond the verbal for any other universal.

Such nominalism has sometimes been interpreted to mean that the one thing cats have in common is the name 'cat', but this account of it makes it at once absurd. To begin with, it is not the case that all cats share this name. Only those cats which are spoken of in English are called 'cats'. If we followed this interpretation strictly the universal 'cat' and the universal 'chat', being different words, would be different universals. In the second place, if it be granted that cats really have one quality in common, namely, having the name 'cat', there seems to be no inherent objection to their having other qualities in common, for instance, a liking for fish. The door is open for the realist.

The nominalist, however, would no doubt object to this interpretation. If we do deny the theory of common qualities, he would say, we do deny it, and two cats must not be supposed to have a common quality in being both called 'cat'. What Hobbes really meant was that universals only come into being with classifying, and that classifying is a verbal technique. In the physical world each object is individual and different from every other. Yet in using a general word we know how to speak of many of them at one and the same time. We have learnt the use of language and part of that learning consists in knowing how to use general words. Now it is here and here only that the universal comes into being, when we classify, using general words for the purpose. It thus belongs essentially to the verbal.

In examining this theory it must first be admitted that the nominalist has the right to use the term 'universal' as he chooses and may use it as a synonym for the general word, and only in this way. This is a matter of convention, and though it is true that normally the word has been used in other ways, yet it may be thus used if the nominalist chooses. But when he goes on to imply that classifying is merely using general words and is solely a verbal matter he is surely on less firm ground. One would have thought it obvious that a classifying is a grouping and grouping is not the same thing as using a general word. Grouping may well proceed without the use of a general word. Very young children group things together manipulatively before they begin to speak. Ribot's deaf-mutes grouped things together though they had no words. Normally we group things together because we discover recurrences. In any case, grouping is not just using a general word. Yet this appears to be the nominalist position as now interpreted, and it is obviously false.

But the nominalist might argue that he is prepared to admit a grouping other than the using of the general word, as long as it is understood that the grouping is wholly arbitrary and that it is not the consequence of the observation of recurrences in nature.

He could not admit the latter without giving the case away to the realists. But we may group things together arbitrarily, he might say. Take any four objects; there is nothing to prevent our grouping them together into a class and now giving them a name. The universal would come into being only in the classifying; no recurrence, no common quality and no resemblance between the objects, would be presupposed.

Now it is a question whether we can ever find four objects of which we can say, 'These have nothing whatsoever in common'; but even if we could it would be agreed that any grouping on this basis would be most unusual. And yet the nominalist, to maintain his position, has to hold that *all* grouping is of this kind. He denies that there is any non-verbal universal element, acquaintance with which guides us in our grouping. But this is an impossible position. In normal grouping we are guided by observing recurrences in our experience and by the empirical suggestion of natural sorts. We did not entirely arbitrarily decide on the constituent members of the cat-group. We might conceivably have done so. A linguistic dictator could enact that henceforth the word 'cat' was to be the name for all the objects that he had put together at a certain place, and perhaps along with creatures which we now call 'cats' he had also included objects that we now call 'bicycles' and 'tomatoes'. We should then have to call them all 'cats'. But this would prove nothing about the way we have in fact come to use the word 'cat' and nothing about universals. The nominalist has to disprove that there are *universalia in rebus* and our ordinary usage of the term 'cat' suggests that there are. For ordinarily the entities covered by the term 'cat' have not been determined by any such arbitrary fiat, but by experience. We have become accustomed to the recurrence of a creature that is domesticated, purrs, likes fish, has fur, and so on. Our classifying is guided by the recurrences. It will not help us to ignore these recurrences or to refuse to call them universals. Yet if we recognize them, nominalism as a positive theory is no longer possible.

The nominalist might seek to defend himself in still another way. Do we not, he might ask, use words significantly in conceptual thinking without having in mind any of the realist's recurrences, and does not this fact support the nominalist case? All we make use of in these circumstances is the word itself, and if there is a universal present in our thought it must be verbal. But this again, we must reply, gives no real support to a thorough-going nominalism. We may use such a word as 'cat' in imageless thinking but obviously not all its uses are of this kind, and even when it is so used we use the word significantly in speaking and thinking because we have learnt from experience how the word should be used, though we do not now explicitly recall these experiences. Thus it would be erroneous in the extreme to suppose that such occasional uses of words in imageless thinking justify the nominalist thesis.

Finally, it must be admitted that there are words in use which operate, as it were, solely within the verbal, and which do not presuppose recurrences or common qualities, for instance, the words 'but' and 'or'. Yet the presence of such words in speech is hardly a justification of nominalism, for the nominalist would certainly not be prepared to admit that his theory applies to such words only, if it applies to them at all. Sometimes, it is true, nominalism is presented as if it were simply the theory that words can be used without reference to a world other than the verbal. But a moment's reflection will show that this doctrine, which I in no way dispute, is not a theory of universals.

To sum up, if nominalism is the doctrine that the members of a class share one thing in common and one thing only, the name, then its absurdity soon becomes apparent. If, on the other hand, it is the assertion that classifying is a purely verbal process and involves no prior knowledge of common features or relations which are non-verbal, then it is false. On either interpretation strict nominalism seems wholly unacceptable.

89. But, if nominalism on either of these interpretations is rejected, it must not be assumed that every doctrine which has been described as 'nominalist' must thereby be rejected. On the contrary these doctrines may well be accepted even when nominalism is denied.

For instance, the 'elimination' or 'abolition' of the class by the authors of *Principia Mathematica* is sometimes supposed to establish nominalism. But this is not so. The claim is made that classes can be eliminated in favour of quantification and propositional functions, and there is a sense in which this is true. But this reduction in no way establishes nominalism. For, as I ventured to point out in my British Academy Lecture,[1] in 'For all *x*'s, if *x* is human then *x* is mortal' we are still left with the universals human and mortal and there is no suggestion that these universals are 'abolished'. That is to say, if *Principia Mathematica* 'abolishes' the class it leaves the problem of universals very much where it finds it. It certainly offers no nominalist theory of, for instance, the universal human.

There are other doctrines described as nominalist which a realist could accept without giving up his realism. Indeed, the present tendency to describe all philosophers who are not 'platonist' as 'nominalist' paradoxically puts many who are realists, but not platonists, into the 'nominalist' camp.[2] Even 'the renunciation of abstract entities' which was the mark of nominalism according to the celebrated article 'Steps towards a Constructive Nominalism' by Quine and Goodman in 1947[3] is something of which a realist might well approve. This article opened, 'We do not believe in abstract entities. No one supposes that abstract entities—classes, relations, properties, etc.—exist in space-time; but we mean more than this. We renounce them altogether.' Unfortunately, no analysis is provided of the key phrase 'abstract entities', though classes, relations, and properties are said to be instances. No one, it is said, supposes that they exist in space-time but, unlike the authors, most people apparently suppose that they do exist—not in space-time but,

[1] *Our Knowledge of Universals*, 1945, § 4.

[2] This regettable tendency in modern logic and philosophy leads to considerable confusion. In his Geneva lecture (1934) entitled 'On Platonism in Mathematics', Paul Bernays describes Hilbert's axioms system (as contrasted with Euclid's) as 'platonist'. This may possibly be the source of the modern dichotomy. It would be good if logicians reconsidered their use of 'platonist' and 'nominalist'. For Bernays's lecture cf. *L'enseignement mathematique*, vol. 34 (1935), pp. 52–69, translated for Bencarref and Putnam, *Philosophy of Mathematics*, 1964, pp. 274–86.

[3] *Journal of Symbolic Logic*, vol. 12, pp. 105–22.

presumably, as objects for the mind, as Lockean internal accusatives. But if 'renouncing abstract entities' is renouncing internal accusatives, and if all who do renounce them are nominalists, then many realists are nominalists; for a realist may certainly reject the doctrine of internal accusatives and yet remain a realist.

Both writers have moved away from this position since 1947; Quine does not consider himself a nominalist,[1] and Goodman, though still a nominalist, has varied his emphasis. He now holds 'that the nominalist insists on the world being described as composed of individuals, that to describe the world as composed of individuals is to describe it as made up of entities no two of which have the same content, and that this in turn is to describe it by means of a system for which no two distinct entities have exactly the same atoms'.[2] Yet nominalism in this sense too might be accepted by a realist. Certainly it is good Aristotelian realist doctrine that what exist are individuals; further the realist accepts the identity of indiscernibles, if this is Goodman's point, from which it follows that no two distinct individuals can be identical in all respects. If the point is, however, that individuals can never have anything in common then Aristotelian realists would reject this theory. But it is not clear whether Goodman is saying this. If he is, what account would he give of the quality of *ultramarine*? The empirical evidence is that we have in the ultramarine of these two pieces of silk an instance of an identical quality in the Aristotelian realist sense.

Unlike Goodman, Quine is prepared to recognize classes. He admits the difficulties, particularly the paradoxes that follow if we do recognize them. 'Yet the admission of classes as values of variables of quantification brings power that is not lightly to be surrendered.'[3] What he is not prepared to recognize is the attribute, and he refuses to recognize it because of its 'referential opacity' and even more because of our inability to identify 'attributes attributed by two open sentences'. The

[1] Cf. *Word and Object*, p. 243, n. 5.

[2] Bencareff and Putnam, *Philosophy of Mathematics*, 1964, p. 203. Reprinted from Goodman's *The Problem of Universals*, 1956.

[3] *Words and Objects*, p. 266.

'referential opacity' of most attributes must be granted, though in defence of Aristotelian realism the case of *ultramarine* should again be studied. It must also be granted that anyone who looks at human thinking from the standpoint of modern logical theory finds difficulty with intensional entities. Yet in my view classes presuppose attributes; to admit classes is to presuppose rules or principles for classifying, and these principles I take to be the attributes and the universals which we speak of in terms of general locutions or open sentences.

90. We must now consider the theory which emerges from our discussions up to the present, but before doing so a word should be said about certain problems which I take to be, in this connexion, secondary, but which are sometimes held to be central. It is occasionally argued or implied that the problem of universals consists (*a*) in distinguishing between token words and type words, (*b*) in distinguishing between determinables and determinates, or (*c*) in making clear the nature of quantification. These three problems are important, particularly the third, and require attention; but in my view the problem of universals is different from all three and is not to be identified with any one of them.

Thus while it is necessary to recognize the difference between token and type words it is surely obvious that the key to the understanding of universals is not to be found in the recognition of this difference. The distinction may be illustrated in the following way. If we confine ourselves for the moment to written, rather than spoken, words then the word 'problem', let us say, occurs more than once on this page. Each appearance is a token word and is numerically different from every other appearance of this word. None the less the printed shape of the various token words is the same and this enables us to use it as a type word. It need not be identically the same, similarity is enough. If we now proceed to say that though there are many appearances of the word 'problem' on this page yet it is one and the same word that appears, we are then thinking of the type word. This distinction, it should be noted, applies to proper names as much as to general words; we can distinguish between the token word 'Peter' and the type word. And this fact at once suggests that we should not expect to find here any special insight into our use of general words. It is important for any language theory that the same shape can recur, and that we know how to make use of this recurrence. The recurrence of shapes is itself an instance of a universal, in one sense of that term. But the simple distinction between token word and type word throws no light on the nature of the universal. No doubt if we began to inquire into the use of the type word we should find universals involved in some cases of its use, but that inquiry would take us farther than the distinction itself.

In the same way the distinction between determinables and determinates is relevant to the problem of universals, though again I cannot agree that making this distinction solves the problem. With occasional straining, it is possible no doubt to speak of each and every quality as a determinable and a determinate; for instance, colour is a determinable and red and blue are determinates, or, again, red is a determinable and the various shades of red are determinates. Relations do not lend themselves so easily to this treatment, though we may say, for instance, that being to the left of is a determinate of the determinable, spatial relation. And we can always say that such and such a relation is a determinate of the determinable, relation. In the case of things, men, tables, dragons, the division would presumably follow the lines of the traditional genus-species division. In this way it might be possible to speak of all universals as either determinables or determinates. But I should still hold that the distinction presupposes universals and does not itself provide a solution of the problem of universals. For if we consider a determinate, say ultramarine, the realization that it is a determinate is subsequent to the realization that ultramarine is a common quality, yet our awareness of the universal in this case is one with the latter realization. I am here speaking of the distinction in empiricist terms. Admittedly, if it was meant that we know the final nature of things, knowing that the real consists of so many determinables which are the ultimate metaphysical forms or principles explanatory of all being, this doctrine would certainly be of the first importance and could not be said to be secondary. But, presumably, those who draw our attention to this distinction do not do so because they have metaphysical knowledge of this kind, but because experience has taught them that some qualities lend themselves to the determinable-determinate distinction. Clearly in their case the solution of the problem of universals cannot be identified with the making of this distinction. The same holds true of the distinction between species and genus.

Thirdly, I believe it a mistake to identify the theory of universals with quantification theory, that is to say, with the logic of the use of such quantifiers as 'all', 'some', and 'any'. It is true that the language of traditional logic itself sometimes suggests this identification. In particular, when the quantifier 'all' is used in a sentence, as in 'All men are mortal', the proposition is traditionally called a 'universal proposition'. Such language makes it easy to suppose that the problem of universals is one about our use of 'all' and is related to the problem of numbers, so that mathematical logicians alone can solve it. *In my opinion quantification presupposes the universal.* Not that it is necessary for the logician to set down a theory of universals before explaining quantification, although perhaps it would be best if he did proceed in that order. Most often, however, he assumes universals without presenting a theory of universals. To resolve 'All men are mortal' into 'For all *x*'s, if *x* is human then *x* is mortal' is to explain the quantification with the help of the variable *x*, but also with the presupposition of universals, namely, those involved in the use of the general words 'human' and 'mortal'. The fact that resolution is possible in this way makes it clear that the theory of universals cannot be identified with quantification theory, though the two are related. No doubt a thorough and complete quantification theory would include a solution of the problem of universals, but it would also contain over and above this solution, the explanation of our use of such words as 'all' and 'some'. This is a problem pre-eminently for the mathematical logician and is bound up with theory of number.

91. I turn then to the final question: what sort of theory of universals is suggested by the argument of this book? The approach has been from the study of thinking and it has become increasingly clear that our adult human thinking is possible only because of our ability to speak in general terms. It is also clear that part of the explanation of how we are able to use general words successfully lies in a natural fact, and it is with this fact that I begin.

The world around us, as revealed in experience, is populated by beings and things which, while being individual and distinct, have yet much in common. Not only in our thinking but in our general behaviour our conduct rests upon the assumption that individual beings, for instance, individual human beings, have many features in common. The tailor, cutting out ready-made suits, knows the general run of men's sizes; the teacher has a rough idea of the capacities of next year's freshmen; and the mother who believes her baby to be unique, as he certainly is, reads with avidity the nursing-book which is written on the assumption that all babies are more or less alike. So, too, with animals, plants, and all living things; we see the individuals but find in them common features; and it is these common features which concern us in our zoological, veterinary, and botanical sciences. This then is the fact with which we start; our thinking rests in part on the observation of recurrences. Here is part explanation of our successful use of general words. The same features recur in different individual beings and individual things and we are aware of this fact.

By universals, then, I mean, in the first place, recurrences found in the natural world. To that extent the theory here put forward is realist. In dealing with universals we are not confined to a world of imaginative or logical constructions and are certainly not concerned with words only. On the contrary, our thinking rests upon foundations empirically given; it is because our experience is what it is that we think as we do and use general words in the way we do. We are able to say that an object we saw yesterday was ultramarine, and that this present object is ultramarine, and that possibly the next object we shall see will be ultramarine, because ultramarine is a shade which recurs in the natural world observed by us. Accordingly when we speak and think, using such general words as 'ultramarine', we are not turning away from the real, that is to say, from the experienced real, but are speaking and thinking about it.

As we examine these recurrences more closely, however, we see that they are of two sorts, identities and resemblances. We may first consider identities. In a previous chapter I have shown that we can quite safely speak of identities in this context, and that we fail to do justice to the facts if we speak of resemblance or similarity only, even of close similarity. The colour of this postage stamp does not resemble the colour of the second stamp but is identical with it; to speak of resemblance here would be to speak falsely. We do observe identical qualities and there are *universalia in rebus*. These qualitative identities are one and the same not only through a passage of time, as a thing may be said to be identical with itself, but also as contemporaneously present at different places. This is their distinguishing feature: one and the same shade of red is here *and* there, in two places at one and the same time.[1]

On considering this matter, however, as has been seen, a very important and very necessary qualification must be borne in mind. The identity is an *observed* identity and nothing more is being claimed for it. Admittedly, what I now take to be identical might turn out to be distinguishable, given more acute sensory powers. There is the disturbing fact that occasionally we find ourselves unable to distinguish the shade *a* from the shade *b* and the shade *b* from the shade *c* and yet we can distinguish between the shades *a* and *c*. What is experienced as indistinguishable is clearly not necessarily identical in the metaphysical sense ('really' identical). None the less, some queer results follow if real identity of quality be denied; for instance, there would be, apparently, as many shades of colour as there are coloured things and this certainly appears absurd. However, fortunately,

[1] Blanshard, *Reason and Analysis*, p. 393, refers to such universals as 'specific universals'.

it is not necessary for us to come to any final decision on this metaphysical point. The question whether there are or are not metaphysically identical qualities does not affect our theory of universals. The latter begins with the observing of qualities which, so far as we can see, are identical. When we say that these are *universalia in rebus* it is understood that the *res* in question are things experienced by us.

Qualities are not the only discoverable identities, there are also relations. The relation of being to the left of, for instance, is one and the same relation in contexts A and B, and no language except that of identity fits the case. To take another example, this line stands perpendicularly upon the other line, so forming a right angle. That relation is precisely the same wherever I find it. The importance of such identical relations as these in our thinking need not be emphasized. Unlike identical qualities they are not universals *in*, but universals *between*, things, not *in rebus* but *inter res*. Yet they are in the world experienced by us, quite as concretely as are the qualities. They too are discovered. It is true that just as in the case of qualities I may see two qualities to be identically the same but later by looking more closely am able to distinguish between them, so I may see one line to fall perpendicularly on another, thus forming a right angle, but later discover, for example, on measuring the angle with a protractor, that though it looks a right angle yet the protractor shows it to fall short of 90 degrees. But the fact remains that I began by seeing one line fall perpendicularly on another. Here is a relation which is constantly recurring in my experience; I look around me at this moment and see many lines falling perpendicularly on other lines in this room. Here is the recurrence and, in that sense of the term, the universal, though not a recurring, identical quality but a recurring, identical relation. So universals are identical relations as well as identical qualities.

92. Now in so far as universals are identities of this kind there can be no objection to speaking of them as objects of which we are aware; that is to say, they are recurrences which we observe. Having observed them we know how to use our observations as

principles in accordance with which we group and classify. On the basis of this classification we know what to expect if something is said to be so and so and we learn how to use the relevant general words significantly. The tokens, the sounds used in spoken language and the shapes in written, are a convention of the language used, but our successful use of them rests on our acquaintance with natural recurrences.

But this is only a beginning. The next step in the theory comes with the realization that the recurrences examined thus far, namely, identical qualities and relations, are not the only recurrences in our experience. Certain qualities are similar without being identical and the similarities recur. For instance, shades of blue which are not identical but similar constantly recur and we learn to speak of the colour 'blue', covering by this token all shades of blue, as a class of colours. Behind the use of 'ultramarine' lies the observation of the identical shade, but behind that of 'blue' lies the observation of identical shades together with the observation of likenesses between them. In the same way certain relations are similar to one another and the recurrence of these similarities suggests new classifications. But once similarities are introduced we cannot stop with qualities and relations. For *things* are similar, and we classify on the basis of the similarity of things. Men are roughly alike, so are the different cats we meet, and the different spades we see. And not only things but processes and situations are similar. Once again parliamentary candidates seek to win our favour, once again the postman walks up the path or the sun sinks over the horizon. The recurrence of these similarities is as useful a basis for classification as is the recurrence of identical qualities and relations. Here too are universals. Perhaps it is not so easy to pinpoint them in this case as in the case of ultramarine. They are recurring likenesses. Sometimes, as in the case of the family face, we are aware of 'overall' likenesses between objects though we cannot single out any identical (or even resembling) quality which they all possess. But they are amongst the likenesses we observe and use, along with other likenesses, as empirically based principles of grouping. So recurring similarities as well as identities are universals, and we consciously use them to classify and order our experience, and are thus able to use a further set of general words successfully.

To hold that the recurring similarity is a universal, along with the recurring identical quality or identical relation, is to go beyond Aristotelian realism. Nor can the latter be maintained by the argument that all similarities must rest in the end on identities, for this, as we have seen, is not the case. Sometimes, it is true, two objects are similar because they have identical qualities; at other times we find no identical qualities and yet the objects are similar. Moreover, simple qualities can be similar where there is no possibility of an underlying identical quality. It follows that a recurring similarity that does not, so far as we can see, rest upon an identity, can none the less be a basis for grouping. Thus while our theory begins with the Aristotelian realist position it soon leaves it behind. Yet, it should also be added, if we begin in this way, if we say that the universal on which grouping rests may be the recurring identity, we already rule out nominalism. Indeed, we rule out nominalism when we say that we group on the basis of an observed similarity. It is curious that nominalists, whilst recognizing that their theory is incompatible with realism, appear to think that it is compatible with the doctrine that we group on the observation of similarities. Yet if we group objects as they are found to resemble one another, then we begin not with so many individuals, as the nominalists wish to say, but with so many *resembling* individuals. The resemblance or similarity is as much objective or natural fact as is the identity of common qualities and common relations. In other words, the Resemblance theory is as unsatisfactory a foundation for nominalism as is the Identity theory. In both cases a universal in nature is presupposed. Thus in asserting that universals are recurring similarities as well as recurring identities our theory is shown to be different from both Aristotelian realism and nominalism.

93. Thus far we have been speaking of the universal mainly as the natural recurrence, the recurring identity or similarity. But the other sense of the word has already emerged according to which a universal is a principle of grouping enabling us to determine the limits of the group and providing a standard whereby to recognize a member of the group when we come across one. Ultramarine is a shade of colour that recurs in our experience, but we use it consciously as a principle for grouping, as when we divide things into those which are ultramarine and those which are not. From this point forward in our statement of the theory it is this second sense of the term 'universal' which more and more engages our attention.

Not all principles of grouping have been gained in the way that ultramarine has been gained and not all of them are used in the way in which it is used. Some of the principles which guide us are far more ambiguous and in using them we are less conscious of what we are doing. Our thinking is carried on at different levels. Thinking on a high level, which is throughout logical and precise, where the justification of every step taken is wholly clear, where nothing is taken for granted and nothing implied of which the mind is not fully conscious—such thinking is very different from normal thinking. Normally our thinking is loose, much is assumed and much vaguely implied and the mind is more passive than active, more controlled than controlling. Now part of the explanation of such loose thinking is to be found in the character of the principles which then guide us in classifying. Our familiarity with certain recurrences in experience has brought into being various habits; we group without being fully conscious of the principle on which we group, indeed, without being fully conscious that we are grouping, and when we do later come to reflect upon this grouping we realize that the principles used were vague and lacked precision.

Traditional conceptualism was at fault in its failure to recognize the occurrence of such primitive classifying. It was justified in its view that not all the universals guiding our thought were universals of the same kind as ultramarine, that such a universal as human, for instance, could not be adequately accounted for in strictly realist terms. But its doctrine that all non-observable universals were of necessity conscious fabrications, conscious compoundings of the observable universals, was false. The classificatory principles essential to our thinking and our use of general words are, as Hume hinted, frequently of a more primitive kind. Experience of houses, tables, and men has given us principles of classification before we become conscious of these principles. Before we ever consciously frame an imaginative concept of, and before we are able to give the precise meaning of, 'house', 'table', and 'man', we know how to use these words. But when we reflect upon these primitive principles and when we seek to clarify them, it is then we realize the extent to which our thought is dominated by them. For we are here concerned not merely with house, man, table, but also with such important categorial notions as substance, cause, space, time, and the rest, whose further analysis proves so difficult. They too are originally gained in this way and must be included amongst these primitive principles. Moreover, it is here that we find the explanation of our primitive inductions, namely, in our acquiring principles of grouping or class-determinants, not as the product of conscious and purposive fabrication, but as the consequence of the working of hidden mental processes.

These primitive principles of grouping are the universals which lie at the base of so much of our normal thinking. They cannot be neglected. Yet it is also necessary to admit as universals the consciously formulated principles with which the conceptualists concerned themselves. They are framed out of observed identical qualities or relations or similarities. They also include elements found to be present in the more primitive principles, though the conceptualists had not understood this point. In framing these principles we define the boundaries of our group more precisely, if arbitrarily, and set down the limits, so that henceforth we have no difficulty in recognizing any member and are able to exclude from the class any object lacking in any of the requisite and essential characters. These are imaginative constructions and the primary purpose of the constructing is to make clear to ourselves the vague principles which, we find, guide us in grouping and classifying. But such construction does not consist entirely in clarificatory analysis. In addition there is what may be termed free fabrication. We construct in imagination such objects as dragons, mermaids, chimaeras, and so on. We combine elements isolated by abstraction in an order we freely choose, and bring into being new imaginative creations. Now these too are used as principles of classification, though the classes in this case have no members (unless we regard drawings and paintings of, for instance, mermaids as members of the class). Nevertheless, the principle in this case is as genuinely a universal as any other, in the sense that it would, for instance, enable us to recognize a mermaid if we saw one. In addition to the creation of imaginative objects we create imaginative situations involving various relations. It is as easy to imagine the situation in which the dragon is slain as it is to imagine the dragon itself. Slaying the dragon, running the hundred yards in nine seconds, conquering cancer, linking the planets by air communication—all such imagery may serve as principles of classification. And it is obvious that universals such as these, imaginative and hypothetical though they may be, play a highly important part in human thinking.

94. Lastly, we must consider the thinking which is predominantly verbal rather than imaginative. In imaginative thinking the universal is exemplified in the use of an image or of images as a principle of grouping together with all the accretions necessary to the use. Since imaginative thinking is rarely wholly non-verbal, one of these accretions is likely to be language. We have now to consider the situation in which the major part of the thinking is verbal and in which images, if they are present at all, are few and faint.

The more intellective and abstract thinking is usually supposed to be predominantly verbal, relying less and less on imagery as it develops. We are agreed that it is mistaken to speak of such thinking in terms of apprehending abstract entities, or as the conceiving of a concept which is an internal entity and of which the general word is the name. We reject too the view that the universal is a concept in this sense. We are not to look for the universal amongst the internal accusatives of the traditional conceptualist.

In the case of predominantly verbal thinking, therefore, we cannot look to the image or to the concept (as defined traditionally) for our theory. In what direction then should we look? Clearly, in the direction of general words. Just as consideration of the use of imagery in the more imaginative thinking gives us understanding of the universal in that thinking, so too does consideration of the use of general words give us understanding in the case of verbal thinking. Suppose, for instance, we examine our use of the general word 'proposition'. Our use of it, we say, is determined by what we think is and is not a proposition, by what we suppose can or cannot complete the open sentence '. . . is a proposition'. If we proceed to explain what we take the word 'proposition' to mean, by saying, for instance, that it is a form of words in which something is affirmed or denied about something, what we are doing then is explaining in other words the principle which rules our thinking in our use of the word. Our thought is in terms of a class that is determined by a principle. Of *x*, *y*, and *z* we can say that each is a series of words in which something is affirmed or denied about something, that is, on this definition, each is a proposition; whereas the series of words *a* is not determined in this way and is accordingly not a proposition. Now this principle is the universal we seek.

The universal is not an image and it is not a concept, that is, an abstract, internal entity. Nor is there any suggestion that it is a word, or even a general word. It is a principle of classification. Such principles rule our thought as we use imagery and general words to think about our world, to classify the objects within it, and to relate the classes with one another. Without the principles we should be tied to immediate experience, but with them significant general statements, science and what Quine has called 'eternal sentences', become possible.

95. Our conclusion then is that a universal is a principle of grouping or classifying. But a little earlier (§ 91) it was said that a universal is a natural recurrence. How are we to relate these two statements? I argue that both of them are necessary for an adequate theory of universals.

Philosophers are free to define the word 'universal' as they choose, and some are content to say that the universal is a common quality *in rebus* and to leave it at that. The term 'common quality' is interpreted either in a narrow sense to cover identical qualities and relations only or in a wider sense to cover resemblances as well. In either case the universal is a natural recurrence. As far as it goes I accept this account of the universal, and find in it the foundation upon which to build a theory of thinking. But it is inadequate; for to say that ultramarine, for example, is a universal, in the sense of being a common quality, leaves something important unsaid, namely, that since it is a common quality it can be used as a principle of grouping. Now this too is part of what is meant when we say that ultramarine is a universal. It is a universal as being a natural recurrence, but also as being a principle of grouping.

But not every principle of grouping is also an observed natural recurrence. On the one hand, familiarity with the features of our world, as opposed to the fully conscious apprehension of a common quality, has disposed us to classify in certain ways. On the other we use imagery which we ourselves have fabricated, for instance, the image of the unicorn, to provide us with a basis for grouping. Again verbal description, which may be vague or precise, provides us with principles. Thus there are many ways in which we acquire principles of grouping in addition to the use of common qualities directly observed.

We cannot then simply say that a universal is a natural recurrence. Any principle of grouping is a universal and we cannot identify principle of grouping with natural recurrence. This is an avowal that the question 'What is a universal?' cannot be answered in one sentence, but needs two. *Universals are natural recurrences*; *universals are principles of grouping or classifying.*

At the same time it would seem to be the case that the fundamental basis of all generalizing and grouping is this observation of natural recurrences. The use of general words would seem to rest finally on this observation, even though the full explanation of our principles of grouping involves more than reference to this observation alone. In this way our thinking is always linked to the experienced world. There is admittedly a metaphysical problem in the existence of these natural occurrences which this book does not attempt to solve. What is the final explanation of the recurrences in nature? It might be said that this is the real problem of universals and that the one attempt to tackle it thus far is the attempt made by the advocates of the theory of Forms. Certainly, this is not the question which has concerned us in this book. Here we have been concerned with a less ultimate problem, that of analysing in phenomenological terms the universal element in thinking, and that of making clear the factors which lie behind our use of general words in thinking. This problem is one that can be solved at the phenomenological level, even if certain ultimate questions are left unanswered.

Our purpose is to prepare the way for a satisfactory theory of thinking. An adequate theory of universals, as I conceive it, is necessary for the further theory of thinking. I do not suggest that the theory of universals contains the whole analysis of thinking; at most it is part of that theory. Thinking involves the successful use of general words and the theory of thinking explains how general words are used. In this part of its task the latter theory is one with that of universals, as here conceived. But clearly there are other problems in the theory of thinking. An obvious problem is that of presenting an adequate account of classes. We have here considered merely a preliminary problem, that of principles presupposed in classifying, and we regard these as universals. I have referred also to the important element of steering and purposeful control which is present in the thinking of intelligent man, and this element needs examination. There is further the question of the nature of insight and of the inferences which rest upon it, together with the whole question of the relation between thinking and knowing. These, and many other matters, need to be discussed in the full theory of thinking. But their discussion lies outside the scope of this book.

INDEX OF SUBJECTS

INDEX OF SUBJECTS

INDEX OF PERSONS

INDEX OF PERSONS